THE *NEW* ILLUSTRATED
DINOSAUR
DICTIONARY

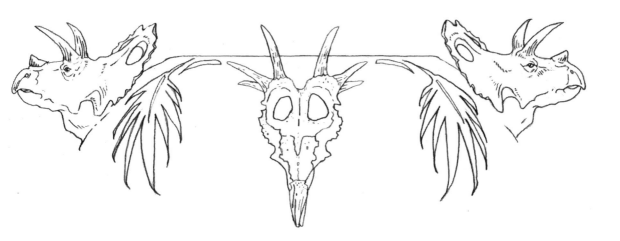

THE *NEW* ILLUSTRATED
DINOSAUR
DICTIONARY

BY HELEN RONEY SATTLER

With a foreword by
JOHN H. OSTROM, PH.D.
Curator of Vertebrate Paleontology
Peabody Museum of Natural History
Yale University

ILLUSTRATED BY JOYCE POWZYK

LOTHROP, LEE & SHEPARD BOOKS NEW YORK

Carnotaurus

First Revised Edition

1 2 3 4 5 6 7 8 9 10

Library of Congress Cataloging in Publication Data
Sattler, Helen Roney.
The new illustrated dinosaur dictionary / by Helen Roney Sattler with a foreword by John H. Ostrom ;
illustrated by Joyce Powzyk.—1st rev. ed., [2nd ed.]
p.   cm. Rev. ed. of: The illustrated dinosaur dictionary. 1st ed. © 1983. Includes bibliographical
references. Summary: A dictionary with entries for all known dinosaurs and other animals of the Mesozoic Era, as well as general topics relating to dinosaurs. ISBN 0-688-08462-1.—ISBN 0-688-10043-0
(pbk.) 1. Dinosaurs—Dictionaries. [1.Dinosaurs—Dictionaries. 2. Extinct animals—Dictionaries.]   I.
Powzyk, Joyce Ann, ill. II. Sattler, Helen Roney. Illustrated dinosaur dictionary. III. Title. QE862.D5S226
1990 567.9'1'03—dc20
90-3313 CIP AC

ACKNOWLEDGMENTS

I would like to express my deepest appreciation and thanks to John H. Ostrom, Curator of Vertebrate Paleontology, Peabody Museum of Natural History, Yale University, for reading the completed manuscript and for his many valuable comments and criticisms along the way.

I also extend thanks to Donald Baird, Edwin H. Colbert, Walter P. Coombs, Jr., John Horner, James A. Jensen, Wann Langston, Jr., James H. Madsen, Jr., Walter L. Manger, George Olshevsky, Dale A. Russell, and Louis Jacobs for their contributions by way of conversations or correspondence. I am grateful also to the following authors for information gleaned from their papers published in scientific journals and books: R. M. Alexander, Luis Alvarez, Walter Alvarez, Donald Baird, Robert T. Bakker, Rinchen Barsbold, J. F. Bonaparte, M. K. Brett-Surman, A. J. Charig, Sankar Chatterjee, Edwin H. Colbert, W. W. Crompton, Philip J. Currie, Peter Dodson, James O. Farlow, Peter Galton, Stephen Jay Gould, M. J. Heaton, John Horner, Sohan L. Jain, James A. Jensen, M. John Kaye, Richard A. Kerr, S. M. K. Kurzanov, Wann Langston, Jr., Douglas A. Lawson, John S. McIntosh, James H. Madsen, Jr., Jean L. Marx, Ralph E. Molnar, William J. Morris, Elizabeth Nicholls, George Olshevsky, Halszka Osmolska, John H. Ostrom, Jaime Eduardo Powell, A. K. Rozhdestvensky, Dale A. Russell, Loris S. Russell, Albert Santa Luca, William Lee Stokes, John E. Storer, J. Willis Stovall, Hans-Sieter Sues, William Swinton, Samuel P. Welles, Ruport Wild, P. Yadagiri, Zi-kui Zhao, and others

Acknowledgments

too numerous to mention. I also thank Carol Gill, Rosalia Purdum, Malinda Shirley-Sattler, and Robert Sattler for their tireless assistance in obtaining reference material. I also extend thanks to Carl Masthay for his tremendous help in editing the etymologies and, finally, to all the editors and other people who have spent so much time and hard work in producing this book.

CONTENTS

FOREWORD

Why a dictionary of dinosaurs? This question can be answered easily. The answer, of course, is that there are so many people of all ages all over the world who are fascinated with dinosaurs. Dinosaur enthusiasts need a handy, quick reference book that will tell them the difference between *Tyrannosaurus* and *Scutellosaurus* or *Secernosaurus.* If you have not heard of either of these, or of *Minmi* or *Mussaurus,* one of the main reasons you will enjoy this book is obvious. It tells you about these and many other recently identified dinosaur kinds that have yet to be "discovered" by other writers of popular dinosaur books.

Helen Sattler's diligent research has produced the most comprehensive book on dinosaurs for the nonscientist that I know of. She has done a superb job of tracking down all the latest discoveries from places like Argentina, China, Mongolia, Brazil, and many others. This book can be depended on to give you accurate, up-to-the-minute information on the subject. And, though dictionaries are not usually purchased for casual reading, it is an additional bonus that *The Illustrated Dinosaur Dictionary* is both an up-to-date reference and a readable book.

Dinosaurs have been known to the world for only a little more than a century and a half, and new discoveries, new knowledge, and new hypotheses come forward almost every day. Of the approximately three hundred fifty dinosaur kinds included in the dictionary, *almost one hundred were discovered and named in just the last twenty years.* These latest discoveries, and all those that were made before, were the result of strenuous and costly expeditions to many parts of the world. The search for new dinosaurs and other forms of ancient life will continue as long as the public and the scientist are intrigued by the curious creatures of the past. Indeed, the curiosity of the paleontologist, and the excitement of search and discovery, guarantee future finds.

John H. Ostrom, Ph.D.
Curator of Vertebrate Paleontology
Peabody Museum of Natural History
Yale University

INTRODUCTION

In this book you will find an alphabetical listing of your favorite dinosaurs, plus information on many that will be new to you. You will also find the names of some of the animals that lived with the dinosaurs, or are mistaken for dinosaurs, and definitions of some of the terms that you come across when reading about dinosaurs and can't find in a regular dictionary. In fact, in this book you can find out just about anything there is to know about dinosaurs.

The word *dinosaur* means "terrible lizard" (it comes from the Greek words *deinos,* "terrible," and *sauros,* "lizard"). These prehistoric animals were originally thought to be gigantic reptiles. Today the word *dinosaur* is used to name a group of extinct animals classed as reptiles because of their reptilian skulls. However, some scientists now think that it is possible that dinosaurs were not true reptiles—at least not in the sense of modern reptiles such as lizards and turtles.

Dinosaurs were actually two kinds of animals, Saurischia and Ornithischia. The two were no more closely related to each other than they were to crocodiles or to the extinct flying reptiles (pterosaurs). Both the saurischian and the ornithischian dinosaurs are thought to have evolved from reptilian ancestors called thecodonts. Dinosaurs in both groups probably were scaly, egg-laying animals that walked in an erect posture like mammals. They did not crawl along close to the ground like modern reptiles. Some scientists now think that dinosaurs were warm-blooded, like today's mammals and birds, and capable of rapid movement. Today's reptiles are cold-blooded and generally slow moving. There is evidence suggesting the possibility that many dinosaurs gave some kind of care to their young. Some scientists have proposed that dinosaurs should be removed from the class Reptilia and placed in a separate class called Dinosauria or Archosauria.

The saurischians, or "lizard-hipped" dinosaurs, are divided into two groups. The theropods were bipedal (two-legged) meat eaters. The sauropodomorpha included the sauropods, gigantic quadrupedal (four-legged) plant eaters, and the pro-sauropods. Prosauropods were sometimes bipedal and sometimes quadrupedal. Most ate plants, but some may have eaten meat also.

There were four kinds of ornithischians, or "bird-hipped" dinosaurs. Those that walked on two legs most of the time are called ornithopods. The plated dinosaurs are called steg-osaurs, the armored dinosaurs are called ankylosaurs, and the horned dinosaurs are called ceratopsians. Some scientists separate the ornithischians into five groups instead of four. They put the dome-headed dinosaurs, or pachycephalosaurs, in a group by themselves. Other scientists consider the pachycephalosaurs to be a subdivision (family) of the ornith-opods.

The period of the earth's history in which dinosaurs lived is called the Mesozoic Era. It began 225 million years ago and ended 65 million years ago. This era is divided into three periods: the Triassic (the earliest), the Jurassic, and the Cre-taceous (the latest). Dinosaurs evolved around the middle of the Triassic Period and became extinct at the close of the Cretaceous Period.

During the 140 million years that dinosaurs existed, many different kinds evolved. We know this because we have found their fossilized remains and tracks. In this book you will find

Classification of Dinosaurs

CLASS REPTILIA

Subclass *Archosauria*	Triassic to present
Order *Thecodontia*	Triassic
Suborder *Proterosuchia*	Primitive thecodonts; Early Triassic
Suborder *Pseudosuchia*	Dinosaur ancestors; Triassic
Suborder *Aetosauria*	Heavily armored plant eaters; Triassic
Suborder *Phytosauria*	Phytosaurs; Triassic
Order *Crocodilia*	Crocodiles; Triassic to present
Order *Pterosauria*	Flying reptiles; Jurassic to Late Cretaceous
Order *Saurischia*	"Lizard-hipped" dinosaurs; Triassic through Cretaceous
Suborder *Theropoda*	Bipedal meat eaters; Triassic through Cretaceous
Infraorder *Coelurosauria*	Small theropods
Infraorder *Carnosauria*	Large theropods
Suborder *Sauropodomorpha*	Triassic to Cretaceous
Infraorder *Prosauropoda*	Forerunners of the *Sauropoda*
Infraorder *Sauropoda*	Huge quadrupedal plant eaters
Order *Ornithischia*	"Bird-hipped" dinosaurs; mainly plant eaters
Suborder *Ornithopoda*	All bipedal; some duck-billed; Triassic to Cretaceous
Suborder *Stegosauria*	Plated; quadrupedal; Jurassic and Cretaceous
Suborder *Ankylosauria*	Armored; quadrupedal; Cretaceous
Suborder *Ceratopsia*	Horned; quadrupedal; Late Cretaceous
Suborder *Pachycephalosauria*	Dome-headed; bipedal; Late Cretaceous

information about more than three hundred fifty different dinosaurs.

This is an exciting time in the history of dinosaur study. New discoveries are made every year; new facts are unearthed almost daily. Four brand-new dinosaur graveyards have recently been found: one in China, one in Alberta, Canada, one in Texas, and one in Nova Scotia. It will take many years for scientists to dig out all the fossils, and it will take many more years to clean them and fit them together like the pieces of giant jigsaw puzzles. But when the work is finished, you can be sure there will be many more new and interesting dinosaurs to read about.

You can also be sure that new facts about old dinosaurs will be uncovered, giving us a better understanding of some that are now poorly known. New information about well-known dinosaurs may cause scientists to change their thinking about some of them, just as new information changed scientific opinions in the past. We know a great deal about dinosaurs now, but there is much more to be learned.

HOW TO USE THIS BOOK

Just about everything there is to know about dinosaurs can be found in this book, which has been organized to make the information as readily accessible as possible. All the dinosaurs that have been named to date and many of the animals that are sometimes confused with dinosaurs are listed alphabetically in boldface capital letters. The meaning of each animal name and a guide to its pronunciation are given.* Approximate measurements and estimated weights are also provided.

In addition to classification and detailed description, there is also information on the amount of evidence we have on each of the creatures. It's interesting as well as important to know whether assumptions and theories have been based on the discovery of an entire skeleton or on a small fragment of bone or a footprint.

There are also definitions of terms frequently encountered when reading about dinosaurs that either aren't in regular dictionaries or may not be defined in a way to reveal the term's relationship to dinosaurs, as is the case with *endotherm.* You may also look up specific items, such as *feet, hands, extinction, young,* or *parental care,* and find discussions of facts and theories concerning them.

For your convenience, the dictionary is cross-referenced. You can find more information about the terms that are set in small capital letters within an entry by referring to the separate entries for those terms.

Black-and-white line drawings accompany the dinosaur entries as well as the entries for many of the other animals discussed. These drawings are designed to point up the distinguishing features of each animal. Dinosaurs, however, were flesh-and-blood animals that lived and breathed and interacted with the flora and fauna in their territories in much the same way animals in the wild do today. The Pictorial Age of the Dinosaurs section will help you visualize dinosaurs as creatures living in their natural habitats. These color pages contain a chart showing animal relationships from the Paleozoic Era to the present, with special emphasis on the Mesozoic Era. There is also a page of maps showing the positions of the continents during these ancient times.

The Reference, by Location, of Dinosaur Discoveries contains entries for continents, countries, and individual states, provinces, or regions. This index will be of special value to anyone who wants to know the names of dinosaurs that have been discovered in a particular area.

*To simplify the updated pronunciation guide while keeping it as accurate as possible, the following system has been used:
    ay = bake
    a = hat
    ah = father
    aw = saw
    ee = feet
    e or eh = met
    y or eye = hide
    i or ih = hit
    oh = hole
    o = plod
    oo = boot
    yu = use
    u or uh = must
The syllable on which the greatest stress is laid appears in capital letters.

RELATIONSHIPS OF ANIMALS

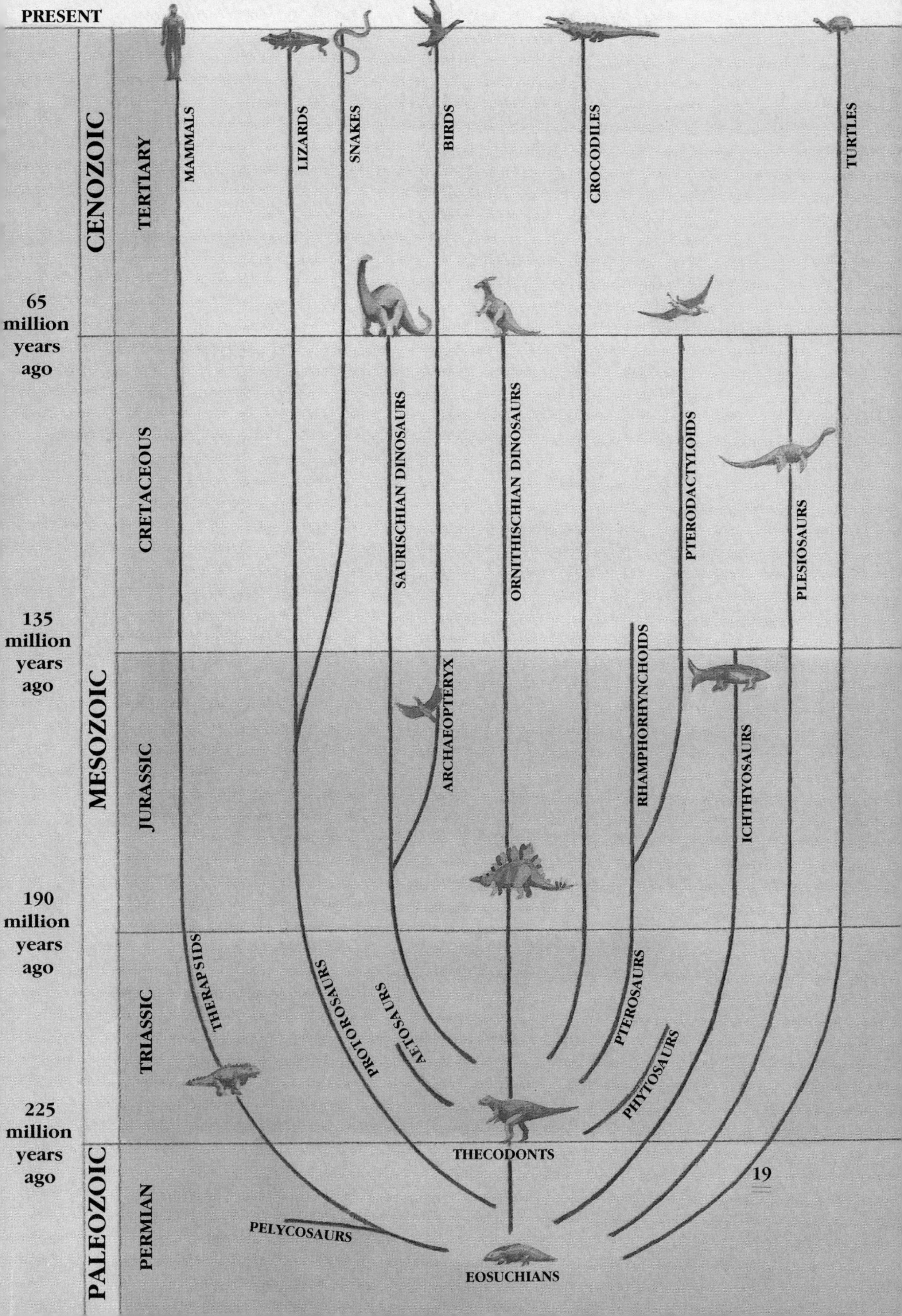

PRESENT

CENOZOIC

TERTIARY

65 million years ago

MESOZOIC

CRETACEOUS

135 million years ago

JURASSIC

190 million years ago

TRIASSIC

225 million years ago

PALEOZOIC

PERMIAN

MAMMALS

LIZARDS

SNAKES

BIRDS

CROCODILES

TURTLES

SAURISCHIAN DINOSAURS

ORNITHISCHIAN DINOSAURS

PTERODACTYLOIDS

PLESIOSAURS

ARCHAEOPTERYX

RHAMPHORHYNCHOIDS

ICHTHYOSAURS

THERAPSIDS

PROTOROSAURS

AETOSAURS

PTEROSAURS

PHYTOSAURS

THECODONTS

PELYCOSAURS

19

EOSUCHIANS

Coelophysis

Scutellosaurus

Chindesaurus

Dilophosaurus

Anchisaurus

Segisaurus

21

Shunosaurus

Huayangosaurus

Xiaosaurus

Lufengosaurus

Gasosaurus

23

young Brachiosaurus

Ceratosaurus

Elaphrosaurus

Brachiosaurus

Dryosaurus

25

EARLY CRETACEOUS PERIOD — EUROPE

Eustreptospondylus

two young Pleurocoelus

Altispinax

Iguanodon

Baryonyx

Hypsilophodon

27

Albertosaurus

Nanotyrannus

Struthiomimus

Pachyrhinosaurus

28

LATE CRETACEOUS PERIOD —
CANADA

Parasaurolophus

Euoplocephalus

Dromiceiomimus

Kritosaurus

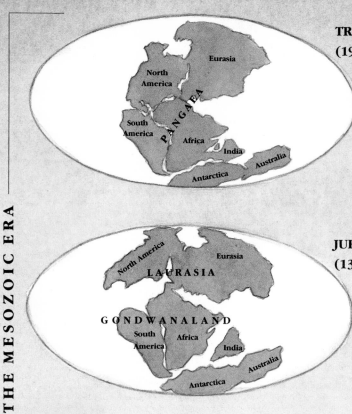

TRIASSIC PERIOD
(190–225 million years ago)

The first dinosaurs appeared during the last third of the Triassic period. The last dinosaurs died out near the end of the Cretaceous period, about sixty-five million years ago.

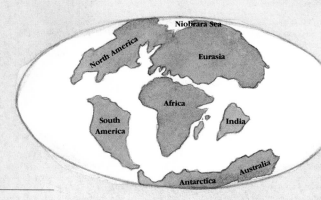

JURASSIC PERIOD
(135–190 million years ago)

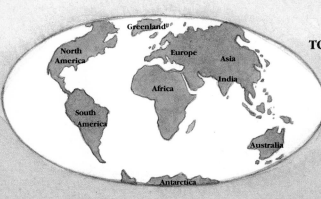

CRETACEOUS PERIOD
(65–135 million years ago)

TODAY

At the beginning of the Mesozoic era, 225 million years ago, all land on the earth was clumped together into one big supercontinent called Pangaea. The land gradually broke up and drifted apart, as these maps indicate. Although continental drift is still going on, the movement is very slow. The continents were positioned as they are today millions of years before humans appeared.

THE *NEW* ILLUSTRATED
DINOSAUR
DICTIONARY

A

ABELISAURUS (ay-bel-ih-SAWR-us) "Abel's Lizard" (Named in honor of Robert Abel, director of the Museum of Natural Sciences of Argentina, + Greek *sauros* = lizard)

A large Late Cretaceous CARNOSAUR found in Patagonia, Argentina. It is known from an almost complete skull that is 36 inches (91 cm) long. This BIPEDAL meat eater had large eyes and a deep, broad skull. It lived at the same time as the TYRANNOSAURIDS but was more closely related to CARNOTAURUS.

Classification: Carnosauria, Theropoda, Saurischia

ABRICTOSAURUS (ah-brik-to-SAWR-us) "Wide-awake Lizard" (Greek *abriktos* = wakeful + *sauros* = lizard, because it did not hibernate)

A primitive ORNITHOPOD found in Late Triassic deposits of South Africa. This BIPEDAL plant eater is known from a fairly well preserved skull that was similar to that of HETERODON-TOSAURUS, except it did not have large tusks. It has been suggested that it may have been a female *Heterodontosaurus,* but this cannot be proved.

Classification: Heterodontosauridae, Ornithopoda, Ornithischia

ACANTHOPHOLIS (ah-kan-THOF-o-liss) "Spiny Scales" (Greek *akantha* = spine, thorn + *pholis* = scale, referring to its armor)

33

A small Early Cretaceous ANKYLOSAUR (armored dinosaur). The slim body of this animal was covered with small plates like those on a turtle's back. Its neck and shoulders were armed with SPIKES; the TAIL was clubless. This four-legged plant eater may have grown to be 14 feet (4.3 m) long. It is known only from a fragmentary skeleton found in southern England.

Classification: Nodosauridae, Ankylosauria, Ornithischia

Acanthopholis

ACROCANTHOSAURUS (ak-ro-KANTH-o-sawr-us) "High-spined Lizard" (Greek *akro-* = high + *akantha* = spine + *sauros* = lizard, referring to the spines on its vertebrae)

A CARNOSAUR of Early Cretaceous North America. This 40-foot (12-m) meat-eating relative of ALLOSAURUS walked on two legs. It had a large head with sharp, sawlike TEETH. Projections up to 17 inches (43 cm) long grew on its vertebrae. These SPINES were probably embedded in a thick ridge of muscle. *Acrocanthosaurus* is the only known American dinosaur with such high spines. It is known from a skull and most of a skeleton found in Oklahoma and Texas.

A recent flood in Texas uncovered some footprints that

Acrocanthosaurus

scientists think were made by *Acrocanthosaurus*. *Acrocanthosaurus* FOSSILS have been found in similar rock nearby. The three-toed footprints were made by 15 individuals traveling at a high speed. Scientists have calculated that they were running about 25 miles (40 km) per hour. These TRACKS provide evidence that *Acrocanthosaurus* traveled in HERDS.

Classification: Carnosauria, Theropoda, Saurischia

AEGYPTOSAURUS (ee-JIP-toh-sawr-us) "Egyptian Lizard" (Named for Egypt, where it was found, + Greek *sauros* = lizard)

A name given to a few SAUROPOD bones found in Late Cretaceous rock in Egypt. This huge four-legged plant eater is thought to have been quite similar to DIPLODOCUS. Although its bones were destroyed in World War II, its discovery is important because it shows that sauropods were living on the African continent in Late Cretaceous times.

Classification: Sauropoda, Sauropodomorpha, Saurischia

AETONYX (ee-TON-ix) "Eagle Claw" (Greek *aëtos* = eagle + *onyx* = claw, because its CLAWS were like those of an eagle)

This dinosaur is now believed to be the same as MASSOSPONDYLUS.

aetosaurs or **Aetosauria** (ee-to-SAWR-ee-ah) "Old Lizards"
(Latin *aeto-* = aged + Greek *sauros* = lizard, because they
were very early REPTILES)

Not DINOSAURS, but a suborder of THECODONTS. Aetosaurs
were heavily armored REPTILES that lived during the TRIASSIC
PERIOD. Their crocodile-shaped bodies were covered with ar-
madillolike bony plates, and curved, serrated spikes protruded from their sides. They were four-legged OMNIVORES
with piglike snouts. Aetosaurs probably roamed throughout
LAURASIA. They have been found in Germany, Scotland, and
the western United States. They ranged in size from the 3- to
4-foot (90- to 120-cm) AETOSAURUS to a 15-foot (4.5-m) DES-
MATOSUCHUS that was found in Arizona. STAGONOLEPIS was about
9 feet (2.5 m) long. This animal was found in Scotland.

AETOSAURUS (EE-to-sawr-us)
See AETOSAURS.

age

No one knows for sure how old dinosaurs lived to be.
Some scientists think they lived to a great age—possibly until
they were 100 or 200 years old. These scientists think that
the huge dinosaurs may have continued to grow throughout
their lives and that that is why they got so large. (See SIZE.)
Growth rings on dinosaur bones show that some were 120
years old when they died.

AGROSAURUS (AG-ro-sawr-us) "Field Lizard" (Greek *agros*
= field + *sauros* = lizard, referring to the place where it
was found)

An Early Jurassic COELUROSAUR. This small, meat-eating dinosaur is known only from a few bones, a CLAW, and a bro-

ken tooth found in Queensland, Australia. It was BIPEDAL and probably resembled COELURUS. Its exact SIZE is unknown.

Classification: Coelurosauria, Theropoda, Saurischia

ALAMOSAURUS (AL-ah-mo-sawr-us) "Alamo Lizard" (Named for the Ojo Alamo rock formation, where it was found, + Greek *sauros* = lizard)

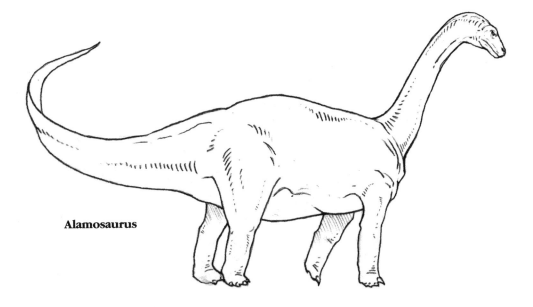

Alamosaurus

A SAUROPOD whose FOSSILS have been found in western Texas, New Mexico, and Utah. This huge four-legged plant eater lived in Late Cretaceous times; it was one of the last of the sauropods to live in North America. (See EXTINCTION.) It is known only from a few bones, but scientists think it resembled DIPLODOCUS. It may have grown to be 50 feet (15 m) long.

Classification: Sauropoda, Sauropodomorpha, Saurischia

ALBERTOSAURUS (al-BER-to-sawr-us) "Alberta Lizard"

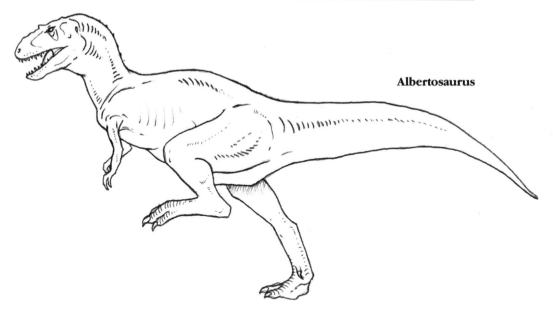

Albertosaurus

(Named for Alberta, Canada, where it was first found, + Greek *sauros* = lizard) Also called GORGOSAURUS.

A large CARNOSAUR of Late Cretaceous North America. This dinosaur is better known as *Gorgosaurus,* but *Albertosaurus* is the preferred name (even though it was given to just a partial skull) because it is the older name. The two are now considered to be the same animal, although *Gorgosaurus* may be a smaller species.

Albertosaurus was a close relative of TYRANNOSAURUS but was smaller and lived several million years earlier. *Albertosaurus* weighed 3 tons (2.7 metric tons), stood 11 feet (3.4 m) tall at the hips, and measured 30 feet (9 m) from its snout to the tip of its TAIL. Like *Tyrannosaurus,* it was a meat eater with a huge head; long, sharp, saw-toothed TEETH; and two-fingered HANDS. Its arms were quite short but were longer than those of *Tyrannosaurus. Albertosaurus* ran on powerful hind legs and was probably swifter than *Tyrannosaurus.* (See SPEED.) Its FEET were armed with long CLAWS.

Scientists have found more FOSSILS of *Albertosaurus* than of any other Late Cretaceous carnosaur. Remains of this animal have been discovered in various areas of the western United States and in Baja California, as well as in Alberta, Canada. Similar types of dinosaurs lived in Mongolia during Late Cretaceous times.

Classification: Carnosauria, Theropoda, Saurischia

ALECTROSAURUS (ah-LEK-tro-sawr-us) "Unmarried Lizard" (Greek *alektros* = unmarried or alone + *sauros* = lizard, because it was unlike any other Asian meat eater known at the time)

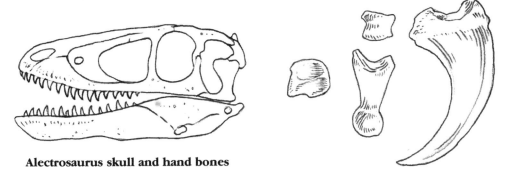

Alectrosaurus skull and hand bones

A large Late Cretaceous CARNOSAUR. This BIPEDAL meat eater was closely related to TYRANNOSAURUS but was more slender. It is known only from an upper arm, HAND, shin, and foot found in Mongolia. It had very long finger CLAWS. Its exact SIZE is unknown.

Classification: Carnosauria, Theropoda, Saurischia

ALGOASAURUS (AL-go-ah-sawr-us) "Algoa Lizard" (Named for Algoa Bay in South Africa, where it was found, + Greek *sauros* = lizard)

An Early Cretaceous SAUROPOD whose FOSSILS were found

in South Africa. Only a few bones of this four-legged plant eater have been found, but *Algoasaurus* is thought to be closely related to DIPLODOCUS and was probably about the same SIZE.

Classification: Sauropoda, Sauropodomorpha, Saurischia

ALIORAMUS (ah-lee-o-RAH-mus) "Different Branch" (Latin *alius* = different + *ramus* = branch, because it was a different kind of TYRANNOSAUR)

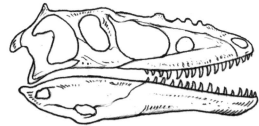

Alioramus

A Late Cretaceous CARNOSAUR whose FOSSILS were found in Mongolia. This two-legged meat eater was a close relative of TARBOSAURUS and resembled that dinosaur, but was smaller. *Alioramus* belonged to the tyrannosaur family, and like all tyrannosaurs, it had a large head, long TEETH, and short arms with two-fingered HANDS and five small CRESTS on its long snout. It was about 20 feet (6 m) long.

Classification: Carnosauria, Theropoda, Saurischia

allosaurids or **Allosauridae** (al-o-SAWR-ih-dee) "Different Lizards" (Named after ALLOSAURUS) Also commonly called allosaurs.

A family of CARNOSAURS. These BIPEDAL meat eaters were medium to very large in size—20 to 45 feet (6 to 13.5 m) long. They had strong, heavy bodies and large, narrow skulls with strong brow ridges. Their arms were quite short, but strong. The HANDS had three fingers and the FEET three forward-pointing toes and a dewclaw. Allosaurids lived in North America and Asia during Late Jurassic and Early Cretaceous times. ACROCANTHOSAURUS, ALLOSAURUS, CHILANTAISAURUS, INDO-SAURUS, and PIATNITZKYSAURUS are members of this family.

allosaurs (AL-o-sawrz)
See ALLOSAURIDS or ALLOSAURIDAE.

ALLOSAURUS (AL-o-sawr-us) "Different Lizard" (Greek *allos* = different + *sauros* = lizard, because its vertebrae were different from those of all other dinosaurs) Also called AN-TRODEMUS.

One of the largest Jurassic CARNOSAURS of North America. An average *Allosaurus* weighed about 4 tons (3.6 metric tons) and measured 35 feet (10.5 m) from the tip of its nose to the end of its TAIL. The largest known was 45 feet (13.5 m) long. When *Allosaurus* stood upright, it was 16.5 feet (5 m) tall.

Like all THEROPODS, *Allosaurus* walked on two legs with its heavy TAIL stretched out behind for balance. Its strong legs were built for SPEED; they had powerful muscles and heavy bones. Although its arms were short, each finger on its three-

Allosaurus

fingered HANDS was armed with a sharp CLAW that could be up to 6 inches (15 cm) long. The three long toes on its FEET were equipped with eaglelike talons.

This meat eater had a strong neck. Its huge 3-foot (90-cm)-long head had heavy bony knobs, or ridges, above its eyes; its enormously powerful jaws were filled with saberlike TEETH 2 to 4 inches (5 to 10 cm) long. The jaws were hinged like those of a snake, so *Allosaurus* would have been able to swallow huge hunks of meat whole. Scientists have found APATOSAURUS vertebrae with *Allosaurus* tooth marks on them, evidence of a Jurassic feast!

Allosaurus remains have been found in North America; FOSSILS found in Africa and Asia may also be those of *Allosaurus*. It is one of the best-known carnosaurs. Sixty individuals—from juveniles to adults—were found at one site in Utah. A middle-size species has been found in Australia.

Classification: Carnosauria, Theropoda, Saurischia

ALTISPINAX (al-tih-SPY-nax) "High Spines" (Latin *altus* = high + *spina* = spine, referring to the high spines on its vertebrae)

Altispinax

The first CARNOSAUR with a fin on its back to be discovered. It is known only from some worn TEETH and three midback vertebrae. On these vertebrae were very long projections similar to, but shorter than, those of SPINOSAURUS. They were, however, somewhat longer than those of ACROCANTHOSAURUS. This two-legged meat eater lived in England in Early Cretaceous times. It may be the same as *Acrocanthosaurus*.

Classification: Carnosauria, Theropoda, Saurischia

AMBLYDACTYLUS (am-bly-DAK-tih-lus) "Blunt Finger" (Greek *amblys* = blunt + *daktylos* = finger, because the fingers were short)

Name given to HADROSAUR footprints found in British Columbia, Alberta, and Utah. The prints of the HANDS show the webbing between the fingers. These are the most abundant footprints found in British Columbia.

AMMONITE (AM-o-nite) "Horn of Ammon" (From Greek, because its shape resembles that of the horns of Ammon, an Egyptian god)

Not a DINOSAUR, but a flat, coiled mollusk that lived in the oceans of the MESOZOIC ERA. This relative of the modern nautilus, octopus, and squid ranged in size from less than an inch (2.5 cm) to 6 feet (1.8 m) in diameter. These sea animals disappeared at the end of the era along with the dinosaurs and many other life forms. (See EXTINCTION.) Its FOSSILS have been found in many Mesozoic marine deposits around the world.

AMMOSAURUS (AM-o-sawr-us) "Sand Lizard" (Greek *ammos* = sand + *sauros* = lizard, because it was found in sandstone)

Ammosaurus

An early North American PROSAUROPOD. It had a long neck and TAIL. Its head was small, and its TEETH were flat or peg-like. Its FEET were broad. Most of the time this 7-foot (2 m) plant eater walked on all fours, but it was capable of walking on two legs. It is one of the earliest-known North American dinosaurs. *Ammosaurus* probably lived all over North America during very late Triassic or Early Jurassic times. It is known from fairly complete material; remains have been found in both Connecticut and Arizona.

Classification: Prosauropoda, Sauropodomorpha, Saurischia

AMTOSAURUS (AHM-to-sawr-us) "Amtgay Lizard" (Named for the Amtgay site, where it was discovered, + Greek *sauros* = lizard)

A large ANKYLOSAUR whose FOSSILS were recently found in Mongolia. This creature lived during the Late CRETACEOUS PERIOD. Like all ankylosaurs, it walked on four legs and ate plants, and its back was covered with bony ARMOR PLATES. Its TAIL is unknown. This dinosaur is known only from a partial braincase and the back of a skull. It was a contemporary of TALARURUS and was probably closely related to that dinosaur, but was somewhat larger.

Classification: Ankylosauridae, Ankylosauria, Ornithischia

AMYGDALODON (ah-MIG-dah-lo-don) "Almond Tooth" (Greek *amygdale* = almond + *odon-* = tooth, because its teeth were almond-shaped)

One of the earliest known SAUROPODS. This giant four-footed plant eater had a long neck and TAIL. It lived in southern Argentina during Middle Jurassic times. Little is known about it because a complete skeleton has not been found, but from the few bones that have been recovered, it appears that this dinosaur was a member of the CETIOSAURID family and was somewhat larger than TITANOSAURUS. It is one of the only certainly known Jurassic dinosaurs from South America.

Classification: Sauropoda, Sauropodomorpha, Saurischia

ANATOSAURUS (ah-NAT-o-sawr-us) "Duck Lizard" (Latin *anato* = duck + Greek *sauros* = lizard, because it had a wide, ducklike bill) Also called TRACHODON.

A Late Cretaceous HADROSAUR. This duck-billed dinosaur is one of the best-known dinosaurs—only its color is unknown. Many skeletons and several SKIN impressions have been found. The skin had a rough, pebbly texture. Fossilized stomach contents show that it ate shrubs, evergreen needles, fruits, and seeds. This indicates that *Anatosaurus* was a land dweller, not a water dweller as scientists first thought. It ran on two

Anatosaurus

legs with its body held horizontally, balanced by a long TAIL stretched out behind.

Anatosaurus belonged to the HADROSAURINE group of hadrosaurs. It had a flat head, webbed forefeet, and up to 1,000 closely packed TEETH in its horny bill. It grew to be 14 feet (4.3 m) tall and 30 feet (9 m) long. It weighed up to 3.5 tons (3.2 metric tons). *Anatosaurus* lived in North America and in England and was one of the last of the duckbills to become extinct. (See EXTINCTION.)

Classification: Hadrosauridae, Ornithopoda, Ornithischia

ANCHICERATOPS (ANG-kee-sayr-ah-tops) "Similar Horned Face" (Greek *anchi-* = near + *keratops* = horned face, because it was similar to other CERATOPSIANS)

Anchiceratops

A Late Cretaceous ceratopsian. This 16-foot (4.9-m) ORNITHISCHIAN had a horny beak and three HORNS on its face—a short stubby one on its nose and two long ones above its eyes. *Anchiceratops* was a long-frilled ceratopsian. Its bony FRILL covered the neck to the shoulders. This four-legged plant eater was very common in Alberta, Canada.

Classification: Ceratopsidae, Ceratopsia, Ornithischia

anchisaurids or **Anchisauridae** (ang-kee-SAWR-ih-dee) "Near Lizards" (Named after ANCHISAURUS)

A primitive family of PROSAUROPODS. They were relatively small, 8 to 10 feet (2.4 to 3 m) long, and were lightly built. They had lightweight bones, long necks and TAILS, and long, slender fingers and toes. Anchisaurids could walk on either two or four legs. They may have eaten both meat and plants; they had bladelike TEETH suitable for tearing meat and other teeth suitable for grinding plants. Anchisaurids lived from Middle to Late Triassic times and have been found almost all over the world. ANCHISAURUS, EFRAASIA, and THECODONTO-SAURUS were members of this family.

ANCHISAURIPUS (ANG-kee-sawr-ih-pus) "Near Lizard Foot" (Greek *anchi-* = near + *sauripous* = lizard foot, because it was originally believed that these footprints were made by ANCHISAURUS)

A name given to three-toed footprints made by a small, 12-foot (3.7-m), BIPEDAL meat-eating dinosaur as it walked from the shore into shallow water during Early Jurassic times 180 million years ago. These footprints were found in the Connecticut Valley in the eastern United States. Scientists now know the prints could not have been made by *Anchisaurus,* because *Anchisaurus* was a PROSAUROPOD. These footprints are typical of THEROPODS; the middle toe is longer than the other

Anchisauripus tracks

two. Prosauropods have four forward-pointing toes; the first toe is quite short, and toe number three is slightly longer than two and four.

ANCHISAURUS (ANG-kee-sawr-us) "Near Lizard" (Greek *anchi-* = near or close to + *sauros* = lizard, because it was an early dinosaur and was close to the REPTILIAN ancestors) Sometimes called YALEOSAURUS.

Anchisaurus

A PROSAUROPOD resembling AMMOSAURUS but with narrower FEET and a slightly smaller head. It was about 8 feet (2.5 m) long. *Anchisaurus* was basically QUADRUPEDAL but may sometimes have run two-legged. It may have eaten both plants and meat. FOSSILS of this dinosaur have been found in Connecticut, Arizona, South Africa, and Germany. It probably lived all over the world from Late Triassic to Early Jurassic times. It is one of the oldest dinosaurs in geological time to be discovered in North America, and it is known from very complete material. At one time it was thought that this dinosaur was a THEROPOD, because of its thin-walled bones and serrated TEETH.

Classification: Prosauropoda, Sauropodomorpha, Saurischia

ankylosaurids or **Ankylosauridae** (ang-kyl-o-SAWR-ih-dee) "Armored Lizards" (Named after ANKYLOSAURUS)

One of the two families of ANKYLOSAURS. The backs, heads, and TAILS of these four-legged plant eaters were covered with thin bony plates, or scutes. Ankylosauridae ranged in size from 15 to 30 feet (4.5 to 9 m) long. They have been found in North America, Asia, and Antarctica. This group had triangular heads, small spikes on their sides (or none at all), and clubbed TAILS. AMTOSAURUS, ANKYLOSAURUS, EUOPLOCEPHALUS, PINACOSAURUS, SAICHANIA, SAUROPLITES, TALARURUS, and TARCHIA were ankylosaurids.

ankylosaurs or **Ankylosauria** (ang-kyl-o-SAWR-ee-ah) "Armored Lizards" (Named after ANKYLOSAURUS)

The suborder of armored ORNITHISCHIAN dinosaurs. It consisted of two families—ANKYLOSAURIDAE and NODOSAURIDAE. They ranged in size from 6 feet (1.8 m) to 30 feet (9 m) long. These four-legged plant eaters lived on every continent including Antarctica throughout the CRETACEOUS PERIOD. Their backs, heads, and TAILS were covered with bony plates, or scutes, somewhat like those of a turtle, but they were flexible except over the shoulders and hips. The Nodosauridae—the most primitive—had thick scutes, pear-shaped heads, large spikes on their sides, and clubless tails. Ankylosauridae had thin oval scutes, triangular heads, small spikes on their sides (or none at all), and clubbed tails.

ANKYLOSAURUS (ang-KYL-o-sawr-us) "Stiffened Lizard" (Greek *ankylo-* = stiffen + *sauros* = lizard, because of its stiffened dermal armor) Sometimes mistakenly called EUOPLOCEPHALUS.

One of the largest and best-known of the ANKYLOSAURS.

Ankylosaurus

The body, head, and TAIL of this "REPTILIAN tank" were covered with bony plates set close together in thick, leathery SKIN. A row of short SPIKES protected each side of the body. The TAIL was short and thick and ended in a bony club. This peaceful plant eater lived in western North America during the CRETACEOUS PERIOD. It was 25 feet (7.5 m) long, 6 feet (1.8 m) wide, and over 4 feet (1.2 m) tall. It weighed about 5 tons (4.5 metric tons). *Ankylosaurus* was one of the very last kinds of dinosaurs to die out. (See EXTINCTION.) It is known from fairly complete material found in Montana.

Ankylosaurus is sometimes called *Euoplocephalus,* but it is now believed that these were two different animals.

Classification: Ankylosauridae, Ankylosauria, Ornithischia

ANODONTOSAURUS (an-o-don-to-SAWR-us) "Toothless Lizard" (Greek *an-* = without + *odonto-* = teeth + *sauros* = lizard, because its jaw was without teeth)

A very primitive toothless ANKYLOSAUR of the NODOSAURIDAE family found in Late Cretaceous rock in Alberta, Canada. It is known only from a skull, jaw, and several scutes. The skull is 1.25 feet (40 cm) long and 1 foot (30 cm) wide. This armored dinosaur is now considered by some to be the same as EUOPLOCEPHALUS.

Classification: Nodosauridae, Ankylosauria, Ornithischia

ANOMOEPUS (an-o-MEE-pus) "Different Foot" (Greek *anomoios* = different + *pous* = foot, because these footprints were different from others found in the same area)

Name given to Late Triassic or Early Jurassic dinosaur footprints found in the Newark Basin of Connecticut, in Glen Canyon, Arizona, and in Europe. Both the three-toed hind FEET and five-fingered forefeet left impressions, indicating the animal that made them was at least sometimes QUADRUPEDAL. Scientists believe the TRACKS were made by an ORNITHOPOD

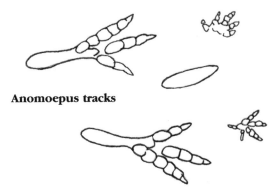

Anomoepus tracks

because there are no CLAW marks. When found, these tracks were important, because no ORNITHISCHIAN dinosaur bones and only a few isolated TEETH had been found in Triassic rock in North America. But now a recent discovery in Arizona has changed that. SCUTELLOSAURUS has been identified as a Late Triassic ornithischian.

ANSERIMIMUS (an-ser-ih-MYM-us) "Goose Mimic" (Latin *anser* = goose + *mimus* = mimic, because it was birdlike)

A small THEROPOD found in Late Cretaceous deposits of Mongolia. It is known from an incomplete skeleton including a shoulder blade, a partial HAND, and a partial foot. The CLAWS on its hand were flattened. This dinosaur was closely related to the ORNITHOMIMIDS and was probably a fast runner.

Classification: Coelurosauria, Theropoda, Saurischia

Antarctic dinosaurs The remains of several Cretaceous dinosaurs have been found in areas that lay below the Antarctic Circle when they were alive. They were all small species. It is unknown whether this was because of the harsh climate or for some other reason. A small, unnamed ANKYLOSAURID was found on James Ross Island, Antarctica. It is too incomplete to be clearly identified but is important because it is the first ANKYLOSAURID found outside of GONDWANALAND.

FOSSILS of four dinosaurs were found in Victoria, Australia, which was below the Antarctic Circle during the CRETACEOUS PERIOD. One was a small species of ALLOSAURUS only 7 feet (2 m) tall. The other three were HYPSILOPHODONTS: ATLASCOPCO-SAURUS, FULGUROTHERIUM, and LEAELLYNASAURA. They were between 6.5 and 10 feet (2 and 3 m) long. Most are known from very scant material, but at least one had large, well-developed eyes and probably could see well in the dark.

ANTARCTOSAURUS (ant-ARK-to-sawr-us) "Southern Lizard" (Greek *antarktikos* = southern + *sauros* = lizard, because it was found at the southern tip of South America)

A Late Cretaceous SAUROPOD. This plant-eating QUADRUPED has been found in India as well as in South America. A nearly complete skeleton was found in Argentina. It was about the SIZE of APATOSAURUS but was more similar in build to DIPLODOCUS. The skull is over 2 feet (60 cm) long. The presence of *Antarctosaurus* in both India and South America raises an interesting question as to when these two continents separated. (See GONDWANALAND.)

Antarctosaurus

Classification: Sauropoda, Sauropodomorpha, Saurischia

ANTRODEMUS (an-tro-DEE-mus) "Cavern-framed" (Greek *antron* = cavern + *demas* = frame of body, referring to the hollows in its vertebrae)

Another name frequently used for ALLOSAURUS. Actually, there is disagreement among scientists as to whether *Antrodemus* and *Allosaurus* are the same animal. The name *Antrodemus* was based on such scanty material that it is difficult to determine for sure.

Classification: Carnosauria, Theropoda, Saurischia

APATOSAURUS (ah-PAT-o-sawr-us) "Deceptive Lizard" (Greek *apatelos* = deceptive + *sauros* = lizard, because its chevron bones were deceptively like those of MOSASAURUS) Also called BRONTOSAURUS.

One of the largest of the Late Jurassic SAUROPODS. This giant four-legged plant eater had a long neck and TAIL. It measured 75 feet (23 m) from the tip of its nose to the end of its 30-

Apatosaurus

foot (9.1-m) whiplike tail. It stood 15 feet (4.6 m) tall at the hips and weighed about 30 tons (27.2 metric tons). It had a small, long-snouted, horselike head, and elephantlike FEET and legs. The front legs were shorter than the hind legs. The TEETH were small and peglike. The BRAIN was about the size of an adult human's fist.

For a long time scientists thought *Apatosaurus* was too heavy to walk on land and assumed that it was a water dweller. However, recent bone studies prove that its legs could have supported its weight. It was probably a plains and forest dweller, and it probably traveled in HERDS. It ate twigs and the needles of pine, fir, and sequoia trees. Its 20-foot (6-m) neck—which had 14 or 15 vertebrae and was longer than its body—allowed it to browse on the very tops of trees.

For protection *Apatosaurus* relied on its SIZE and tough, leathery SKIN. (See DEFENSE.) It lived in many areas of western North America from Montana to Baja California, as well as in Europe. Several nearly complete skeletons have been found, but only one head.

Classification: Sauropoda, Sauropodomorpha, Saurischia

ARALOSAURUS (ar-ahl-o-SAWR-us) "Aral Lizard" (Named for the U.S.S.R.'s Aral Lake + Greek *sauros* = lizard)

A HADROSAUR (duck-billed dinosaur) that lived during Late Cretaceous times in what is now the U.S.S.R. Very little is known about this BIPEDAL plant eater because only an incomplete skull has been found. However, it is important because from it scientists learned that the TEETH in the upper and lower jaws of hadrosaurs were quite different from one another. This has made it possible to identify many teeth as hadrosaurian that were previously unidentifiable.

Classification: Hadrosauridae, Ornithopoda, Ornithischia

ARCHAEOPTERYX (ahr-kee-OP-ter-ix) "Ancient Wing" (Greek *archaio-* = ancient + *pteryx* = wing, because it was an ancient bird)

Not a dinosaur, but a crow-sized Jurassic bird—until 1986 the oldest bird known. Although more recent than PROTOAVIS, it is more primitive. Many scientists once believed *Archaeopteryx* was the first step in the evolution of birds from small COELUROSAURS. *Archaeopteryx* looked very much like a tiny dinosaur with feathers and wings. It probably could fly, but not far. Three clawed fingers extended from the front of each wing. The tail was long and bony, and the jaws were lined with teeth. *Archaeopteryx* probably ate insects. Its FOSSILS have been found in West Germany. These fossils were formed in

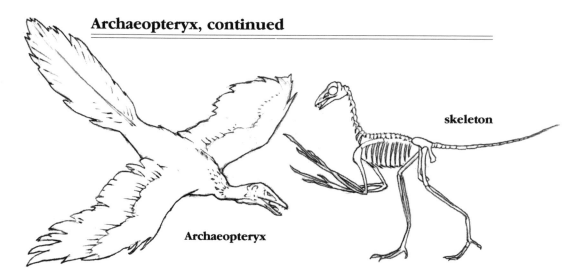

skeleton

Archaeopteryx

fine-grained limestone; they clearly show the impressions of the long feathers on the wings and tail. The first *Archaeopteryx* specimen ever found is owned by the Natural History Museum in London. It is considered the most valuable fossil in the world.

ARCHAEORNITHOMIMUS   (ahr-kee-or-NITH-ih-my-mus) "Ancient Bird Mimic" (Greek *archaio-* = ancient + *ornitho-* = bird + *mimos* = mimic, because it was birdlike)

An early ORNITHOMIMID ("ostrich dinosaur"). It lived during Late Cretaceous times. This dinosaur was BIPEDAL; it had three-fingered HANDS with nearly straight CLAWS. The toe claws, however, were curved. *Archaeornithomimus* probably ate insects and small animals. Its FOSSILS have been found in both the western United States and Mongolia, but it is known only from fragments, and its SIZE is unknown.

Classification: Coelurosauria, Theropoda, Saurischia

archosaurs or **Archosauria** (ahr-ko-SAWR-ee-ah) "Ruling Lizards" (Greek *archos* = ruler + *sauros* = lizard, because they were the dominant life form of the MESOZOIC ERA)

A subclass of REPTILIA; a group of higher vertebrates (animals with backbones) including the CROCODILIANS, DINOSAURS, PTEROSAURS, and THECODONTS. Since birds are now thought to be descendants of dinosaurs, some scientists propose that Archosauria should be raised to class level and that it should include birds.

ARGYROSAURUS (ahr-JY-ro-sawr-us) "Silver Lizard" (Greek *argyros* = silver + *sauros* = lizard, because it was found in Argentina, or "Silver Land")

A massive SAUROPOD, larger than APATOSAURUS, that lived in Argentina during Late Cretaceous times. Only the legs and a few vertebrae have been recovered, but these are quite similar to those of DIPLODOCUS, and *Argyrosaurus* may be a Cretaceous descendant of that dinosaur. Like all sauropods, *Argyrosaurus* was a four-legged plant eater.

Classification: Sauropoda, Sauropodomorpha, Saurischia

ARISTOSAURUS (ah-RISS-toh-sawr-us) "Best Lizard" (Greek *aristos* = best + *sauros* = lizard, because of the completeness of the specimen)

A small, Late Triassic PROSAUROPOD found in South Africa. This four-legged plant eater is known from a skeleton that is complete except for the skull. It was 5 feet (1.5 m) long.

Classification: Prosauropoda, Sauropodomorpha, Saurischia

ARISTOSUCHUS (ah-RISS-toh-sook-us) "Good Crocodile" (Greek *aristos* = good or best + *souchos* = crocodile, because at first it was thought to be CROCODILIAN)

A small COELUROSAUR. This two-legged meat eater lived during Late Jurassic or Early Cretaceous times. It is known only from fragments found on the Isle of Wight, but it is thought to be closely related to COELURUS or ORNITHOLESTES and probably resembled them.

Classification: Coelurosauria, Theropoda, Saurischia

ARKANSAURUS (ar-kan-SAWR-us) "Arkansas Lizard" (Named for the state in which it was found, + Greek *sauros* = lizard)

The name given to the foot bones of a dinosaur found in Cretaceous sediments in Arkansas. Arkansas was covered by a shallow sea at that time. The bones were probably washed into the sea by floodwaters. This dinosaur was a BIPEDAL meat eater that probably resembled ORNITHOMIMUS. Although *Arkansaurus* has been named and classified as an ORNITHOMIMID, it has not, at this time, been certified. It may be the same as ARCHAEORNITHOMIMUS.

Classification: Coelurosauria, Theropoda, Saurischia

armor plating

The bodies of ANKYLOSAURS were covered with rows of plates, or scutes, that were made of hard, bony material and keeled like the bottom of a boat. In the ANKYLOSAURIDAE these plates were oval and were hollowed out underneath, so they were relatively thin and light. Some rose to form low, pointed cones. These plates did not touch one another. The plates of the NODOSAURIDAE were thicker and heavier than those of the Ankylosauridae. They were solid and flat (or nearly flat) underneath. Some rose to form tall conical spikes. The plates, or scutes, of Nodosauridae contacted or touched each other and were rectangular or square in outline, rather than oval.

There is evidence that some ORNITHOPODS and some SAU-

ROPODS (TITANOSAURIDS) had bony armor plates, similar to those of the ankylosaurids, attached to their SKIN.

STEGOSAURS had two rows of large, thin, leaf-shaped bony plates running down the middle of their backs. Although these were once thought to be DEFENSE mechanisms, it is now believed that they regulated body temperature. These plates contained blood vessels. Wind flowing across the plates would cool the blood flowing through the blood vessels.

armored dinosaurs

See ANKYLOSAURS.

ARRHINOCERATOPS (ah-RYN-o-sayr-ah-tops) "Without a Nose-horn Face" (Greek *a* = without + *rhin-* = nose + *kerat-* = horn + *ops* = face, referring to the small nose horn)

A Late Cretaceous CERATOPSIAN with a very short nose HORN

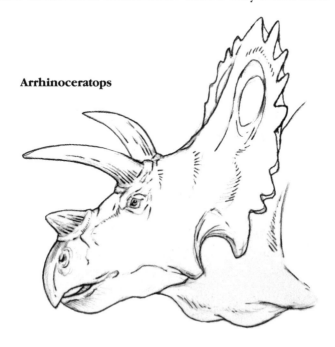

Arrhinoceratops

and two long, slightly forward-curving brow horns. Its long neck shield was armed with SPIKES, and its snout ended in a short, horny beak. This four-legged plant eater is known from a skull found in Alberta, Canada.

Classification: Ceratopsidae, Ceratopsia, Ornithischia

ASTRODON (ASS-tro-don) "Star Tooth" (Greek *astr-* = star + *odon-* = tooth)

Same as PLEUROCOELUS.

Classification: Sauropoda, Sauropodomorpha, Saurischia

atlantosaurids or **Atlantosauridae** (at-lan-toh-SAWR-ih-dee) "Atlas's Lizards" (Named after ATLANTOSAURUS)

A name sometimes used for one of the two major divisions of SAUROPODS. Most PALEONTOLOGISTS now prefer to use the name TITANOSAURIDAE for this group, because *Atlantosaurus* is no longer considered a valid name for a dinosaur.

Atlantosaurinae (at-lan-toh-SAWR-ih-nee) "Atlas's Lizards" (Named after ATLANTOSAURUS)

One of the subfamilies of the TITANOSAURIDAE (ATLANTO-SAURIDAE) SAUROPODS. APATOSAURUS was the only member of this family, and it is now placed in the new DIPLODOCIDAE family.

ATLANTOSAURUS (at-lan-toh-SAWR-us) "Atlas's Lizard" (Named for Atlas, god of strength in Greek and Latin mythology, + Greek *sauros* = lizard)

Name given to the FOSSILS of the first four-footed dinosaur to be discovered in North America. This dinosaur was originally called TITANOSAURUS, but this name had already been given to another dinosaur, so the name was changed to *At-*

lantosaurus. However, it is known from very fragmentary material. Some think it is the same as APATOSAURUS, but there is not enough material to make a definite identification.

Classification: Sauropoda, Sauropodomorpha, Saurischia

ATLASCOPCOSAURUS (at-las-cop-co-SAWR-us) "Atlas Copco Corporation Lizard" (Named in honor of the corporation that provided equipment for excavation + Greek *sauros* = lizard)

A small, Early Cretaceous HYPSILOPHODONT found in Australia. It is known from fragmentary material including a left upper jaw with TEETH. This two-legged plant eater was probably between 6.5 and 10 feet (2 and 3 m) long.

Classification: Hypsilophodontidae, Ornithopoda, Ornithischia

AUSTROSAURUS (OSS-tro-sawr-us) "Southern Lizard" (Latin *auster* = south + Greek *sauros* = lizard, because it was found in Queensland, Australia)

An Early Cretaceous SAUROPOD. This giant, four-legged plant eater was closely related to CETIOSAURUS and probably resembled that dinosaur. It was probably about the same size— about 50 feet (15 m) long—but its forelegs were slightly longer than those of *Cetiosaurus.* This dinosaur is known from parts of six individuals. It is important because it shows that sauropods were living in Australia in Early Cretaceous times. It may have survived into Late Cretaceous times.

Classification: Sauropoda, Sauropodomorpha, Saurischia

AVACERATOPS (a-vah-SAYR-ah-tops) "Ava's Horned Face" (Named for Ava Cole, wife of discoverer, + Greek *keratops* = horned face)

Avaceratops

A 75-million-year-old Late Cretaceous CERATOPSIAN. It was different from all other known horned dinosaurs. It had a solid FRILL. All others had large openings in their frills. Most of a skull and a large part of the skeleton of a 7.5-foot (2.3-m)-long juvenile were found in Montana in the United States. Adults of this four-legged plant eater may have been 12 feet (3.7 m) long. The juvenile was 3 feet (90 cm) tall and may have weighed 400 pounds (181 kg).

Classification: Ceratopsidae, Ceratopsia, Ornithischia

AVIMIMUS (ay-vih-MY-mus) "Bird Mimic" (Latin *avis* = bird + *mimus* = mimic, because it was birdlike)

A small Late Cretaceous COELUROSAUR discovered in Mongolia. It is known from a nearly complete skeleton. This BIPEDAL DINOSAUR was very birdlike. It had long, slim legs, birdlike FEET, short arms, a stubby TAIL, and a long, slender neck. Suggestive evidence indicates that feathers may have been attached on the arm bones. If this proves to be so, then this creature will be classified as a bird, rather than a dinosaur, because only birds have feathers.

Classification: Coelurosauria?, Theropoda?, Saurischia?

B

BACTROSAURUS (BAK-tro-sawr-us) "Staff Lizard" (Greek *baktron* = staff + *sauros* = lizard, because it was the staff, or beginning, of a new line of dinosaurs)

One of the earliest known HADROSAURS (duck-billed dinosaurs). It is known from a nearly complete skeleton and a partial skull. Although we don't know what the top of its head looked like, scientists think that *Bactrosaurus* was close to (if not the) ancestor of the hollow-crested duckbills (the LAMBEOSAURINES. It had robust limbs, high SPINES on its pelvic vertebrae, and other features that are similar to those of the lambeosaurines. This BIPEDAL plant eater evolved in Mongolia about the middle of the CRETACEOUS PERIOD.

Bactrosaurus was 13 feet (4 m) long and 6.5 feet (2 m) tall at the hips. It had fewer teeth than later hadrosaurs.

Classification: Hadrosauridae, Ornithopoda, Ornithischia

BAGACERATOPS (bah-gah-SAYR-ah-tops) "Small Horned Face" (Mongolian *baga* = small + Greek *keratops* = horned face, referring to its overall SIZE)

Bagaceratops

A tiny Late Cretaceous PROTOCERATOPSIAN. This four-legged plant eater was only 3 feet (90 cm) long. It had a small HORN on its nose and a short, solid FRILL, or shield, that protected its neck. Its FOSSILS were found in Mongolia.

Classification: Protoceratopsidae, Ceratopsia, Ornithischia

BAHARIASAURUS (bah-ha-REE-ah-sawr-us) "Baharija Lizard" (Named for Baharija Oasis, near where it was found, + Greek *sauros* = lizard)

Name given to a few bones of a large CARNOSAUR found in Late Cretaceous deposits in Egypt. This BIPEDAL meat eater belonged to the same family as MEGALOSAURUS and probably resembled that dinosaur.

Classification: Carnosauria, Theropoda, Saurischia

BARAPASAURUS (bah-RAH-pah-sawr-us) "Big-leg Lizard" (Indian *bara* = big or massive + *pa* = leg + Greek *sauros* = lizard, referring to the size of the leg bone)

One of the earliest known SAUROPODS. This giant four-legged

plant eater was only slightly smaller than DIPLODOCUS. Unlike most sauropods, it had rather slender limbs. Its TEETH were spoon-shaped. It probably resembled CAMARASAURUS or DIPLODOCUS in shape. It is known from well-preserved material of at least eight or nine individuals. These specimens varied greatly in SIZE, the largest being nearly twice as large as the smallest, suggesting that YOUNG and older animals HERDED together. These FOSSILS were found in Early Jurassic sediments in India.

Classification: Sauropoda, Sauropodomorpha, Saurischia

BAROSAURUS (BAHR-o-sawr-us) "Heavy Lizard" (Greek *baros*

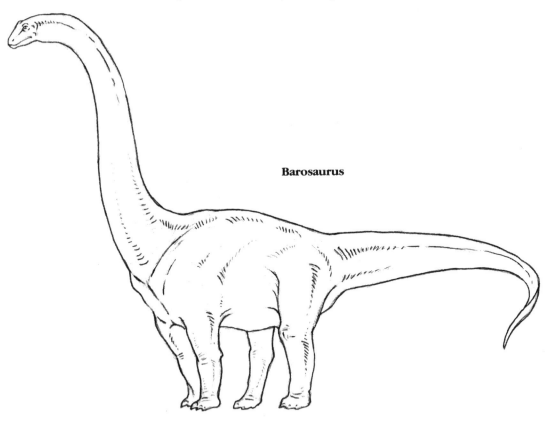

Barosaurus

= weighty, heavy + *sauros* = lizard, referring to its heavy neck bones)

A SAUROPOD that resembled DIPLODOCUS. *Barosaurus* was the same overall length as *Diplodocus* but had a shorter TAIL and a longer neck. This four-legged plant eater measured 90 feet (27 m) from its snout to the tip of its tail. Its neck was 30 feet (9 m) long. *Barosaurus* lived in western North America and East Africa in Late Jurassic times. Three nearly complete skeletons have been found at the Dinosaur National Monument in Utah. Seven GASTROLITHS were found with the bones of one specimen, giving evidence that these animals swallowed FOOD whole and swallowed stones to grind it up.

Classification: Sauropoda, Sauropodomorpha, Saurischia

BARSBOLDIA (bahrz-BOHL-dee-ah) "Barsbold's dinosaur" (Named in honor of Russian PALEONTOLOGIST Rinchen Barsbold)

A 40-foot (12-m)-long Late Cretaceous LAMBEOSAURINE HADROSAUR. This duckbill lived in Central Asia, in what is now the U.S.S.R. It weighed 11 tons (10 metric tons) and was one of the largest-known duckbills. It had a long, hollow tube on top of its head. It walked on two legs and ate plants.

Classification: Hadrosauridae, Ornithopoda, Ornithischia

BARYONYX (bahr-ee-ON-iks) "Strong Claw" (Greek *bary* = heavy, strong + *onyx* = talon, claw, referring to a large CLAW, the first piece that was found)

A large Early Cretaceous THEROPOD discovered in Surrey, England. It is known from about 70 percent of a complete skeleton, including a 12-inch (30.5-cm) claw. *Baryonyx* had a long neck, a long, crocodilelike snout with a CREST on top, and 128 finely serrated TEETH (twice as many as any other

Baryonyx

theropod). Scientists think that *Baryonyx* may have eaten fish, perhaps snatching them from the bank with its long claw. This dinosaur may have been 30 feet (9 m) long, 12 feet (3.7 m) tall on its hind legs, and weighed 1.5 tons (1.4 metric tons).

Classification: Carnosauria, Theropoda, Saurischia

BAVARISAURUS (bah-VAR-ih-sawr-us) "Bavaria Lizard" (Named for Bavaria in Germany, where it was found, + Greek *sauros* = lizard)

Not a DINOSAUR, but a small, fast-running ground lizard of Late Jurassic Germany. This animal had a very long tail and short forelimbs. It probably ran on two legs. A nearly complete specimen of this lizard was found within the skeleton of a COMPSOGNATHUS. It was once thought that this skeleton was an unborn baby *Compsognathus*. We now know it was the last dinner of the little dinosaur, giving proof that *Compsognathus* preyed on small lizards.

BELLUSAURUS (bel-oo-SAWR-us) "Beautiful Lizard" (Latin *bellus* = beautiful + Greek *sauros* = lizard)

A small (possibly juvenile) Middle Jurassic SAUROPOD known from a nearly complete skeleton and 17 individuals found in China. Like those of CAMARASAURUS, the forelegs of this plant eater were the same as its hind legs. This four-legged, long-necked, long-tailed dinosaur may have held its TAIL extended. It was a little over 15 feet (4.8 m) tall.

Classification: Sauropoda, Sauropodomorpha, Saurischia

Beringia (ber-INJ-ee-ah) (Named after the land bridge that spanned the Bering Strait)

During the CRETACEOUS PERIOD, the western part of North America was separated from the eastern part of the continent by a wide, shallow sea. However, the western part of North America was connected with the eastern part of Asia. This land mass is called Beringia.

biped (BY-ped) "two feet" (Latin *bi-* = two + *ped-* = foot)

Any animal that stands or walks on its two hind legs. BIPEDAL means "two-footed." THEROPODS were bipeds; so were ORNITHOPODS such as HADROSAURS and IGUANODONTS. Human beings and birds are also bipeds. Compare with QUADRUPED.

bipedal

See BIPED.

bird-hipped dinosaurs

See ORNITHISCHIANS.

BLIKANASAURUS (blih-KAN-ah-sawr-us) "Blikana Lizard" (Named for Blikana Mountain in South Africa, where it was found, + Greek *sauros* = lizard)

A Late Triassic PROSAUROPOD known only from a partial hind leg and foot. It was related to MELANOROSAURUS, but its legs and FEET were much more robust than those of *Melanoro-saurus*. Extremely stocky limbs indicate a heavily built animal similar to the later sauropods, but it probably was not ancestral to sauropods, because it had five toes. Its fifth toe was much smaller than the other four. *Blikanasaurus* ate plants and walked on four legs.

Classification: Prosauropoda, Sauropodomorpha, Saurischia

BOROGOVIA (bor-o-GOHV-ee-ah) (Named for the borogoves in Lewis Carroll's *Through the Looking Glass)*

A small THEROPOD of the TROÖDONTID family. It was found in Late Cretaceous deposits of Mongolia and is known from a distinctive partial foot.

Classification: Coelurosauria, Theropoda, Saurischia

BOTHRIOSPONDYLUS (bah-three-o-SPON-dih-lus) "Trench Vertebra" (Greek *bothrio-* = little trench + Latin *spondylus* = vertebra, referring to the grooves in its vertebrae)

A large Late Jurassic SAUROPOD. This four-legged plant eater was similar to CAMARASAURUS. Its forelegs were about as long as its hind legs. It is estimated that this dinosaur was about 65 feet (19.8 m) long. It had large TEETH and, like all sauropods, had a long neck and TAIL. It is known only from a few teeth and vertebrae. Its FOSSILS have been found in England and Madagascar.

Classification: Sauropoda, Sauropodomorpha, Saurischia

brachiosaurids or **Brachiosauridae** (brak-ee-o-SAWR-ih-dee) "Arm Lizard" (Named after BRACHIOSAURUS) Sometimes called CAMARASAURIDAE.

A family of SAUROPODS with spatulate (or spoon-shaped) TEETH and forelimbs as long as or longer than the hind. Dinosaurs in this group had only four vertebrae in their pelvic area. These plant eaters were the largest of the dinosaurs—some may have been as much as 100 feet (30.5 m) long or more. Brachiosauridae lived worldwide during Jurassic and Cretaceous times. This family is divided into four subfamilies: CETIOSAURINAE, BRACHIOSAURINAE, CAMARASAURINAE, and EUHELOPODINAE. It has been proposed that these subfamilies be raised to family status. A study is being made to do that.

Brachiosaurinae (brak-ee-o-SAWR-ih-nee) "Arm Lizards" (Named after BRACHIOSAURUS)

A subfamily of BRACHIOSAURID SAUROPODS. In this group the forelegs were longer than the hind. They lived in North America, Europe, Africa, and Asia. BOTHRIOSPONDYLUS, BRACHIOSAURUS, PLEUROCOELUS, REBBACHISAURUS, ZIGONGOSAURUS, and possibly ULTRASAURUS were members of this subfamily. This subfamily may soon be raised to the family level.

brachiosaurs (BRAK-ee-o-sawrs) "Arm Lizards" (Named after BRACHIOSAURUS)

Same as BRACHIOSAURIDS or BRACHIOSAURINAE. This is just a shortened form of the other two names.

BRACHIOSAURUS (BRAK-ee-o-sawr-us) "Arm Lizard" (Greek *brachion* = arm + *sauros* = lizard, referring to its long forelegs)

A gigantic Jurassic SAUROPOD, one of the largest known land animals. A complete skeleton found in Tanzania, now at the Humboldt University Natural History Museum in East Berlin, stands 40 feet (12 m) tall—taller than a four-story building—and is 85 feet (26 m) long. A live *Brachiosaurus* probably

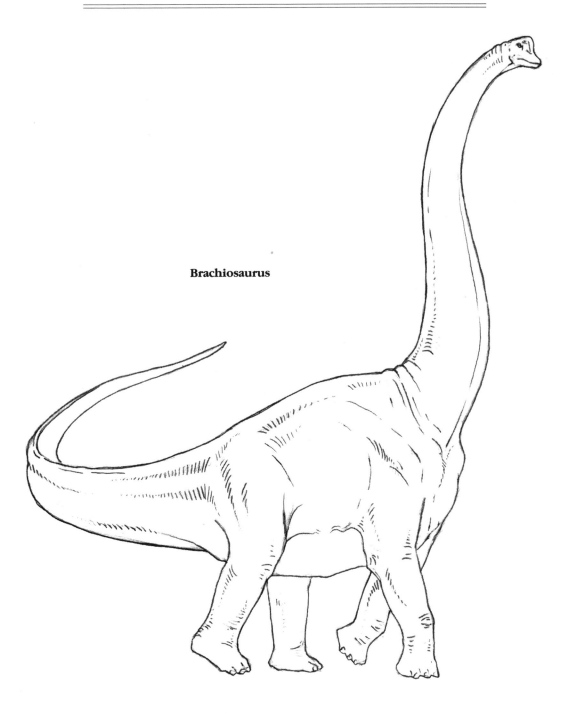

Brachiosaurus

weighed 70 or 80 tons (63.5 to 72.6 metric tons). Its body was more massive than that of any other sauropod. Its neck was 28 feet (8.5 m) long, but its TAIL was short. Unlike most sauropods, *Brachiosaurus* had longer forelegs than hind legs. Its shoulders towered 19 feet (5.8 m) above the ground—higher than a giraffe is tall.

This four-legged dinosaur roamed the forests of the Jurassic world, eating the tops from tall trees. Contrary to popular belief, it could not have lived in deep water—it would not have been able to breathe. The pressure of the water on its lungs would have been too great.

The remains of *Brachiosaurus* have been found in the western United States as well as in Africa and Europe.

Classification: Sauropoda, Sauropodomorpha, Saurischia

BRACHYCERATOPS (brak-ee-SAYR-ah-tops) "Short Horned Face" (Greek *brachy-* = short + *keratops* = horned face, because it was a short-faced CERATOPSIAN)

Name given to the FOSSILS of five small, short-frilled ceratopsians that were found together in Montana. These horned dinosaurs were only 6 feet (1.8 m) long, and are believed to be juveniles. It was first thought that they were young specimens of CENTROSAURUS or MONOCLONIUS, but then a few bones and the skull of an adult ceratopsian were found near the same site. The bones of the adult were nearly twice as large as those of the five juveniles. The adult represented a new GENUS. It had a very large HORN on its nose, short brow horns, and a short, knobbed FRILL. The horns and frills of the juveniles more closely resembled those of the adult than those of *Centrosaurus* or *Monoclonius* and were therefore assigned to the same genus.

Finding five half-grown ceratopsians together near an adult suggests to some scientists that the YOUNG may have received

Brachyceratops

some kind of PARENTAL CARE.

These four-legged plant eaters lived during Late Cretaceous times.

Classification: Ceratopsidae, Ceratopsia, Ornithischia

BRACHYLOPHOSAURUS (brak-ee-LOH-fo-sawr-us) "Short-crested Lizard" (Greek *brachy-* = short + *lophos* = crest + *sauros* = lizard, referring to its small crest)

A Late Cretaceous HADROSAUR (duck-billed dinosaur). *Brachylophosaurus* had a small hump on its nose and a small, thin, bony CREST over the top of its head. It belonged to the HADROSAURINE group of hadrosaurs. This two-legged plant eater was about 16.5 feet (5 m) tall, and, like all hadrosaurs, it ran with its body horizontal and its TAIL extended for balance. *Brachylophosaurus* lived in forests, browsing on leaves and flowering plants. It is known from fairly complete material found in Alberta, Canada.

Classification: Hadrosauridae, Ornithopoda, Ornithischia

brains

Scientists have not found DINOSAUR brains, but they know how large some of them were. Casts formed when mud filled the brain cavities of dead dinosaurs are almost the same size and shape as the dinosaurs' brains. These casts also show the roots of nerves in the brains and help us to understand how well a particular dinosaur could smell or hear. (See SENSORY PERCEPTION.)

Most dinosaurs (like modern REPTILES) had rather small brains in comparison to their body SIZE. The brains of huge SAUROPODS, for example, were only about the size of a modern dog's brain. STEGOSAURUS had a ridiculously small brain. It was only the size of a golf ball and was the smallest, in comparison to the size of the animal, of all the dinosaurs' brains. However, sauropods and *Stegosaurus* were specially adapted to get along without large brains. Each animal had an enlargement in the spinal cord in the region of its hips. This nerve center was larger than the brain itself, and it controlled the dinosaur's hind legs and tail. (This nerve center has sometimes been called a second brain, but it was not.) The brains of ANKYLOSAURS were probably small also, because they had small heads.

Not all dinosaurs had tiny brains. The brains of CERATOPSIANS and THEROPODS were relatively large. Of all the dinosaurs, the DROMAEOSAURIDS ("emu lizards") had the largest brains, in comparison to their body size. The brain of STENONYCHOSAURUS was seven times as large as the brain of any living ARCHOSAUR of similar body weight. Its brain was larger than that of an ostrich, and it was probably at least as intelligent as an ostrich. (Also see INTELLIGENCE.)

The brains of ORNITHOPODS were somewhat larger than those of the ankylosaurs and the ceratopsians.

brontosaurs (BRON-toh-sawrz) "Thunder Lizards" (Named after BRONTOSAURUS)

Another name for SAUROPODS, the largest land animals that ever lived. Any giant, four-legged, plant-eating, land-dwelling

SAURISCHIAN dinosaur may be called a brontosaur. These dinosaurs are also sometimes called CETIOSAURS.

BRONTOSAURUS (BRON-to-sawr-us) "Thunder Lizard" (Greek *bronte* = thunder + *sauros* = lizard, perhaps because its discoverer thought its footfalls would have been thunderous)

The best-known of the dinosaurs. Its correct name is APATOSAURUS, because that name was given first. The FOSSIL bones that were named *Apatosaurus,* in 1877, belong to the same kind of animal as those discovered later, in 1879, and named *Brontosaurus.*

Classification: Sauropoda, Sauropodomorpha, Saurischia

C

CALLOVOSAURUS (cal-LOH-vo-sawr-us) "Callovian Lizard" (Named for the Callovian Rock Formation, from which it was recovered, + Greek *sauros* = lizard)

An ORNITHOPOD of the CAMPTOSAURID family. It lived during Middle Jurassic times in England. This BIPEDAL plant eater was about 9 feet (2.7 m) long and possibly weighed 125 pounds (56.7 kg). It is known from incomplete material and was once thought to be a species of CAMPTOSAURUS.

Classification: Iguanodontidae or Camptosauridae, Ornithopoda, Ornithischia

camarasaurids or **Camarasauridae** (kam-ah-rah-SAWR-ih-dee) "Chambered Lizards" (Named after CAMARASAURUS) Also commonly called CAMARASAURS.

A name sometimes used for the family of spatulate-toothed (spoon-shaped TEETH) SAUROPODS whose forelimbs were as long as or longer than the hind legs. This group is more frequently called the BRACHIOSAURIDAE.

Camarasaurinae (kam-ah-rah-SAWR-ih-nee) "Chambered Lizards" (Named after CAMARASAURUS) Sometimes called CA-MARASAURS.

A subfamily of BRACHIOSAURID SAUROPODS whose forelimbs and hind limbs were nearly equal. Their skulls were large, but the snouts were shorter than those of other sauropods. The necks and TAILS were relatively shorter. These four-legged plant eaters were from 30 to 60 feet (9 to 18 m) long. They lived in North America and Europe from the JURASSIC to the Middle EARLY CRETACEOUS PERIODS. *Camarasaurus* is the only certainly known member of this family.

camarasaurs (KAM-ah-rah-sawrz)
A name commonly used in the place of CAMARASAURIDAE or CAMARASAURINAE.

CAMARASAURUS (KAM-ah-rah-sawr-us) "Chambered Lizard" (Greek *kamara* = chamber + *sauros* = lizard, referring to the holes in its vertebrae)

The most common SAUROPOD in North America during Middle and Late Jurassic times. It also lived in Europe, where it survived into Early Cretaceous times. *Camarasaurus* was one of the smallest sauropods. Its neck was shorter, and its TAIL was *much* shorter, than those of most sauropods; but the tail was more powerful than the tails of other sauropods. *Camarasaurus* grew to be 30 to 60 feet (9 to 18 m) long and

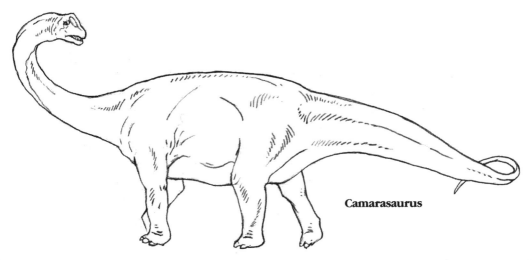

Camarasaurus

15 feet (4.6 m) high at the hips. There were holes in the vertebrae to lighten the weight of the backbone. Its forelegs were nearly as long as its hind legs, making the back almost level. The head of this plant eater was larger and shorter than those of most sauropods. Many skeletons of this dinosaur have been found in the western United States. A complete skeleton of a 17-foot (5.2-m)-long juvenile in nearly perfect condition was found in Utah.

Classification: Sauropoda, Sauropodomorpha, Saurischia

camptosaurids or **Camptosauridae** (kamp-to-SAWR-ih-dee) "Bent Lizards" (Named after CAMPTOSAURUS) Also called CAMP-TOSAURS.

A family of ORNITHOPODS sometimes listed as a subfamily of IGUANODONTS. Their forelegs were much shorter than the hind legs, but they were stout, and the five-fingered HANDS were strong. This makes scientists believe that although these plant eaters were basically BIPEDAL, they probably grazed on all fours. The FEET had four toes. Both fingers and toes were tipped with hooflike nails. Camptosaurid snouts ended in horny beaks. Camptosaurids were very common in North America from Middle Jurassic to Early Cretaceous times. They also lived in England. They ranged from turkey size up to 17 feet (5.2 m). Camptosaurids were quite similar to iguanodonts and were possibly ancestors of that dinosaur family. Two GENERA of Camptosauridae are known: CALLOVOSAURUS and CAMPTOSAURUS.

camptosaurs (KAMP-to-sawrz)
A shortened version commonly used for CAMPTOSAURIDS.

CAMPTOSAURUS (KAMP-to-sawr-us) "Bent Lizard" (Greek *kamptos* = bent + *sauros* = lizard, because when it grazed on all fours, its body had to have been bent)

An early ORNITHOPOD (a two-legged, plant-eating ORNITHISCHIAN). It was an ancestor of the HADROSAURS (duck-billed dinosaurs). Large numbers lived in North America and Europe during the JURASSIC PERIOD, and a few may have lived until Early Cretaceous times. There were many species of *Camp-*

Camptosaurus

tosaurus. Their SIZES ranged from that of a turkey to 17 feet (5.2 m) long and 7 feet (2 m) tall at the hips. This plant eater usually walked on two legs with its body held horizontally, but probably grazed on all fours. Although the forelegs were quite short, they were strong. The HANDS had five fingers, and the snout ended in a horny beak. Many skeletons have been found in Wyoming, Colorado, and Utah.

Classification: Iguanodontidae? or Camptosauridae?, Ornithopoda, Ornithischia

CARCHARODONTOSAURUS　(kar-kar-o-DON-to-sawr-us) "Sharp-toothed Lizard" (Greek *karcharo-* = sharp-pointed + *odonto-* = teeth = *sauros* = lizard)

An Early Cretaceous CARNOSAUR whose FOSSILS were found in Northern Africa. This two-legged meat eater is known only from a few bones and TEETH. It probably resembled MEGALOSAURUS, but it was somewhat smaller—about 26 feet (8 m) long. It had elongated SPINES on its neck vertebrae that may have served as places of attachment for the extra-strong muscles needed to hold up its enormous head. Its teeth were less curved than those of most carnosaurs.

Classification: Carnosauria, Theropoda, Saurischia

carnivore (KAR-nih-vohr) "Meat eater" (Latin *carn-* = flesh + *vorare* = to devour)

Any animal that eats mainly meat. Modern cats, dogs, and bears are carnivores. Carnivores have large, sharp teeth and powerful jaws. Some may, on occasion, eat plant food such as berries or grass. COELUROSAURS and CARNOSAURS were meat-eating (carnivorous) dinosaurs. Compare HERBIVORE; OMNIVORE.

carnivorous (kar-NIV-ohr-us)

See CARNIVORE.

carnosaurs or **Carnosauria** (kar-no-SAWR-ee-ah) "Meat-eating Lizards" (Latin *carn-* = flesh + Greek *sauros* = lizard)

The infraorder of large THEROPODS. All were BIPEDAL meat eaters; all had huge skulls, short necks, heavy bones, chicken-like FEET, powerful TAILS, knifelike TEETH, and (except for the DEINOCHEIRIDS) short front legs. Some scientists think that carnosaurs may have been ENDOTHERMIC (warm-blooded). Carnosaurs lived from Late Triassic to Late Cretaceous times. They have been found on every continent except Antarctica.

There is not complete agreement on how carnosaurs should be divided. In the past, they were divided into four families: MEGALOSAURIDAE, SPINOSAURIDAE, DEINOCHEIRIDAE, and TYRANNOSAURIDAE.

Many scientists think that the Deinocheiridae should be classed as an infraorder rather than as a family of carnosaurs because, unlike all other carnosaurs, they had very long arms and huge CLAWS on their fingers. They have been found only in Cretaceous deposits in Mongolia. Only two are known— DEINOCHEIRUS and THERIZINOSAURUS.

It seems that any carnosaur that could not specifically be identified as belonging to one of the other families was placed in the Megalosauridae. Most of these were known from very fragmentary material. However, many dinosaurs once classed as megalosaurids are now much better known and have been placed in families of their own. Members left in this family ranged from 25 to 30 feet (7.6 to 9 m) long and had massive heads and three or more fingers. Some had elongated SPINES on their vertebrae, but the spines were not as long as those of the SPINOSAURIDS. They lived during the JURASSIC and CRETACEOUS PERIODS in Europe, North America, Africa, Asia, South America, and Madagascar.

Three new families of carnosaurs have been formed from dinosaurs once classed as megalosaurids. The TERATOSAURIDAE—the earliest known carnosaurs—lived in Europe and South America during the TRIASSIC PERIOD. TERATOSAURUS is the best-known of this group. The ALLOSAURIDAE had strong, heavy bodies; large, narrow skulls; strong brow ridges; and three-fingered HANDS. They lived in North America and Asia during Late Jurassic and Early Cretaceous times. ACROCANTHOSAURUS, ALLOSAURUS, and CHILANTAISAURUS are examples of this family. The CERATOSAURIDAE had four fingers and a HORN on the nose. CERATOSAURUS from Late Jurassic North America is the only known member of this family.

The Tyrannosauridae represent the culmination of carnosaur evolution. (See EVOLVE.) These dinosaurs had very short arms and only two fingers on their hands. They first appeared in Mongolia during the early part of Late Cretaceous times. However, most tyrannosaurids lived during the latter part of the Late Cretaceous Period. They have been found in east Asia, western North America, and India. ALBERTOSAURUS, DASPLETOSAURUS, TARBOSAURUS, and TYRANNOSAURUS were Tyrannosauridae.

The Spinosauridae had very long SPINES on their vertebrae—some up to 6 feet (1.8 m) long. These spines may have supported a SKIN fold shaped like a fin that ran along the dinosaur's back. The spinosaurids lived in North Africa during the Cretaceous Period. SPINOSAURUS is the best-known of these. Although some scientists place ALTISPINAX in this family group, it is so poorly known at this time that most scientists place it with the MEGALOSAURS.

Many recent discoveries do not fit neatly into any of these families, and each has been placed in a family of its own.

CARNOTAURUS (kahrn-o-TAWR-us) "Meat-eating Bull" (Latin *carn-* = flesh + *taurus* = bull, referring to its unusual bulllike horns)

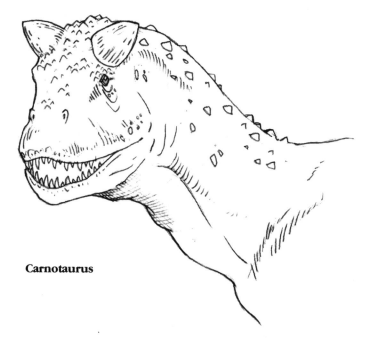

Carnotaurus

A large Late Cretaceous THEROPOD from Patagonia, Argentina, known from a nearly complete skeleton and excellent SKIN impressions. The impressions of the pebbly skin are the first ever found of a meat-eating dinosaur. *Carnotaurus* had a short snout and two large, bull-like HORNS on its head. This two-legged dinosaur was about 40 feet (12.2 m) long. It is a close relative of ABELISAURUS.

Classification: Carnosauria, Theropoda, Saurischia

CATHETOSAURUS (ka-THET-o-sawr-us) "Upright Lizard"

(Greek *kathetos* = perpendicular, upright + *sauros* = lizard, because the finder believed it could rear up on its hind legs)

A 30-foot (9-m)-long SAUROPOD closely resembling CAMARASAURUS found in Late Jurassic deposits of Colorado. This dinosaur is known from an almost complete skeleton, missing only the skull, hind limbs, left forefoot, and end of the TAIL. It had specialized structures in its spine and pelvis that may have enabled it to stand on its hind legs. The skeleton shows TOOTH marks of both large and small CARNIVOROUS dinosaurs.

Classification: Sauropoda, Sauropodomorpha, Saurischia

Cenozoic (sen-o-ZOH-ik) **Era** "New Life" (Greek *kaino-* = new + *zoikos* = life)

The "age of mammals"—the geological age following the MESOZOIC ERA. It began 65 million years ago and continues to the present. This is the time during which mammals became dominant. It is the era in which we are living.

CENTROSAURUS (SEN-tro-sawr-us) "Horned Lizard" (Greek *kentron* = sharp point, spur + *sauros* = lizard, because of the horn on its nose)

Centrosaurus

A CERATOPSIAN (horned dinosaur) of Late Cretaceous North America. This four-legged plant eater was very similar to MONOCLONIUS, but the 18-inch (46-cm) HORN on its nose curved forward rather than to the rear as did the horn of *Monoclonius*. Its FRILL was knobbed, and in the center of the back edge there were two long, hooklike projections. Some scientists consider this dinosaur a species of *Monoclonius*. Eighteen separate individuals have been found in Alberta, Canada, suggesting that ceratopsians traveled in large HERDS.

Classification: Ceratopsidae, Ceratopsia, Ornithischia

CERATOPS (SAYR-ah-tops) "Horned Face" (Greek *kerat-* = horned + *ops* = face, referring to the horns)

Name given to a pair of small brow HORNS found in Late Cretaceous rocks in Montana. *Ceratops* is probably a juvenile specimen of another CERATOPSIAN.

Classification: Ceratopsidae, Ceratopsia, Ornithischia

ceratopsians or **Ceratopsia** (sayr-ah-TOP-see-ah) "Horned Faces" (Named after CERATOPS)

The suborder of ORNITHISCHIAN dinosaurs with HORNS on their faces. Ceratopsians resembled rhinoceroses and possibly ran like them. However, ceratopsians had neck FRILLS, or shields, and much longer and heavier TAILS than rhinoceroses. Some ceratopsians were pig size; others were quite large. They probably ate CYCAD and palm leaves, nipping off leaves with their parrotlike beaks and chopping them up with their scissorlike TEETH.

There were three families of ceratopsians: the PSITTACOSAURIDAE, the PROTOCERATOPSIDAE, and the CERATOPSIDAE. The Psittacosauridae were the most primitive group and are thought to be the ancestors of all ceratopsians. They had parrotlike beaks, large heads, and the faintest hint of a frill. They were mainly BIPEDAL. The Protoceratopsidae were almost completely QUADRUPEDAL and were the smallest of the four-legged ceratopsians. They had very small horns on their noses or none at all. They had very short neck frills. There were two kinds of Ceratopsidae. Some had short nose horns, long brow horns, and long frills. Others had long nose horns, short brow horns, and short frills.

The Ceratopsians seem to have EVOLVED in Mongolia. They were the last group of dinosaurs to evolve and were among the last to become extinct. (See EXTINCTION.) Most of these Late Cretaceous dinosaurs have been found in North America, but a few kinds have been found in Mongolia. PROTOCERATOPS, MONOCLONIUS, STYRACOSAURUS, TOROSAURUS, and TRICERATOPS are some of the best-known of this group.

ceratopsids or **Ceratopsidae** (sayr-ah-TOP-sih-dee) "Horned Faces" (Named after CERATOPS)

A family of the CERATOPSIA (horned dinosaurs). Members of this family had HORNS on either their snouts or their brows, and sometimes on both. They had FRILLS extending back over their necks. These four-legged plant eaters were from 12 to 25 feet (3.5 to 7.5 m) long. They lived in North America during the Late CRETACEOUS PERIOD. There were two kinds of ceratopsids. One group, the short-frilled ceratopsians, had short shields that did not reach the shoulders, long nose horns, and short brow horns. BRACHYCERATOPS, CENTROSAURUS, MONOCLONIUS, PACHYRHINOSAURUS, and STYRACOSAURUS were members of this group. Long-frilled ceratopsians had shields that extended back to or over the shoulders, short nose horns,

and long brow horns. ANCHICERATOPS, ARRHINOCERATOPS, CHAS-
MOSAURUS, PENTACERATOPS, and TOROSAURUS were members of
this group.

CERATOSAURUS (sayr-AT-o-sawr-us) "Horned Lizard" (Greek
kerat- = horned + *sauros* = lizard, referring to its nose
horn)

A 20-foot (6-m) Jurassic CARNOSAUR. It was related to ALLO-
SAURUS and resembled that dinosaur, but it had a bladelike
HORN on its nose, and four-fingered HANDS. *Ceratosaurus* is
the only known SAURISCHIAN with a horn. Like *Allosaurus,*
Ceratosaurus had a huge head, saberlike TEETH, bony knobs
above its eyes, and short front legs. This powerful hunter
walked on two legs with its long, heavy TAIL extended to bal-
ance its head. Its FOSSILS have been found in western North
America and in Tanzania. A complete skeleton was found in
Colorado.

Classification: Carnosauria, Theropoda, Saurischia

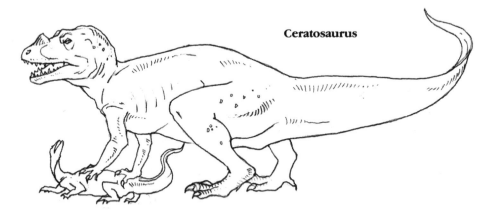

Ceratosaurus

CETIOSAURISCUS (seet-ee-o-sawr-ISS-kus) "Whalelike Lizard" (Modified from CETIOSAURUS, because it was once thought
to be a species of *Cetiosaurus*)

Cetiosauriscus

A Late Jurassic SAUROPOD. It was a relative of DIPLODOCUS, and like that dinosaur, it probably had a long neck and a long whiplike TAIL. It grew to be 50 feet (15 m) long and weighed about 10 tons (9 metric tons). Its incomplete skeleton was found in England. It was a four-legged plant eater.

Classification: Sauropoda, Sauropodomorpha, Saurischia

cetiosaurs or **Cetiosaurinae** (seet-ee-o-SAWR-ih-nee) "Whale Lizards" (Named after CETIOSAURUS)

A subfamily of BRACHIOSAURIDAE SAUROPODS. These were the most primitive sauropods. They lived from Early Jurassic to Early Cretaceous times and have been found in Europe, South America, North America, Africa, and Australia. They ranged in size from 45 to 72 feet (13.7 to 22 m) long. Their forelegs and hind legs were nearly equal in length. AMYGDALODON, AUSTROSAURUS, CETIOSAURUS, HAPLOCANTHOSAURUS, OHMDENOSAURUS, PATAGOSAURUS, and VOLKHEIMERIA were cetiosaurs.

CETIOSAURUS (SEET-ee-o-sawr-us) "Whale Lizard" (Greek *keteio-* = sea monster + *sauros* = lizard, because of its size and supposed marine habitat)

A very early Middle Jurassic SAUROPOD from England, Europe, and Africa. It was the first giant four-legged plant-eating SAURISCHIAN discovered. It resembled its relative CAMARASAURUS, but its vertebrae were spongy instead of hollow as were those of later sauropods. It was 45 feet (13.7 m) long and weighed about 10 tons (9 metric tons). It is known from a partial skeleton.

Classification: Sauropoda, Sauropodomorpha, Saurischia

CHAMPSOSAURUS (KAMP-so-sawr-us) "Crocodile Lizard" (Greek *champsos* = crocodile + *sauros* = lizard, because it resembled a crocodile)

Not a DINOSAUR, but a large EOSUCHIAN. (Eosuchians were sprawling REPTILES that resembled the gavials or crocodiles of today but were more closely related to lizards.) *Champsosaurus* lived in North American freshwater lakes and streams throughout the CRETACEOUS and into the TERTIARY PERIOD. It was 6 to 8 feet (1.8 to 2.5 m) long, and it was a meat eater. It probably ate small dinosaurs.

CHAOYOUNGOSAURUS (chah-o-YAHNG-o-sawr-us) "Chao and Young's Lizard" (Named for Zhao Minchen and Young Chung Chien, now Yang Zhongian, + Greek *sauros* = lizard)

A PACHYCEPHALOSAUR found in Late Jurassic deposits of China. This unusual dome-headed dinosaur is known only from fragments. It is one of the earliest known pachycephalosaurs and has been placed in its own family. *Chaoyoungosaurus* walked on two legs and ate plants.

Classification: Pachycephalosauridae, Ornithopoda or Pachycephalosauria, Ornithischia

CHASMOSAURUS (KAZ-mo-sawr-us) "Opening Lizard" (Latin *chasma* = opening + Greek *sauros* = lizard, referring to the openings in its FRILL)

A medium-size CERATOPSIAN. This horned dinosaur was about 16 feet (4.9 m) long and weighed about 2.5 tons (2.3 metric tons). It had a small HORN on its nose and two fairly long, upward-curving horns on its brow. Very large holes through the bone lightened the weight of the very long FRILL, or shield, that stretched back over the neck and shoulders. These holes are technically called fenestrae. SKIN impressions show that *Chasmosaurus* had rows of buttonlike scales down its back. These scales were 2 inches (5 cm) across. This four-legged plant eater ate ground plants that it cropped with a horny, parrotlike beak. Many FOSSILS of *Chasmosaurus* have been discovered in Late Cretaceous sediments in Alberta, Canada.

Classification: Ceratopsidae, Ceratopsia, Ornithischia

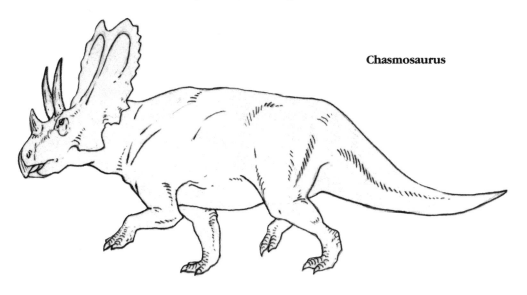

Chasmosaurus

CHENEOSAURUS (KEEN-ee-o-sawr-us) "Goose Lizard" (Greek *chen* = goose + *sauros* = lizard, referring to its gooselike bill)

A small Late Cretaceous HADROSAUR whose FOSSILS were found in Alberta, Canada. This duck-billed dinosaur had a rather large skull and a low, hollow CREST. Some scientists believe it was a young HYPACROSAURUS or LAMBEOSAURUS. Others disagree; they believe it was a different dinosaur. This bipedal plant eater is known only from a skull, some leg bones, and a few vertebrae.

Classification: Hadrosauridae, Ornithopoda, Ornithischia

CHIALINGOSAURUS (chee-ah-LING-o-sawr-us) "Chia-ling Lizard" (Named for the Chia-ling River, near which it was found, + Greek *sauros* = lizard)

A STEGOSAUR (plated dinosaur) that lived in China during Late Jurassic times. It was very similar to KENTROSAURUS but perhaps was an earlier GENUS. It had smaller, more platelike spikes than *Kentrosaurus* and was more slender. Like all stegosaurs, *Chialingosaurus* was a QUADRUPEDAL plant eater. It is known from incomplete material.

Classification: Stegosauridae, Stegosauria, Ornithischia

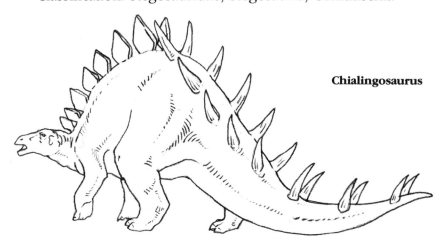

Chialingosaurus

Chilantaisaurus

CHILANTAISAURUS (chee-LAHN-tah-ee-sawr-us) "Chilant'ai Lizard" (Named for Lake Chilant'ai in Inner Mongolia, near which it was found, + Greek *sauros* = lizard)

A CARNOSAUR with great hooked CLAWS and three-fingered HANDS. This large BIPEDAL meat eater was related to, and probably resembled, ALLOSAURUS or CERATOSAURUS; however, it had a less distinct brow ridge than those dinosaurs. *Chilantaisaurus* lived during Late Jurassic and Early Cretaceous times. It is known only from fragments found in Mongolia and China.

Classification: Carnosauria, Theropoda, Saurischia

CHINDESAURUS (chin-deh-SAWR-us) "Chinde Lizard" (Named for the rock formation, Chinde Point, where it was found; Navaho *chinde* = ghost + Greek *sauros* = lizard)

A Late Triassic PROSAUROPOD—the oldest known dinosaur. It was discovered in the Petrified Forest of Arizona, where it lived 225 million years ago. This four-legged plant eater was about the SIZE of a German shepherd dog and weighed about 200 pounds (91 kg). It had a long neck and TAIL and may have been an ancestor of PLATEOSAURUS. It is known from a complete leg, several thighs, ribs, vertebrae, and other bones, possibly from more than one individual.

Classification: Prosauropoda, Sauropodomorpha, Saurischia

CHINGKANKOUSAURUS (ching-KAHNG-ko-sawr-us) "Chingkankou Lizard" (Named for the place in China where it was found + Greek *sauros* = lizard)

Name given to the shoulder blade of a large CARNOSAUR. This bone resembles the shoulder blade of TYRANNOSAURUS. It was found in Late Cretaceous deposits in eastern China. Like all carnosaurs, *Chingkankousaurus* was a BIPEDAL meat eater.

Classification: Carnosauria, Theropoda, Saurischia

CHIROSTENOTES (ky-ROSS-ten-o-teez) "Narrow Hand" (Greek *cheir* = hand + *steno-* = narrow)

A Late Cretaceous COELUROSAUR. It is known from most of a skeleton minus the skull. Its HANDS are similar to those of ORNITHOLESTES but are larger and narrower. The FOSSILS of this small meat eater were found in Alberta, Canada.

Classification: Coelurosauria, Theropoda, Saurischia

CHUBUTISAURUS (choo-VOOT-ih-sawr-us) "Chubut Lizard" (Named for Chubut Province in Argentina, where it was found, + Greek *sauros* = lizard)

A large Late Cretaceous SAUROPOD. It is known only from fragments found in Argentina. It is important because it shows that these huge animals were living in South America in Late Cretaceous days. Like all sauropods, *Chubutisaurus* was a giant four-legged HERBIVORE with a long neck and TAIL.

Classification: Sauropoda, Sauropodomorpha, Saurischia

CLAOSAURUS (CLAY-o-sawr-us) "Broken Lizard" (Greek *klao* = broken + *sauros* = lizard, referring to the position of the skeleton when it was found)

One of the oldest known North American HADROSAURS (duck-billed dinosaurs). It was much smaller than later duckbills—only 12 feet (3.7 m) long. Its unusual FEET and TEETH suggest that this HADROSAURINE (flat-headed hadrosaur) was one of the earliest. The small, pointed teeth were broader than those of later hadrosaurs and were set in single rows rather than in banks. The hind feet had a trace of a first toe, as did the feet of IGUANODONTS.

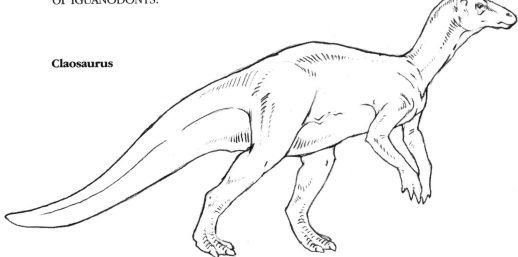

Claosaurus

FOSSILS of *Claosaurus* have been found in Kansas and Wyoming. One complete skeleton found in Kansas shows the animal frozen in what was apparently a running position, with the body held horizontally, the TAIL outstretched, and the head thrown back. This important discovery provided strong evidence that hadrosaurs did run in this position, rather than upright, as had previously been thought. *Claosaurus* was a plant eater. It lived during Late Cretaceous times.

Classification: Hadrosauridae, Ornithopoda, Ornithischia

claws

All dinosaurs had claws of some sort on their FEET and HANDS. The THEROPODS had long, sharp, talonlike claws, similar to those of an eagle. These were on both the hands and the feet. The claws of CARNOSAURS often were quite long, ranging in length from 5 inches (13 cm) to 12 inches (30 cm). These claws were used to capture and hold prey while the enormous TEETH ripped them apart. The DROMAEOSAURIDS such as DEINONYCHUS and VELOCIRAPTOR had a sicklelike claw on each foot. These were used to rip open the bellies of their prey while the finger claws gripped the head or body. *Deinonychus*'s "sickle blade" was 5 inches (13 cm) long. DEINOCHEIRUS had 12-inch (30-cm) claws.

The ORNITHOMIMIDS probably used their bearlike claws to dig up REPTILE EGGS, rip open logs, or rake leaves in search of insects and ground animals.

SAUROPODS had one or more long claws on each forefoot and three or more on their hind feet. These may have been used for digging their bowl-shaped NESTS in sand or mud.

ORNITHISCHIANS had blunt, hooflike claws that served the same purpose as hooves on animals today—to protect the ends of the toes. IGUANODON had a unique spikelike claw on each thumb. It was probably used as a defensive weapon.

COELOPHYSIS (see-lo-FYS-iss) "Hollow Form" (Greek *ko-ilos* = hollow + *physis* = form, referring to its hollow bones)

A Late Triassic COELUROSAUR. This small two-legged meat eater is one of the earliest and most primitive North American THEROPODS known. It was only 10 feet (3 m) long, counting the long, slender TAIL that it carried stretched out behind. It stood 3 feet (90 cm) tall at the hips and weighed about 100 pounds (45 kg). Its head was small, but it had very long

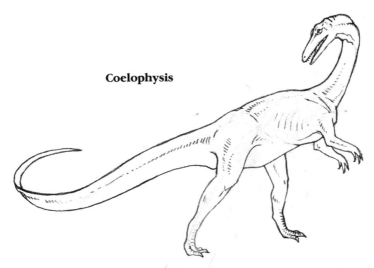

Coelophysis

jaws. The neck was long and slender. The legs were also long and slender; the bones were hollow like those of a bird. The FEET had three long forward-pointing toes and a dewclaw. The arms were short, like those of most other theropods, and the three-fingered HANDS could grip prey.

Some scientists think that *Coelophysis* was warm-blooded because it was apparently an active animal and capable of running very swiftly. *Coelophysis* probably lived in family groups. Whole families—from very small juveniles to adults— have been found together in New Mexico. This seems to indicate that the parents gave some care to their YOUNG. Two adult skeletons were found with the remains of tiny *Coelophysis* skeletons inside their rib cages. This may mean that *Coelophysis* gave birth to live young, but more likely it means that adults sometimes ate the young. Traces of *Coelophysis* have been found in the eastern United States as well as in New Mexico. PODOKESAURUS may be the same as this dinosaur.

Classification: Coelurosauria, Theropoda, Saurischia

coelurids or **Coeluridae** (see-LOOR-ih-dee) "Hollow Tails"
(Named after COELURUS)

   A family of small, lightweight COELUROSAURS. This group were
2.5 to 6 feet (.76 to 1.8 m) long. They had hollow bones;
their forelegs were long and slender. These BIPEDAL meat eaters lived from Late Jurassic to Early Cretaceous times in North
America, England, and possibly Australia. COELURUS, ORNITHO-
LESTES, and MICROVENATOR were members of this family.

coelurosaurs or **Coelurosauria** (see-loor-o-SAWR-ee-ah)
"Hollow-tailed Lizards" (Named after COELURUS + Greek
sauros = lizard, referring to their hollow bones)

   The infraorder of small THEROPODS. Some scientists believe
that these BIPEDAL meat eaters were the ancestors of birds.
They had hollow bones like birds, were fleet-footed, and had
delicate, birdlike builds. Most had three-fingered HANDS. Some
had quite large BRAINS in comparison to their body size, and
these were the most intelligent of the dinosaurs. Some scientists believe that coelurosaurs were ENDOTHERMIC (warm-
blooded).

   Many kinds of coelurosaurs lived throughout the world,
and they existed through most of the MESOZOIC ERA. This was
the longest-lived of all dinosaur groups. Some coelurosaurs
were no larger than a chicken, and others were larger than
ostriches.

   The Coelurosauria have been divided into eight families.
The PROCOMPSOGNATHIDAE were the most primitive group. They
were about 4 feet (1.2 m) long and had four-fingered hands
and four toes. Their necks were long and flexible. They have
been found in Late Triassic Germany. PROCOMPSOGNATHUS is
the best-known member of this family.

The PODOKESAURIDAE were small, very early coelurosaurs. They had short necks and forelegs. Their hands had five fingers. Their hind legs were long. Podokesauridae ranged from cat size to 10 feet (3 m) long or more. This family lived from the very earliest Late Triassic times to very early Jurassic times. They have been found in North America, South America, Africa, Europe, and Asia. COELOPHYSIS, HALTICOSAURUS, and PODOKESAURUS were members of this family, and some people think DILOPHOSAURUS belongs in this family instead of in the CARNOSAURS.

The SEGISAURIDAE were quite similar to the COELURIDAE but were more primitive and had collarbones. Their vertebrae and the long bones of their body were solid instead of hollow. Segisauridae were rabbit size and in many respects resembled THECODONTS. They lived during Late Triassic and Early Jurassic times.

The Coeluridae were small, and lightweight because they had hollow bones. Their front legs were long and slender. Coeluridae ranged from 30 inches to 6 feet (76 cm to 1.8 m). They lived from the Late TRIASSIC to the Early CRETACEOUS PERIODS in North America, South America, England, and possibly Australia. COELURUS, ORNITHOLESTES, and MICROVENATOR are members of this family.

The COMPSOGNATHIDAE had small, pointed heads, flexible necks, hollow bones, and two-fingered hands. They were about the size of a chicken. They lived in Europe in Late Jurassic times. COMPSOGNATHUS is the best-known member of this family.

The ORNITHOMIMIDAE resembled ostriches in shape, but had long TAILS, three toes instead of two, and arms instead of wings. They ranged from ostrich size to 20 feet (6 m) long and lived in North America, Israel, Asia, and Africa in Late Cretaceous times. DROMICEIOMIMUS, GALLIMIMUS, and STRUTHIOMIMUS were members of this family.

The DROMAEOSAURIDAE were advanced coelurosaurs. They had large brains, huge eyes, and sicklelike CLAWS on their inner toes. They were about man size and lived in North America, South America, and Asia during Cretaceous times. DEINONYCHUS, DROMAEOSAURUS, STENONYCHOSAURUS, and VELOCIRAPTOR were members of this family. It has been proposed that this family be raised to infraorder—the DEINONYCHOSAURIA—because they are so different from other Coelurosauria.

The OVIRAPTORIDAE closely resembled birds. They were toothless and were lightly built, with hollow bones. Their skulls were unusually short and deep and had large brain cavities. They were about 5 feet (1.5 m) long and lived during Cretaceous times in Mongolia. OVIRAPTOR is the best-known of this family.

Several new discoveries have been placed in separate families of their own.

COELUROSAURUS (see-LOOR-o-sawr-us) "Hollow Lizard" (Greek *koilos* = hollow + *sauros* = lizard, referring to its hollow bones)

A Late Cretaceous COELUROSAUR, now most often called *Coelosaurus* (SEE-lo-sawr-us). This two-legged meat eater is known only from a few FOSSIL bones found in New Jersey. It may be the same as STRUTHIOMIMUS.

Classification: Coelurosauria, Theropoda, Saurischia

COELURUS (see-LOOR-us) "Hollow Tail" (Greek *koilos* =

hollow + *oura* = tail, referring to the hollow vertebrae in its TAIL)

A small COELUROSAUR of Late Jurassic North America. This BIPEDAL meat eater has long been considered to be the same as ORNITHOLESTES. However, new studies of several more FOSSIL bones of *Coelurus* show that the two are probably different GENERA. The TAIL bones of *Coelurus* were more hollow than those of *Ornitholestes,* and some of the vertebrae and foot bones were longer and more complex.

It is estimated that *Coelurus* was 6 feet (1.8 m) long and 3 feet (90 cm) tall. It is known only from several vertebrae, foot and leg bones, and parts of the pelvis found in Wyoming.

Classification: Coelurosauria, Theropoda, Saurischia

COLORADIA (kohl-oh-RAH-dee-ah) (Named for the Los Colorados Formation of La Roja, Patagonia, Argentina, where it was found)

Coloradia skull

A very early Jurassic or Late Triassic PROSAUROPOD known from a skull and jaws. The skull resembles that of PLATEOSAURUS but was wider at the back, and the snout of this dinosaur was shorter. It has been suggested that this four-legged plant eater may be the adult form of MUSSAURUS, because a baby *Mussaurus* was found in the same formation, but this has not been confirmed.

Classification: Prosauropoda, Sauropodomorpha, Saurischia

coloration

Scientists know almost everything about how dinosaurs looked except their color. They think that some dinosaurs may have been dull greens or browns, similar to living crocodiles and alligators. Some may have been brightly colored like some modern Gila monsters and iguanas. Their SKIN texture was quite similar to that of these animals.

COLUMBOSAURIPUS (ko-lum-bo-SAWR-ih-pus) "Columbian Lizard Foot" (Named for British Columbia, where it was found, + Greek *sauripous* = lizard foot)

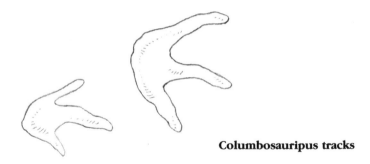

Columbosauripus tracks

Name given to COELUROSAUR footprints found in Early Cretaceous deposits of British Columbia, Canada. The FEET that made these TRACKS had three toes. The toes were tapered and ended in long CLAWS, similar to those of ORNITHOMIMIDS. Only hind feet left tracks, so the animal was obviously BIPEDAL.

COMPSOGNATHUS (komp-SOG-nath-us) "Elegant Jaw" (Greek *kompos* = elegant + *gnathos* = jaw)

One of the smallest known adult dinosaurs. *Compsog-*

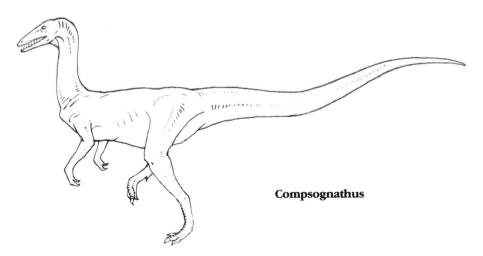

Compsognathus

nathus was about the SIZE of a chicken. Only baby dinosaurs are smaller. This tiny COELUROSAUR lived in Europe during the Late JURASSIC PERIOD. It was BIPEDAL and had long, delicate, birdlike legs; a small, pointed head; and a flexible neck. Like all coelurosaurs, it had hollow bones and was fleet-footed. Its TEETH were sharp, and its short arms were equipped with two-fingered HANDS with which it could catch and hold prey. It probably ate insects and small REPTILES or mouselike mammals. This coelurosaur was very birdlike, and it is possible that it had feathers.

A complete skeleton of *Compsognathus* was found in Germany. It had the skeleton of a smaller reptile within its body. Scientists once believed that this skeleton was a baby *Compsognathus*. It has now been shown that the skeleton was a young BAVARISAURUS—a small, fast-running ground lizard—that was the last meal for the *Compsognathus*. This discovery provides proof of the agility and swiftness of this little predator.

Classification: Coelurosauria, Theropoda, Saurischia

CONCHORAPTOR (konch-o-RAP-tor) "Conch Seizer" (Greek

konche = shell + Latin *rapere* = to seize, because it was assumed that this dinosaur ate mollusks)

A small THEROPOD closely related to OVIRAPTOR. It is known only from a birdlike skull that was 4 inches (10 cm) long. It was found in Late Cretaceous deposits of Mongolia. Its jaws were toothless and it apparently had a horny beak that may have been used to crush mollusks.

Classification: Coelurosauria, Theropoda, Saurischia

CORYTHOSAURUS (ko-RITH-o-sawr-us) "Helmet Lizard" (Greek *korythos* = helmet + *sauros* = lizard, referring to the shape of its CREST)

A LAMBEOSAURINE HADROSAUR. This Late Cretaceous dinosaur measured 30 feet (9.1 m) from the tip of its ducklike bill to the end of its long, heavy TAIL. It weighed 2 to 3 tons (1.8 to 2.7 metric tons). A hollow, helmet-shaped crest adorned its long, narrow head, and hundreds of TEETH lined its jaws. Its SKIN had a pebbly surface, similar to the texture of a football. Three rows of larger bumps, or tubercles, covered the belly.

Corythosaurus

Corythosaurus was a BIPEDAL land dweller and probably a fast runner. It ate twigs, leaves, and pine needles. A nearly complete skeleton has been found in Alberta, Canada.

Classification: Hadrosauridae, Ornithopoda, Ornithischia

crests

Some DINOSAURS and PTEROSAURS had bony crests on their heads. The purpose of these crests is not known.

The best-known crested dinosaurs are the HADROSAURS (the duckbills), but not all hadrosaurs had crests. Among those that did, the crests varied greatly in size and shape. Some were only a small hump, while others were larger and hatchet-shaped, and still others were very long tubes. Some hadrosaur crests were of solid bone while others were hollow.

It was once thought that hollow crests served as snorkels, allowing the animals to hide or travel underwater. But it is now known that they could not have been used for this purpose—there were no openings in the top of them. The nostrils of LAMBEOSAURINES (hollow-crested hadrosaurs) were on the tip of their snouts, just as they were in all other duckbills.

It has also been suggested that the hollow crests were air storage spaces, but the crests were much too small to hold enough air for the lung capacity of these large animals.

More recent theories suggest that the crests were resonating chambers that made the hadrosaurs' voices louder. Or the hollow crests may have improved the animals' sense of smell.

In some lambeosaurines, air passages ran from the nostrils up into the hollow crest before descending into the throat. Some scientists suggest these crests may have been an adaptation that allowed these hadrosaurs to breathe and eat at the same time. Since these animals probably ate almost continuously, this would have been very useful.

Solid crests may simply have marked different species, as the horns of antelope do today. Or they may have been sex characteristics—males having larger crests than females.

DILOPHOSAURUS, a large meat-eating dinosaur, had a double crest. It is the only known THEROPOD with a crest. This crest consisted of two large bladelike ridges that ran lengthwise along the top of its head.

PTERANODON, a PTEROSAUR, had a long crest on the back of its head. This FLYING REPTILE's crest may have been used as a brake when the creature landed, or it may have acted as a rudder. It might have been a sexual characteristic, since some did not have crests.

Cretaceous (kreh-TAY-shus) **Period** (From Latin *creta-* = chalk, referring to the chalk deposits of southeast England, which are of this age)

The last of the three periods of the MESOZOIC ERA. It began about 135 million years ago and ended 65 million years ago. At the end of this geological time interval, the dinosaurs became EXTINCT.

Little is known about the dinosaurs of the first half of the Cretaceous Period. Not many exposed outcroppings of Early Cretaceous rocks containing FOSSILS have been found. It is in the Late Cretaceous deposits that the most dinosaurs have been found.

crocodilians or **Crocodilia** (crok-o-DIL-ee-ah) (From Greek *krokodeilos* = crocodile)

Not dinosaurs, but an order of ARCHOSAURS. This is the order to which modern alligators, crocodiles, and gavials belong. They first appeared in very late Triassic or Early Jurassic times and have continued to live successfully to the present day. The crocodilians were close cousins of dinosaurs. They EVOLVED from the same branch of REPTILES, the THECODONTS. ORNITHISCHIANS and SAURISCHIANS were no more closely related to one another than they were to crocodilians.

cycad or **Cycada** (SY-kad-ah)

The dominant order of plants in the MESOZOIC ERA. It had palmlike crowns from which stems of fernlike leaves grew. It flourished from the TRIASSIC to the CRETACEOUS PERIODS, and one species exists in subtropical areas of the world today. Cycad plants were probably an important part of the diet of some plant-eating dinosaurs.

D

DACENTRURUS (dah-sen-TROO-rus) "Very Spiked Tail" (Greek *da* = very + *kentron* = spike + *oura* = tail, referring to the SPINES on its TAIL) Also called OMOSAURUS.

A Jurassic STEGOSAUR. It was quite similar to STEGOSAURUS,

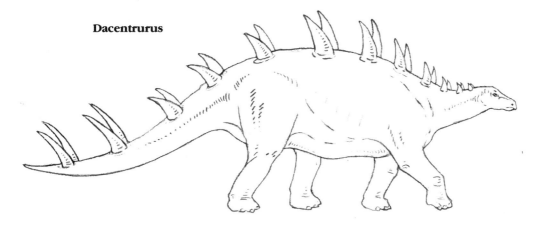

Dacentrurus

Dacentrurus, continued

but it had two rows of huge spikes running along its back and tail instead of plates, and its forelegs were somewhat longer than those of *Stegosaurus*. *Dacentrurus* was also smaller than *Stegosaurus;* it was only 15 feet (4.5 m) long.

This four-legged plant eater is known from a nearly complete skeleton found in England and from other finds in England and Portugal. Dinosaur eggs found in Portugal are thought to be those of this dinosaur.

Classification: Stegosauridae, Stegosauria, Ornithischia

DASPLETOSAURUS (dahs-PLEE-toh-sawr-us) "Frightful Lizard" (Greek *daspletos* = frightful + *sauros* = lizard, because of its fearsome TEETH)

A large Late Cretaceous CARNOSAUR. This two-legged, heavy-bodied dinosaur was a close relative of TYRANNOSAURUS but was not as large. It measured 30 feet (9 m) long and may have weighed 7,000 pounds (3,175 kg). Like *Tyrannosaurus,*

Daspletosaurus

it had very short arms and two-fingered HANDS. A skeleton of this meat eater, lacking only the hind limbs, was found in Alberta, Canada.

Classification: Carnosauria, Theropoda, Saurischia

DATOUSAURUS (DAH-toh-sawr-us) "Lizard from Datou" (Named for the place where it was found + Greek *sauros* = lizard)

This primitive, Middle Jurassic SAUROPOD was more than 45 feet (14 m) long. Its skull was big and heavy but shorter than that of SHUNOSAURUS. The nostrils were in front of the face and the TEETH were spade-shaped. This four-legged plant eater had five toes on each foot. Jaws, vertebrae, a pelvic girdle, leg bones, and the FEET were found in China.

Classification: Sauropoda, Sauropodomorpha, Saurischia

defense

Dinosaurs defended themselves in many ways. The necks of CERATOPSIANS were covered with heavy shields, or FRILLS, and enormous HORNS grew on the brows or snouts. Few predators would have dared to attack them. The spikelike thumbs of IGUANODON may have been defense weapons—perhaps they were used to gouge out the eyes of a CARNO-SAUR.

The ANKYLOSAURS developed the most effective method of protection. Their bodies were encased in bony plates and SPINES from head to TAIL—only their bellies were bare. When threatened, they simply flattened to the ground. They were so huge that it would have been impossible for a predator to turn them over. In addition, some had long spikes on their sides, whereas others had macelike clubs or spikes on the ends of their tails.

The tails of other dinosaurs were also effective defense weapons. STEGOSAURS' tails were armed with long spikes, and the long, whiplike tails of some SAUROPODS could have been very useful in warding off an attacker.

HERDING was probably the most important means of defense for unarmed plant-eating dinosaurs. Herding, along with SPEED, keen EYESIGHT and hearing, and an excellent sense of smell were the only means of defense of the ORNITHOPODS. (See SENSORY PERCEPTION.) SIZE may have been a means of defense for the sauropods.

The THEROPODS probably depended upon speed, good eyesight, superior INTELLIGENCE, and, in some, enormous size to protect them from enemies such as larger carnosaurs, PHYTOSAURS, or crocodiles.

deinocheirids or **Deinocheiridae** (dy-no-KY-rih-dee) "Terrible Hands" (Named after DEINOCHEIRUS)

A family of THEROPODS. Deinocheirids have been found only in Cretaceous deposits of Mongolia. These theropods had very long arms and huge CLAWS on their fingers. They are sometimes listed as a family of CARNOSAURS and sometimes as COELUROSAURS. Only two kinds are known, DEINOCHEIRUS and THERIZINOSAURUS. No one knows how large these dinosaurs were, but they may have been as large as TYRANNOSAURUS or even larger. Some scientists think this group should be a separate infraorder of theropods because they are so different from all other theropods.

DEINOCHEIRUS (dy-no-KY-rus) "Terrible Hand" (Greek *deinos* = terrible + *cheir* = hand, because its HANDS were huge and had vicious CLAWS)

A gigantic Late Cretaceous CARNIVORE with arms and hands

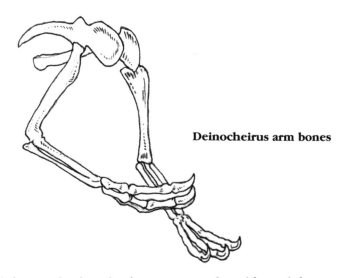

Deinocheirus arm bones

9 feet (3 m) long. The hands alone were 2 feet (60 cm) long, and each had three enormous fingers capable of grasping and holding prey. We know that *Deinocheirus* was BIPEDAL, because its forelimbs could not have been used for walking. Each finger was armed with a terrible, 8- to 12-inch (20- to 30-cm) hooklike claw. *Deinocheirus* was perhaps the most dangerous animal of Late Cretaceous times. Only the arms, hands, shoulders, and a few rib fragments of this giant creature have been found. These are similar to those of STRUTH-IOMIMUS but were more than three times as large! If the rest of the animal matched its hands, this meat eater may have been 25 feet (7.5 m) tall and more than 45 feet (13.5 m) long. It may even have been larger than TYRANNOSAURUS. Its FOSSILS were found in the Gobi Desert of Mongolia.

Classification: Coelurosauria, Theropoda, Saurischia

DEINODON (DY-no-don) "Terror Tooth" (Greek *deinos* = terrible + *odon-* = tooth, because it had very long fangs)

Name given to a jaw and twelve enormous curved and serrated TEETH found in Montana in 1856 and the Gobi Desert
in 1987. This CARNOSAUR may have been a species of ALBER-
TOSAURUS. It lived in Late Jurassic times.

Classification: Carnosauria, Theropoda, Saurischia

deinodonts or **Deinodontidae** (dy-no-DON-tih-dee) "Terror Teeth" (Named after DEINODON)

A name sometimes used for the important CARNOSAURS of
Late Cretaceous times, including ALBERTOSAURUS, DASPLETO-
SAURUS, TARBOSAURUS, and TYRANNOSAURUS. Most deinodonts
were large, but one was no larger than a large dog.

deinonychosaurs or **Deinonychosauria** (dyn-on-ik-o-
SAWR-ee-ah) "Terrible Claw Lizards" (Named after DEIN-
ONYCHUS + Greek *sauros* = lizard)

A proposed new infraorder of THEROPODS. Some scientists
believe that DROMAEOSAURS do not fit under either the CAR-
NOSAURS or COELUROSAURS. In these dinosaurs the hind legs
and skulls were highly specialized for SPEED and savage attack. Their FEET were equipped with sicklelike CLAWS, and their
TAILS were carried rigidly out behind, strengthened by bundles of bony rods that lay along the vertebrae. This infraorder would include all of the DROMAEOSAURIDAE family:
CHIROSTENOTES, DEINONYCHUS, DROMAEOSAURUS, and VELOCIRAP-
TOR. These dinosaurs lived only in Cretaceous times. Not all
scientists agree that this new classification is needed.

DEINONYCHUS (dyn-ON-ik-us) "Terrible Claw" (Greek *deinos* = terrible + *onychos* = claw, referring to the lethal
CLAWS on its feet)

A vicious-looking Early Cretaceous THEROPOD. This lightly-

Deinonychus

built, fleet-footed BIPED was 9 feet (2.7 m) long, 5 feet (1.5 m) tall and weighed about 175 pounds (80 kg). Its long TAIL was held rigidly out behind by a bundle of bony rods running along the vertebrae. *Deinonychus* had a short neck, a large head, excellent EYESIGHT, and sharp, serrated TEETH. Its forelegs were half as long as its hind. It had long, powerful, grasping HANDS; each hand had three fingers equipped with long, sharp claws. The second toe of each foot was equipped with a powerful 5-inch (13-cm) sickle-shaped claw the *Deinonychus* probably used to slash open the bellies of its prey.

Deinonychus probably hunted in packs and attacked animals much larger than itself. Like all theropods, it was probably ENDOTHERMIC (warm-blooded). The FOSSILS of this formidable dinosaur were found in Montana. It is classified in the DROMAEOSAURIDAE, but some think it should be in a group of its own, the DEINONYCHOSAURIA. Its hips were OPISTHOPUBIC instead of lizardlike.

Classification: Coelurosauria, Theropoda, Saurischia

DENVERSAURUS (DEN-ver-sawr-us) "Denver Lizard" (Denver + Greek *sauros* = lizard, because it was found in the Denver Museum of Natural History collection)

A 3-ton (2.7-metric-ton), 20-foot (6-m) ANKYLOSAUR that lived in South Dakota during the Late Cretaceous. It was closely related to NODOSAURUS and, like that dinosaur, did not have a club on its TAIL. This four-legged plant eater was covered head to tail with ARMOR PLATES and had long spikes on the shoulders.

Classification: Nodosauridae, Ankylosauria, Ornithischia

DESMATOSUCHUS (dez-mat-o-SOOK-us) See AETOSAURS.

diapsid or **Diapsida** (dy-APS-ih-dah) "Two Arches" (Greek *di* = two + *apsides* = arches, referring to two openings in the skull)

A subclass of REPTILIA. Members of this group have two openings behind each eye socket in their skull. There are two kinds of diapsids: snakes and lizards form one group, and the ARCHOSAURS—CROCODILIA, DINOSAURS, PTEROSAURS, and THECODONTS—form the other. Many suggest that dinosaurs were not true reptiles, but partly because they had diapsid skulls, dinosaurs are still classed as reptiles.

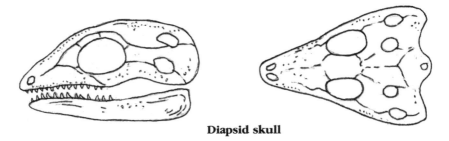

Diapsid skull

Dicraeosaurinae (dy-cree-o-SAWR-ih-nee) "Forked Lizards" (Named after DICRAEOSAURUS)

A former subfamily of TITANOSAURIDAE SAUROPODS. These were

quite similar to the DIPLODOCINAE but were smaller, and their vertebrae were nearly solid instead of having hollow spaces. *Dicraeosaurus* is the only known member of this subfamily. Under a new reorganization of sauropods, this subfamily has been placed under the DIPLODOCIDAE.

DICRAEOSAURUS (dy-CREE-o-sawr-us) "Forked Lizard" (Greek *dikraios* = forked + *sauros* = lizard, referring to the forked spines on its vertebrae)

Dicraeosaurus

A SAUROPOD of Late Jurassic Tanzania and Egypt. This four-legged dinosaur was similar to DIPLODOCUS but was smaller—it was 40 feet (12 m) long, 10 feet (3 m) tall, and weighed about 6 tons (about 5.4 metric tons). *Dicraeosaurus* was a plant eater. It had a moderately long neck and a very long TAIL with forked vertebral SPINES like those of *Diplodocus,* but in *Dicraeosaurus* the vertebrae were nearly solid. This dinosaur is known from an almost complete skeleton.

Classification: Sauropoda, Sauropodomorpha, Saurischia

diet
See FOOD.

DILOPHOSAURUS (dy-LOH-fo-sawr-us) "Two-crested Lizard" (Greek *di* = two + *lophos* = crest + *sauros* = lizard, because it had two CRESTS)

A Late Triassic or Early Jurassic THEROPOD with two high crests running lengthwise along the top of its large head. *Dilophosaurus* was a medium-size dinosaur—it was about 20 feet (6 m) long. This BIPEDAL meat eater had short arms and powerful legs built for SPEED. There were three fingers on its HANDS and four toes on its FEET (however, only three toes reached the ground). Its fingers and toes were armed with sharp CLAWS. The FOSSILS of this dinosaur were found in Arizona. It is known from a nearly complete skeleton. Although this dinosaur was originally classed as a CARNOSAUR, it is now thought to be a large COELUROSAUR.

Classification: Coelurosauria, Theropoda, Saurischia

Dilophosaurus

DIMETRODON (dy-MET-ro-don) "Two-measure Teeth" (Greek *di* = two + *metron* = measure + *odon-* = tooth, referring to the fact that it had TEETH of two different sizes)

Not a DINOSAUR, but a PELYCOSAUR, an ancestor of the mammallike REPTILES. *Dimetrodon* had a great sail 2 to 3 feet (60 to 90 cm) high along its back. This sail may have helped regulate its body temperature. *Dimetrodon* was 10 feet (3 m) long and was a four-legged CARNIVORE. It is the largest-known meat eater of the PERMIAN PERIOD. It had become EXTINCT by the beginning of the MESOZOIC ERA. Its FOSSILS have been found in Texas.

DIMORPHODON (dy-MORF-o-don) "Two-form Teeth" (Greek *di* = two + *morphe* = shape + *odon-* = tooth, referring to the fact that it had TEETH of two different shapes)

Not a DINOSAUR, but one of the earliest FLYING REPTILES—a very primitive PTEROSAUR. It was a member of the RHAMPHO-RHYNCOID family and had an enormous head and a long, naked tail. The fourth finger of each hand was very long and supported the wing. *Dimorphodon* was about 3 feet (90 cm) long. FOSSILS of this pterosaur have been found in England. It lived from Early to Late Jurassic times.

dinosaurs or **Dinosauria** (dy-no-SAWR-ee-ah) "Terrible Lizards" (Greek *deinos* = terrible + *sauros* = lizard, because of their giant size and because at first these animals were thought to be lizardlike)

The name given to two separate kinds of EXTINCT animals—the SAURISCHIA and the ORNITHISCHIA—both orders of the ARCHOSAURIA, a subclass of REPTILIA. These two kinds of animals were no more closely related to each other than they were to crocodiles. However, they both were scaly, egg-laying animals that walked erect, like mammals, instead of sprawling like modern reptiles. Some may even have taken care of their YOUNG. They were possibly warm-blooded (EN-DOTHERMIC), and many were capable of moving very rapidly. These characteristics are not typical of reptiles, and some scientists suggest that dinosaurs should be removed from the reptilian class and placed in a separate class. However, they are still classified as reptiles because of their very reptilian skulls. (See DIAPSID.)

Dinosaurs lived from Middle Triassic times to the end of the CRETACEOUS PERIOD. As a group they existed for about 140 million years.

diplodocids or **Diplodocidae** (dih-plo-DOH-sih-dee) "Double Beamed" (Named after DIPLODOCUS)

A family of SAUROPODS that had peglike TEETH. It includes all those having "double-beamed," or Y-shaped, SPINES on their TAIL vertebrae similar to those found in *Diplodocus.* These bones may have provided extra protection for major blood vessels along the tail or extra muscle attachment. These four-legged plant eaters were from 40 feet (12 m) to 90 feet (27 m) long.

Diplodocids lived during Late Jurassic times in North America, Europe, Asia, and Africa, but some also lived during the CRETACEOUS PERIOD. APATOSAURUS, BAROSAURUS, CETIOSAUR-ISCUS, DICRAEOSAURUS, DIPLODOCUS, MAMENCHISAURUS, and NE-MEGTOSAURUS belong in this family based on a new study and reorganization of the sauropods.

Diplodocinae (dih-plo-DOH-sih-nee) "Double Beamed" (Named after DIPLODOCUS)

One of the subfamily groups of the TITANOSAURIDAE SAURO-PODS. This group had only five vertebrae in the pelvic area. ALAMOSAURUS, ANTARCTOSAURUS, BAROSAURUS, and DIPLODOCUS were members of this group.

This subfamily has recently been restudied and reorga-nized. Many of the dinosaurs formerly included in this subfamily are now placed in a new family, the Diplodocidae. However, some scientists continue to use this old system.

DIPLODOCUS (dih-PLOD-o-kus) "Double Beam" (Greek *di-plos* = double + *dokos* = beam, referring to the double-beamed chevron bones under the middle part of the tail vertebrae)

A Late Jurassic sauropod with a long, snaky neck, a long, whiplike tail, and front legs shorter than the hind legs. A complete skeleton of this dinosaur has been found. It is the longest dinosaur skeleton ever found. It is 90 feet (27 m) long, and has a 26-foot (8-m) neck and a 45-foot (13.7-m) tail. This *Diplodocus* stood 13 feet (4 m) tall at the hips and probably weighed 25 tons (22.7 metric tons).

The elephantlike feet and legs of this four-legged plant eater indicate that it was a land or swamp dweller. Because its

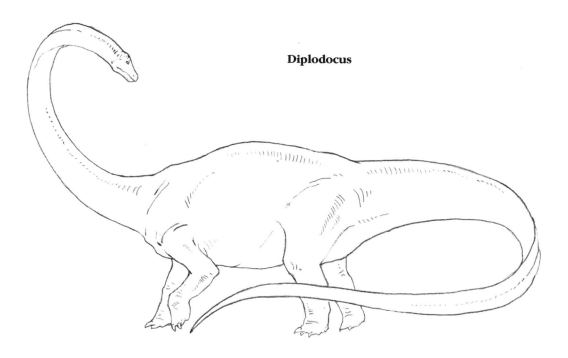

Diplodocus

nostrils were on top of its head, scientists once thought that it lived on the bottom of lakes with only the top of its head above water. It is now known that it could not have breathed in such deep water, because the pressure of the water would have been too great.

Diplodocus may have used its tail as a weapon. The Y-shaped SPINES on the tail vertebrae could have provided extra places of attachment for muscles that made it possible to move the tail from side to side. Its long neck enabled the animal to lift its head to see an approaching enemy from a long distance. Many nearly complete skeletons and several partial ones have been found in the Rocky Mountain states of North America. *Diplodocus* may have lived into Early Cretaceous times.

Classification: Sauropoda, Sauropodomorpha, Saurischia

dome-headed dinosaurs
See PACHYCEPHALOSAURS.

DRACOPELTA (dra-ko-PEL-tah) "Fabulous Lizard with Shield" (Greek *drakon* = fabulous lizardlike animal + Latin *pelta* = shield)

A European ANKYLOSAUR from the JURASSIC PERIOD. This recently discovered armored dinosaur was a NODOSAURID. It had five different types of armor. Like all ankylosaurs, it was a four-legged plant eater.

Classification: Nodosauridae, Ankylosauria, Ornithischia

DRAVIDOSAURUS (dra-VID-o-sawr-us) "Dravid Lizard" (Named for the Dravidanadu Peninsula of India, where it was found, + Greek *sauros* = lizard)

The only known STEGOSAUR from the Middle CRETACEOUS

PERIOD. This plated ORNITHISCHIAN was found in southern India. It is known from a partial skull, a TOOTH, ten ARMOR PLATES, a spike, and several other bones. It resembled STEGOSAURUS more than other stegosaurs, but was smaller. Like *Stegosaurus,* it was a four-legged plant eater. Its back plates were thin and triangular. They ranged from 2 inches (5 cm) to 10 inches (25 cm) in height. The spike is 6 inches (15 cm) long and slightly curved.

Classification: Stegosauridae, Stegosauria, Ornithischia

dromaeosaurids or **Dromaeosauridae** (dro-mee-o-SAWR-ih-dee) "Swift Lizards" (Named after DROMAEOSAURUS) Also called dromaeosaurs.

A family of advanced COELUROSAURS, sometimes called "emu lizards." These agile meat eaters had large BRAINS and huge eyes and had sicklelike CLAWS on their inner toes. They were small, fierce, BIPEDAL predators and were the most "intelligent" of the dinosaurs. (See INTELLIGENCE.) They lived in North America, Asia, and South America from Early to Late Cretaceous times. CHIROSTENOTES, DEINONYCHUS, DROMAEOSAURUS, SAURORNITHOIDES, SAURORNITHOLESTES, STENONYCHOSAURUS, and VELOCIRAPTOR were dromaeosaurs.

Some scientists propose that this family be moved to a new infraorder of THEROPODS—the DEINONYCHOSAURIA.

dromaeosaurs (DROHM-ee-o-sawrz)
See DROMAEOSAURIDS.

DROMAEOSAURUS (drom-ee-o-SAWR-us) "Swift Lizard" (Greek *dromaios* = swift-running + *sauros* = lizard, because it was a fast runner)

An advanced Late Cretaceous COELUROSAUR. This very fleet-

Dromaeosaurus

footed dinosaur was about the SIZE of a man; it weighed only 100 pounds (45 kg). It was a BIPEDAL meat eater and probably a formidable killer—it had razor-sharp TEETH and a 3-inch (8-cm) eaglelike CLAW on the inner toe of each foot. The neck of this fearsome dinosaur was rather long, but thick and powerful. *Dromaeosaurus* had a broad head; its braincase (see BRAINS) was large, and its eyes were huge. FOSSILS of this THEROPOD have been found in Alberta, Canada.

Classification: Coelurosauria, Theropoda, Saurischia

DROMICEIOMIMUS (dro-miss-ee-o-MY-mus) "Emu Mimic" (Latin *Dromiceius* = genus name for emu + *mimus* = mimic, because it resembled a big bird)

A Late Cretaceous ORNITHOMIMID (ostrich dinosaur) about the size of an ostrich. It was closely related to ORNITHOMIMUS and STRUTHIOMIMUS and, like them, looked like an ostrich with a long TAIL. It had a long, slender neck; a birdlike beak; long, slender legs; and huge eyes. But *Dromiceiomimus* had arms with three-fingered HANDS instead of wings. *Dromiceiomimus* was probably one of the most "intelligent" animals of the

Dromiceiomimus

CRETACEOUS PERIOD; its BRAIN was larger than that of an ostrich. This dinosaur was a swift runner that preyed on small animals. Its FOSSILS have been found in Alberta, Canada; the partial skeletons of several individuals make up most of the parts of a whole animal.

Classification: Coelurosauria, Theropoda, Saurischia

DROMICOSAURUS (dro-MIK-o-sawr-us) "Fleet Lizard" (Greek *dromikos* = swift, fleet + *sauros* = lizard, because its long legs indicate it was a good runner)

A very early PROSAUROPOD from South Africa. It lived in the Late TRIASSIC PERIOD. This long-necked, long-tailed dinosaur is known only from the hind legs, fragments of the forelimbs, a few vertebrae, and a few other bones. It is thought to be closely related to THECODONTOSAURUS and possibly resembled that dinosaur. *Dromicosaurus* walked on four legs and ate plants.

Classification: Prosauropoda, Sauropodomorpha, Saurischia

DRYOSAURUS (DRY-o-sawr-us) "Oak Lizard" (Greek *dryo* = oak + *sauros* = lizard, because the top of the TEETH were shaped somewhat like oak leaves)

A small, graceful ORNITHOPOD of the HYPSILOPHODONT family. It was 12 feet (3.5 m) long, 4 feet (1.2 m) tall, and weighed 170 pounds (77 kg). Its small head had a slim, beaklike snout. *Dryosaurus* had five-fingered HANDS and walked on long, slender legs, carrying its body horizontally. It probably could run swiftly. Like all ornithopods, it was a plant eater. *Dryosaurus* lived in western North America, in Europe, and in east Africa from Late Jurassic to Early Cretaceous times. It is known from a nearly complete skeleton found in Utah. DYSALOTOSAURUS is considered to be a species of this dinosaur.

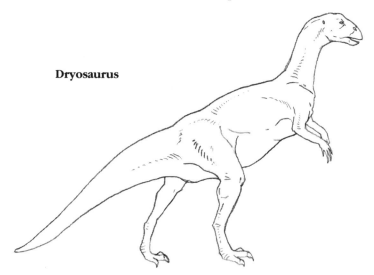

Dryosaurus

Classification: Hypsilophodontidae, Ornithopoda, Ornithischia

DRYPTOSAURUS (DRIP-toh-sawr-us) "Tearing Lizard" (Greek *drypto* = to tear + *sauros* = lizard, referring to its fearsome TEETH and CLAWS) Originally named LAELAPS.

A CARNOSAUR whose remains were found in New Jersey—the only known Late Cretaceous carnosaur from eastern North America. It probably resembled MEGALOSAURUS. Its exact SIZE is unknown, because a complete skeleton hasn't been found,

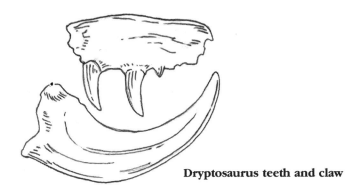

Dryptosaurus teeth and claw

but the bones that have been found suggest it may have been 20 feet (6 m) long. This formidable BIPEDAL meat eater had daggerlike teeth and 8-inch (20-cm), talonlike foot claws.

Classification: Carnosauria, Theropoda, Saurischia

duck-billed dinosaurs or **duckbills**

See HADROSAURS.

DYOPLOSAURUS (dy-OP-lo-sawr-us) "Double-armored Lizard" (Greek *dyo* = two, double + *oplos* = armored + *sauros* = lizard, referring to its two forms of DEFENSE—its ARMOR and its clubbed TAIL)

Name given to Late Cretaceous ANKYLOSAUR bones found in Mongolia and Alberta, Canada. *Dyoplosaurus* is now considered to be the same as EUOPLOCEPHALUS.

Classification: Ankylosauridae, Ankylosauria, Ornithischia

DYSALOTOSAURUS (dis-o-LOH-toh-sawr-us) "Unconquerable Lizard" (Greek *dysalotos* = hard to catch + *sauros* = lizard, referring to its supposed SPEED)

Name given to a complete skeleton of a small HYPSILOPHO-DONT that was found in Late Jurassic rocks in Tanzania. This dinosaur is now considered by some to be the same species as DRYOSAURUS.

Classification: Hypsilophodontidae, Ornithopoda, Ornithischia

DYSTYLOSAURUS (dy-STY-lo-sawr-us) "Two-beamed Lizard" (Greek *dyo-* = two + *stylos* = beam + *sauros* = lizard, referring to the double-beamed bones on the vertebrae)

A large, Late Jurassic SAUROPOD found in Colorado. It is known only from fragments, but the double beams on the vertebrae suggest it was a close relative of *Diplodocus*.

Classification: Sauropoda, Sauropodomorpha, Saurischia

E

ECHINODON (eh-KY-no-don) "Spiky Tooth" (Greek *echino-* = spiky + *odon-* = tooth, referring to the spines on its TEETH)

This name has been changed to SAURECHINODON because another animal had already been given this name.

Classification: Fabrosauridae, Ornithopoda, Ornithischia

ectotherm (EK-toh-therm) "Outside Heat" (Greek *ektos* = outside + *therme* = heat)

A cold-blooded animal; one that gets its body heat from the sun or something else in its environment. Ectotherms control their body temperature by moving into or out of the shade. Snakes, turtles, alligators, and lizards are ectotherms. It has long been thought that the dinosaurs were ectotherms, but now some scientists think that at least some dinosaurs were ENDOTHERMS. Compare HOMOIOTHERM.

ectothermic

See ECTOTHERM.

EDMONTONIA (ed-mon-TOH-nee-ah) (Named for the Edmonton rock formation, where it was found)

A Late Cretaceous ANKYLOSAUR whose nearly complete skeleton was found in Alberta, Canada. Some scientists think that *Edmontonia* was a species of PANOPLOSAURUS. Others do not agree; however, if it is not, they were very similar.

Classification: Nodosauridae, Ankylosauria, Ornithischia

EDMONTOSAURUS (ed-MON-toh-sawr-us) "Edmonton Lizard" (Named for the Edmonton rock formation, where it was found, + Greek *sauros* = lizard)

A HADROSAUR of Late Cretaceous Alberta, Canada. This duck-billed dinosaur was related to ANATOSAURUS and was a member of the HADROSAURINES. It had a heavy body; long, strong legs; short, slender forelimbs; a crestless head with a long, slender nose; and a broad, spoon-shaped beak. Its jaws were packed with hundreds of TEETH. *Edmontosaurus* was one of the largest hadrosaurs—it weighed 3 to 4 tons (2.7 to 3.6 metric tons) and was 32 feet (9.8 m) long. Like all hadrosaurs, it walked on two legs, carrying its body horizontally. It

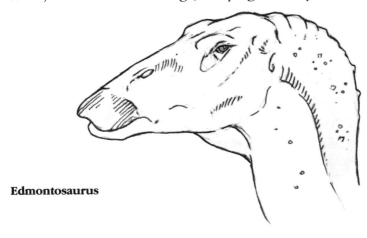

Edmontosaurus

ate tree leaves and pine needles. Many specimens of this dinosaur have been found. *Edmontosaurus* was one of the most abundant animals of its time.

Classification: Hadrosauridae, Ornithopoda, Ornithischia

EFRAASIA (eh-FRAH-see-ah) (Named in honor of E. Fraas, an early German fossil collector)

A PROSAUROPOD recently discovered in Late Triassic Germany. This plant-eating dinosaur resembled ANCHISAURUS. It had a long neck and TAIL and was capable of walking on either two legs or all four.

Classification: Prosauropoda, Sauropodomorpha, Saurischia

eggs

Although it is possible that some dinosaurs gave birth to live YOUNG, most of them certainly reproduced by laying eggs. Scientists' knowledge of dinosaur eggs is based on abundant finds of pieces and, occasionally, of whole eggs; sometimes they have even found complete NESTS of dinosaur eggs. Scientists think that dinosaur eggs probably had brittle shells similar to those of modern crocodiles.

Huge dinosaurs such as SAUROPODS did *not* lay gigantic eggs. If they had done so, the shells would have been too thick to allow air to pass through to the baby dinosaurs inside—nor could the baby dinosaurs have succeeded in breaking out. Eggs believed to be those of the sauropod HYPSELOSAURUS were discovered in France. These were laid in craterlike dirt nests in clutches of five. The eggs were roundish in shape and about 10 inches (25 cm) long—twice the size of an ostrich egg. They had a rough, sandpapery surface. These are the largest dinosaur eggs that are known up to this time.

Protoceratops eggs

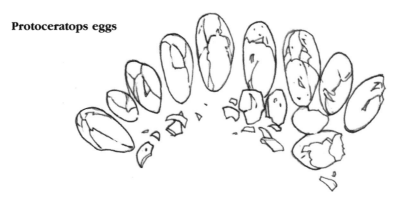

The pig-size PROTOCERATOPS laid its eggs in sand nests, arranging the eggs in three circles, one within another. There were as many as 18 potato-shaped eggs in some nests. These eggs were about 6 inches (15 cm) long and had rough, wrinkled shells. Another *Protoceratops* nest recently found in Mongolia had an even greater number of eggs in it. Scientists think that many females may have shared the same nest. They think it is unlikely that one could have laid that many eggs. The total volume of the eggs was greater than the body of an adult.

The eggs of MAIASAURA, a 30-foot (9.1-m) HADROSAUR, were long and slender and typically egg-shaped. The 8-inch (20-cm)-long eggs were laid in bowl-shaped nests. A nest in Montana contained 15 eggs. The eggs of ORODROMEUS, an 8-foot (2.4-m) HYPSILOPHODONT from the same area, were 6 inches (15 cm) long and were laid in clutches of 24. CAT scans (special X rays) show that these eggs contained skeletons of embryos. Eggs of TROÖDON, a small CARNIVORE, were 4 inches (10 cm) long and were laid in double rows rather than in circular nests. The eggs were oval and had a lumpy surface. They are the first eggs of a carnivorous dinosaur ever found. A single 2-inch by 4-inch (5-cm by 10-cm) egg found in Col-

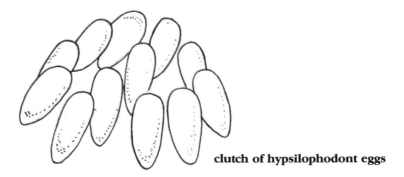

clutch of hypsilophodont eggs

orado may be that of an ALLOSAURUS. It was found with FOSSILS of that dinosaur.

The earliest-known eggs were also found in Colorado. These 145-million-year-old eggs were 8 inches (20 cm) long and 3.5 inches (9 cm) across. The same nesting area had been used at least six different times. Scientists have no idea what dinosaur laid the eggs. Other unidentified dinosaur eggs have been found in Canada and Mongolia.

A clutch of 16 eggs was recently found in China. A footprint believed to have been made by the dinosaur that laid them was impressed upon three of the eggs. These eggs are elongated and nearly pointed on each end.

ELAPHROSAURUS (eh-LAHF-ro-sawr-us) "Lightweight Lizard" (Greek *elaphros* = lightweight + *sauros* = lizard, referring to its hollow bones)

A slender, medium-size, hollow-boned COELUROSAUR—possibly the ancestor of the ORNITHOMIMIDS. This short-legged BIPED was about three times the SIZE of ORNITHOLESTES—larger than most coelurosaurs. It measured 19 feet (5.8 m) from its snout to the tip of its TAIL. It was probably a scavenger, feeding on carcasses of dead animals left by large CARNOSAURS. Many FOSSILS of *Elaphrosaurus,* including one nearly complete skele-

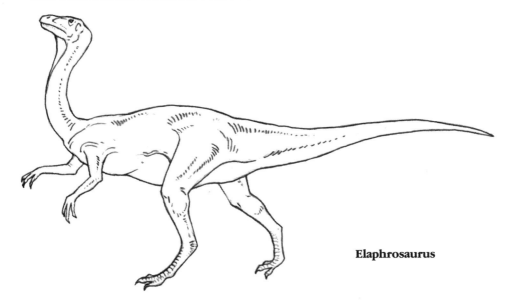

Elaphrosaurus

ton, have been found in Tanzania, Israel, and North America. It lived during Middle and Late Jurassic times.

Classification: Coelurosauria, Theropoda, Saurischia

ELASMOSAURUS (ee-LAZ-mo-sawr-us) "Thin-plated Lizard" (Greek *elasmos* = thin plate + *sauros* = lizard, referring to the platelike bones of its pelvic girdle)

Not a dinosaur, but a long-necked PLESIOSAUR. This marine REPTILE was 43 feet (13 m) long. About half of its length was its head and neck. The neck had 76 vertebrae. *Elasmosaurus* was not built for SPEED; it moved slowly through the Late Cretaceous oceans propelled by narrow, paddlelike flippers. FOSSILS of these fish eaters have been found in North America.

ELMISAURUS (EL-mih-sawr-us) "Foot Lizard" (Mongolian *el-myi* = hind foot + Greek *sauros* = lizard, referring to the foot, which had fused bones)

A small COELUROSAUR found in Late Cretaceous sediments

of Mongolia. It is known only from a foot and a HAND. Based on the SIZE of the FOOT, its height has been estimated to be about 3 feet (90 cm) at the hips. This little dinosaur was closely related to CHIROSTENOTES and probably resembled that dinosaur. It was a BIPEDAL meat eater.

Classification: Coelurosauria, Theropoda, Saurischia

endotherm (EN-doh-therm) "Inner Heat" (Greek *endon* = within + *therme* = heat)

A warm-blooded animal; one whose body temperature does not change with the temperature of its environment. Endotherms generate their own heat internally. They have developed ways of regulating their body temperature—such as perspiring or panting to cool off and shivering to warm up. In these ways, they maintain a high and uniform temperature even when the temperature of their environment is very low or very high. (See HOMOIOTHERM.)

For a long time scientists thought dinosaurs were ECTOTHERMIC (cold-blooded), like modern reptiles. But now some scientists believe that at least some dinosaurs—particularly the THEROPODS—may have been endotherms, like birds and mammals. The great size of SAUROPODS may have been their means of controlling body temperature. The plates on the back of STEGOSAURS, and fins, such as those of SPINOSAURUS, may have been cooling mechanisms. A few dinosaurs may even have had insulating body covering such as fur or feathers like modern mammals and birds have.

There are many reasons to think that dinosaurs may have been endothermic. Dinosaurs had erect posture—that is, they walked with their legs vertical, or nearly so; they did not sprawl like alligators or crocodiles. Many BIPEDAL dinosaurs were swift runners, and they were highly active and very agile animals. The bone tissue of some dinosaurs was similar to that of mammals. And there is evidence that some dinosaurs lived in HERDS and took some care of their YOUNG. Among modern animals only endothermic ones have these characteristics.

endothermic

See ENDOTHERM.

EOCERATOPS (ee-o-SAY-uh-tops) "Dawn Horned Face" (Greek *eos* = dawn + *keratops* = horned face, because it appears to be one of the earlier CERATOPSIANS)

Eoceratops

A ceratopsian similar to MONOCLONIUS. It is known only from a half skull and lower jaw fragments found in Alberta, Canada. The skull is over 3 feet (90 cm) long. *Eoceratops* had a short, slightly forward-curved HORN on its snout and small horns on its brow that curved slightly toward the back. This four-legged plant eater lived during the early part of Late Cretaceous times.

Classification: Ceratopsidae, Ceratopsia, Ornithischia

EODELPHIS (ee-o-DEL-fiss) "Early Opossum" (Greek *eos* = dawn + *delphis* = opossum)

131

Not a DINOSAUR, but a Late Cretaceous marsupial mammal. It was about two-thirds as large as the common modern opossum. Though small, it was a relatively large mammal compared with other mammals living at that time, and it is the largest known marsupial of Late Cretaceous times. This neighbor of the dinosaur is known only from jaw fragments and teeth found in Alberta, Canada, and Montana.

eosuchians or **Eosuchia** (ee-o-SOOK-ee-ah) "Early Crocodiles" (Greek *eos* = dawn + *souchos* = crocodile, because they resembled modern crocodiles)

Not DINOSAURS, but an order of DIAPSID REPTILES that resembled modern gavials or crocodiles but were more closely related to lizards. They are thought to be the ancestors of snakes and lizards. Eosuchians lived from the PERMIAN PERIOD to the TERTIARY PERIOD and lived in many parts of the world. They were meat eaters and probably preyed on insects and the smaller dinosaurs. They ranged in size from 4 feet (1.2 m) to 8 feet (2.4 m). They walked on all fours with a sprawling gait, as modern crocodiles do. CHAMPSOSAURUS and MALERISAURUS were eosuchians.

EPANTERIAS (eh-pan-TAYR-ee-us) See ALLOSAURUS.

FOSSILS of this rare, 50-foot-long Late Jurassic CARNOSAUR have been found in Colorado and Oklahoma. It is currently believed to be the largest and latest species of ALLOSAURUS.

ERECTOPUS (ee-REK-to-pus) "Upright Foot" (Latin *erectus* = upright + Greek *pous* = foot, because the animal apparently walked upright)

Name given to a few FOSSIL bones of a large Early Cretaceous CARNOSAUR. *Erectopus* was probably closely related to

MEGALOSAURUS. Like all carnosaurs, it was a two-legged meat eater. Its fossils were found in northern France, Egypt, and Romania.

Classification: Carnosauria, Theropoda, Saurischia

ERLIKOSAURUS (ER-lik-o-sawr-us) "Erlik's Lizard" (Named after Erlik, legendary Lamaist king of the dead, + Greek *sauros* = lizard. Lamaism is a kind of Buddhist religion practiced in Mongolia.)

An unusual kind of Late Cretaceous dinosaur recently found in Mongolia. Its skull is unlike that of any other known dinosaur. It had a long, slender, toothless beak, but sharp, pointed TEETH lined the sides of its jaws. It had a long neck and TAIL. It may have been partially QUADRUPEDAL. Its four-toed FEET were short and massive with long, narrow CLAWS. *Erlikosaurus* closely resembled SEGNOSAURUS and belonged to the same family, the SEGNOSAURIDAE, but it was smaller.

Classification: Segnosauridae, Segnosauria, Ornithischia.

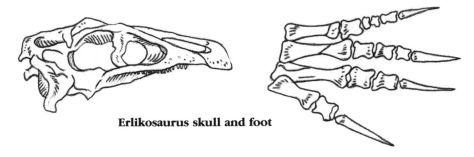

Erlikosaurus skull and foot

ERYOPS (AR-ee-ops) "Drawn-out Face" (Greek *eryein* = drawn-out + *ops* = face, because most of its skull was in front of its eyes)

Not a DINOSAUR, but an Early Permian amphibian whose FOSSILS were found in Texas. Amphibians are born in the water but often live much of their adult lives on land. Toads and frogs are modern amphibians. *Eryops* lived in and near streams and ponds. It ate fish. This long-faced creature was EXTINCT before the dinosaurs appeared.

EUBRONTES (yu-BRON-teez) "True Thunder" (Greek *eu* = good, true + *brontos* = thunder, because it was thought that the footsteps of this large animal would surely be thunderous)

Name given to three-toed dinosaur TRACKS found in Dinosaur State Park in Connecticut and also in Glen Canyon, Arizona. They provide evidence that large THEROPODS lived in North America during very late Triassic and Early Jurassic times. It is speculated that the animal that made the tracks was 20 feet (6 m) long and was a heavy-bodied CARNOSAUR similar to MEGALOSAURUS. Similar tracks have been found in Germany, but no bones of the animal that made them have ever been found.

Some of the Connecticut tracks appear to have been made while the dinosaur was floating in water. Only the tips of the toes made impressions in the mud as the animal pushed itself along. This seems to indicate that some carnosaurs could swim. Before the discovery of these tracks, it was assumed that carnosaurs did not swim.

Eubrontes tracks

Euhelopodinae (yu-heh-lo-POH-dih-nee) "True Marsh Foot" (Named for EUHELOPUS)

A subfamily of BRACHIOSAURID SAUROPODS. They were similar to the CAMARASAURINAE in some ways; their forelimbs were as long as the hind legs and they had short skulls. But Euhelopodinae had relatively longer legs and very long necks. Some may have carried their short TAILS high off the ground. They ranged between 40 to 60 feet (12 to 18 m) in length. This group of four-legged plant eaters has been found only in China and Mongolia. They lived throughout the CRETACEOUS PERIOD. EUHELOPUS, OMEISAURUS, OPISTHOCOELICAUDIA, and TIENSHANOSAURUS are members of this family.

EUHELOPUS (yu-heh-LOH-pus) "True Marsh Foot" (Greek *eu* = true, good + *helos* = marsh + *pous* = foot, probably because it was assumed that this dinosaur lived in marshy

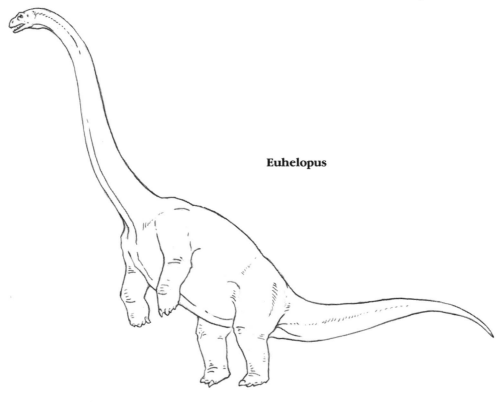

Euhelopus

areas) A new name for HELOPUS. It was renamed because that name was used for another animal.

An Early Cretaceous SAUROPOD 45 feet (13.7 m) long. Two partial skeletons of this long-necked SAURISCHIAN were found in China; together, they provide most of the parts of a whole animal. Its skull was similar to that of CAMARASAURUS, and its forelimbs were as long as its hind. But the neck of *Euhelopus* was much longer than the neck of *Camarasaurus*. Like all sauropods, *Euhelopus* was a QUADRUPEDAL plant eater.

Classification: Sauropoda, Sauropodomorpha, Saurischia

EUOPLOCEPHALUS (yu-op-lo-SEF-ah-lus) "Well-armed Head" (Greek *euoplo-* = well-armed + *kephale* = head, referring to the armor on its head)

A Late Cretaceous ANKYLOSAUR (armored dinosaur). The upper part of its body—from the nose to the TAIL—was covered with bony plates studded with rows of horny spikes 4 to 6 inches (10 to 15 cm) long. The tail ended in a bony club. This plant eater was about 20 feet (6 m) long and 8 feet (2.4 m) wide, and it weighed 3.5 tons (3.2 metric tons). It walked on four short, stout legs with hooflike claws. Its snout ended in a horny beak. The FOSSILS of *Euoplocephalus* have been found in Alberta, Canada.

Euoplocephalus

ANODONTOSAURUS, DYOPLOSAURUS, and SCOLOSAURUS are other names given to fossil remains that are now considered to be the same as *Euoplocephalus*. It was once thought that *Euoplocephalus* was the same as ANKYLOSAURUS, but scientists now believe they were two different animals.

Classification: Ankylosauridae, Ankylosauria, Ornithischia

EUPARKERIA (yu-PARK-ah-ree-ah) (Named in honor of W. K. Parker, English scientist)

Not a dinosaur, but a PSEUDOSUCHIAN (an advanced THECODONT). Some scientists think it may be an ancestor of the ORNITHISCHIAN dinosaurs; others suggest it was an ancestor of the SAURISCHIANS. It was a relatively small animal—5 feet (1.5 m) long—and weighed 40 pounds (18 kg). It had a long TAIL. ARMOR PLATES covered its back. It probably walked on all fours most of the time, but it may have run on two legs, like modern lizards do. This meat eater lived in South Africa during Triassic times.

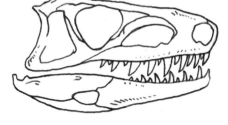

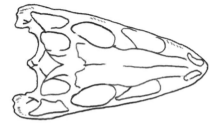

Euparkeria skull

EUSKELOSAURUS (yu-SKEL-o-sawr-us) "Good Leg Lizard" (Greek *eu* = good or true + *skelos* = leg + *sauros* = lizard, because it had strong legs)

A Late Triassic PROSAUROPOD similar to PLATEOSAURUS. It is known from fragmentary material of several individuals. This dinosaur had a long neck and TAIL. It was capable of walking either on four legs or two, and ate plants.

Classification: Prosauropoda, Sauropodomorpha, Saurischia

EUSTREPTOSPONDYLUS (yu-strep-to-SPON-dih-lus) "Well-curved Vertebrae" (Greek *eustreptos* = well-curved + *spondylos* = vertebrae, because its vertebrae were more curved than those of most MEGALOSAURS)

A CARNOSAUR that was very similar to MEGALOSAURUS. It lived about the same time and was about the same SIZE. *Eustreptospondylus* was a meat eater and walked on two powerful

Eustreptospondylus

hind legs. Its forelimbs were very short. Its head was large, and its long jaws were lined with sharp, serrated TEETH. FOSSILS of *Eustreptospondylus* have been found in Middle Jurassic rock in England and Madagascar, and in Late Jurassic rock in Europe and South America. It is known from most of the parts of the skeleton.

Classification: Carnosauria, Theropoda, Saurischia

evolve (ih-VOLV) (From Latin *evolvere* = to unroll)

To change or develop by slow stages. When a plant or animal evolves, it gradually develops new features and adaptations, from one generation to another, that make it better suited to its environment. This usually takes many centuries.

extinction (ek-STINK-shun)

No longer existing. By the end of the MESOZOIC ERA, all the dinosaurs had died out, along with PLESIOSAURS, AMMONITES, certain kinds of plankton, PTEROSAURS, and many kinds of plants. Their extinction appears to have been relatively sudden. Some scientists think it took just a few years. Others think it took thousands of years, or even millions of years. But in terms of geological time, even that is rather sudden.

Extinction is a natural process. It happens all the time. There have been other periods of earth's history in which large numbers of animals died out at one time. Also, during the Mesozoic Era individual species of dinosaurs were dying out from time to time. Even whole families, like the STEGOSAURS, vanished. But never had there been such a massive dying out of so many kinds of plants and animals without leaving any descendants. Only the COELUROSAURS, of all the dinosaurs, left descendants (in the form of birds), and these were only descendants of very early coelurosaurs. There were no large land animals left after the dinosaurs and their contemporaries became extinct.

What caused them all to disappear is not known. Many scientists have studied the problem. Many theories have been proposed.

Some modern PALEONTOLOGISTS believe that excessive radiation plus a cooling of the environment are the most likely reasons for the extinction at the end of the CRETACEOUS PERIOD. Some scientists believe that a supernova exploded near the earth and flooded the earth with excessive radiation for several decades. Others suggest that volcanic activity temporarily destroyed the earth's ozone layer, allowing too much deadly ultraviolet radiation from the sun to reach the earth's surface. Still others suggest that there was a reversal of the earth's magnetic poles. Scientists know that the magnetic poles have reversed a number of times in the history of the earth. While a reversal is occurring, the earth's magnetic field is weak. When its magnetic field is weak, the earth is exposed to large doses of radiation.

Other experts believe that sudden, severe cold weather caused the exterminations. Dinosaurs may have been warm-blooded, but they lacked insulative coverings such as hair or feathers. If temperatures dropped a great deal, they wouldn't have been able to retain enough body heat and would have perished. One theory suggests that sea-floor spreading and the breakup of the supercontinents, LAURASIA and GONDWANALAND, caused changes in the climate. Another suggests that a spillover of water from an arctic ocean reduced the salinity of the world's oceans and affected the climate.

A recently proposed theory suggests that an asteroid from our own solar system collided with the earth. This theory is based on discoveries of unusually high levels of iridium (a metallic element) in clay sediments that mark the very end of the Cretaceous Period. Scientists proposing this theory suggest that the asteroid collision caused a cloud of dust to circle the earth for several years, blocking the sunlight and causing the death of both plants and animals.

Further evidence of such an impact is the discovery of carbon found in clay deposits in five separate sites in Europe and New Zealand. The carbon is thought to be from soot that settled to the ground about the same time as the iridium was deposited. This suggests a worldwide fire that may have been ignited by the impact. High levels of strontium 87 have also been found in fossilized shells of the same period. This suggests that severe acid rain may have helped cause the extinction. The intense heat given off by the meteorite as it plunged through the atmosphere could have caused oxygen and nitrogen to unite, creating nitrogen oxide, which turns to acid rain when mixed with water. Acid rain can kill plants and cause starvation among animals.

This is the only theory with solid evidence to back it up, but it still does not explain why some kinds of animals became extinct, while others (such as turtles, crocodiles, mammals, and birds) survived. Perhaps the real answer will be found in a combination of these theories.

eyesight

Scientists can tell how large a dinosaur's eyes were from the size of the eye sockets in the skull. In general, the larger the eyes, the better the vision. Eyes placed in front of the skull provide better vision than those on the sides of the skull, and widely spaced eyes enable an animal to judge distances more accurately.

Most plant-eating dinosaurs had fairly large eyes. One of

their best DEFENSES was their very good vision. Only the STEG-OSAURS and ANKYLOSAURS had quite small eyes in comparison to their body size. Of the plant eaters, the ORNITHOPODS had the largest eyes. They undoubtedly could see very well. When they saw danger approaching from a distance, they fled. SAU-ROPODS, too, had rather good vision and had the advantage of an extraordinarily long neck, which gave them a much larger range of vision.

Predatory dinosaurs also had large eyes and keen eyesight. Of all the dinosaurs, the DROMAEOSAURS had the largest eyes compared to body size. We know that DEINONYCHUS had to have good eye-and-foot coordination to use its sicklelike CLAW to kill prey. Such coordination requires good vision. STEN-ONYCHOSAURUS probably had the best eyesight of all. Its eyes were forward-directed and spaced far apart, like those of humans. It probably could judge distances very accurately, and probably had good night vision as well. In modern animals the largest eyes are found in nocturnal animals.

F

fabrosaurids or **Fabrosauridae** (fab-ro-SAWR-ih-dee)

"Fabre's Lizards" (Named after FABROSAURUS) Also called fabrosaurs.

A primitive family of Triassic ORNITHOPODS, all resembling FABROSAURUS or LESOTHOSAURUS. They had lightweight bones and no muscular cheeks. A single row of TEETH lined the jaws to the tip of the snout. In other groups, the teeth lined only the side jaws. Fabrosaurs did not have canine teeth like those found in the HETERODONTOSAURS. Fabrosaurs were quite small—

3 to 4 feet (90 to 120 cm) long. Their forelimbs were much smaller than the hind, but were strong, indicating that they could walk either on two feet or on all four. Fabrosaurs first appeared in Late Triassic times. They have been found in Africa and North America. Fabrosaurus, Lesothosaurus, and SCUTELLOSAURUS were fabrosaurs. Some scientists also include SAURECHINODON in this family. It was found in Late Jurassic sediments in England.

FABROSAURUS (FAB-ro-sawr-us) "Fabre's Lizard" (Named in honor of Jean Henri Fabre, French entomologist, + Greek *sauros* = lizard)

An ORNITHOPOD known only from an incomplete lower right jaw that was found in Triassic sediments of South Africa. It is generally described as a small, 3-foot (90-cm) plant eater with a small head; a horny, beaklike jaw with TEETH; short front limbs; five-fingered HANDS; long, slender back legs; and long FEET. This description was based on other FOSSIL material that was once believed to be a species of *Fabrosaurus*. It has now been decided that this other material belonged to a different GENUS and has been named LESOTHOSAURUS. The two are very closely related and probably resembled each other.

Classification: Fabrosauridae, Ornithopoda, Ornithischia

feet

Dinosaur feet came in many shapes and sizes. However, all members of the same group of dinosaurs had similar feet. THEROPODS had birdlike feet, usually with three forward-pointing toes and a dewclaw pointing inward or backward. Their toes were equipped with talonlike CLAWS, like all predators. SAUROPODS had broad, padded, elephantlike feet. The hind feet were equipped with three or more claws, but the

Feet

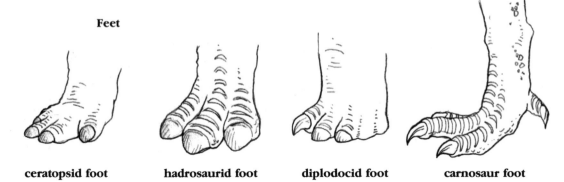

ceratopsid foot   hadrosaurid foot   diplodocid foot   carnosaur foot

front had none or only one. These were the feet of land animals. PROSAUROPODS had four forward-pointing toes on the hind feet with strong claws on the two middle toes. The forefeet were smaller, but strong, and had two clawed fingers and a thumb.

Nearly all of the ORNITHISCHIANS had blunt, hooflike claws on both fore and hind feet. ORNITHOPODS had three or four toes on their hind feet and four or five fingers on their forefeet. The hind feet of STEGOSAURS were also three-toed, while the forefeet had five toes, all ending in hooflike nails. ANKYLOSAURS and CERATOPSIANS had broad feet with hooflike nails, four toes on the hind feet and five on the forefeet.

fins
See SPINES.

flying reptiles
See PTEROSAURS.

food
Most DINOSAURS ate plants. All the ORNITHISCHIANS (ORNITHOPODS, STEGOSAURS, ANKYLOSAURS, and CERATOPSIANS) ate plants.

So did the largest of the dinosaurs, the SAUROPODS (such as DIPLODOCUS, APATOSAURUS, and BRACHIOSAURUS). Some of the PROSAUROPODS (such as HERRERASAURUS and ANCHISAURUS) apparently ate both meat and plants. Small THEROPODS (COELOPHYSIS, TROÖDON, and COMPSOGNATHUS) probably ate insects, small lizards, mammals, eggs, and possibly baby dinosaurs. Larger theropods such as DEINONYCHUS, ALLOSAURUS, and TYRANNOSAURUS preyed on larger animals, including other dinosaurs.

Scientists can usually tell what a dinosaur ate by the kind of TEETH it had. Flat or blunt teeth are generally used for eating plants. Sharp, saw-toothed teeth are used to slice meat.

Scientists found a mummified stomach of an ANATOSAURUS. It contained shrubs and evergreen needles. *Anatosaurus* may have stripped leaves from branches with its ducklike beak in the same manner as modern giraffes.

A fossilized stomach of a sauropod contained parts of large branches but few leaves. Scientists think that these animals ate from the very tops of tall trees that could not be reached by other dinosaurs.

Ceratopsians apparently ate low ground bushes. They were capable of chewing very large and very tough plant material.

The huge sauropods ate twigs and needles from the tops of tall pine, fir, and sequoia trees. One of the big mysteries about sauropods is how they could eat enough to stay alive. Elephants eat 300 to 600 pounds (135 to 270 kg) of food every day. They spend up to 18 hours a day just foraging and eating. The largest sauropod was 15 times as large as an African elephant. Did it eat 15 times as much? We don't know, but probably not.

Prosauropods foraged on smaller trees, while STEGOSAURS,

CERATOPSIANS, and ANKYLOSAURS ate low ground plants and probably CYCAD and fern fronds.

footprints

See TRACKS, TRACKWAYS.

fossil (FAHS-il) (From Latin *fossilis* = dug up)

A piece or trace of a once-living thing—plant or animal—that has been preserved in stone by the replacement of once-living tissues with minerals dissolved in water. Fossils of DINOSAURS may be their actual remains—TEETH, bones, stomach contents—or they may be footprints or SKIN impressions.

Fossils were formed when an animal's body was covered by deep layers of mud or sand soon after it died. It takes millions of years for fossils to form. We know that dinosaurs existed, because scientists have found their fossilized bones. Scientists can tell by the shape of a fossil bone or tooth what kind of animal it belonged to. By studying a dinosaur's bones, they can determine what kind of dinosaur it was. Fossils tell scientists nearly everything about a dinosaur's appearance except its color.

By piecing together entire fossil skeletons, scientists have learned how large the creatures were and how many fingers or toes they had. Scientists know how and where muscles were fastened to the bones, so they can determine how the animal looked when it was alive. Fossilized skin impressions tell them what the skin of that dinosaur looked like. Fossilized TRACKS give information about the habits of the dinosaur. Fossilized EGGS tell how they reproduced. On rare occasions, scientists have even found fossilized stomach contents; these show what some dinosaurs ate.

frills

Bony shields, or frills, covered the necks of CERATOPSIANS. These frills protected the necks, but their primary purpose was to provide a place of attachment for the strong neck and jaw muscles required to support the weight of the animals' huge heads and HORNS. As the size of the skulls and horns increased, the frills became larger to support them. PROTO-CERATOPSIANS had relatively small heads and only suggestions of horns. Their frills were very small. Long-frilled ceratopsians had huge heads and very long brow horns. They had enormous shields that extended back over their shoulders. The frills of the short-frilled ceratopsians were about halfway between these two. Their heads were smaller than those of the long-frilled group, and their brow horns were either very short or nonexistent. Their shields did not even reach to their shoulders. The frills of protoceratopsians and short-frilled ceratopsians were solid or had small holes through the bone, while the enormous frills of long-frilled ceratopsians had large openings in the bone to lighten their weight.

TOROSAURUS had the longest frill. Its skull and frill together measured 8.5 feet (2.6 m) long—one-third of its total body length! The frill was 5.5 feet (1.7 m) wide.

FULGUROTHERIUM (ful-gur-o-THEER-ee-um) "Lightning Beast" (Latin *fulgur* = lightning + Greek *therion* = beast)

A small, Early Cretaceous HYPSILOPHODONT that lived in Australia, when it was below the Antarctic Circle. This two-legged plant eater is known only from several thigh bones found at Victoria and in Asia.

Classification: Hypsilophodontidae, Ornithopoda, Ornithischia

G

GALLIMIMUS (gal-ih-MY-mus) "Rooster Mimic" (Latin *gallus* = rooster + *mimus* = mimic, because it resembled a big bird)

The largest of the ORNITHOMIMIDS ("ostrich dinosaurs"). From the tip of its snout to the end of its TAIL, *Gallimimus* was 20 feet (6 m) long. With its small head, long, toothless, beaklike jaws, and long, slender neck, it resembled a huge ostrich. Like an ostrich, it was BIPEDAL and could run swiftly. It had long, strong legs and three-toed FEET; the toes were armed with sharp CLAWS. The arms were short, and they had three-fingered HANDS. *Gallimimus* probably ate small animals, EGGS, and plants. It is known from several complete skeletons found in Late Cretaceous deposits in Mongolia.

Classification: Coelurosauria, Theropoda, Saurischia

Gallimimus

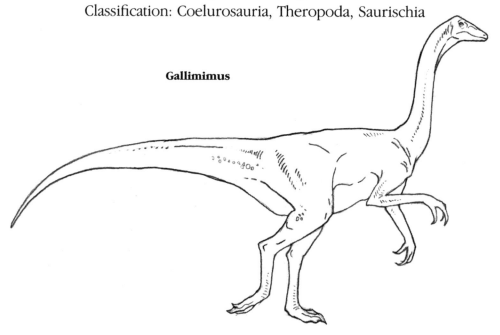

GARUDIMIMUS (gah-roo-dih-MYM-us) "Garuda Mimic" (Named for a fierce mythological bird of Hindu and east Asian literature + Greek *mimos* = mimic)

A very primitive ORNITHOMIMID ("ostrich dinosaur"). It was similar to ORNITHOMIMUS but was more primitive. *Garudimimus* is known from most of a skull and a fragmentary skeleton—a pelvis, an incomplete hind leg, and one foot—found in Middle and Late Cretaceous deposits in Mongolia. The skull is 1 foot (30 cm) long. The total length of this meat eater is estimated to be about 13.5 feet (4 m). It walked on two legs.

Classification: Coelurosauria, Theropoda, Saurischia

GASOSAURUS (GAS-o-sawr-us) "Gas Lizard" (gaso = the combining form of gas + Greek *sauros* = lizard, because it was found on the property of an oil and gas company)

A Middle Jurassic CARNOSAUR from China. This two-legged meat eater probably belongs to the MEGALOSAUR family, because its TEETH are shaped like those of MEGALOSAURUS. *Gasosaurus* was 12 feet (3.5 m) long. It is known from a nearly complete skeleton.

Classification: Carnosauria, Theropoda, Saurischia

gastroliths (GAS-tro-liths) "stomach stones" (Greek *gastros* = stomach + *lithos* = stone)

Small, round stones used to grind FOOD in the gizzards or stomachs of some animals. (Modern birds swallow gravel for this purpose.) Gastroliths found near SAUROPOD FOSSILS have led scientists to speculate that these dinosaurs swallowed vegetation whole and ground it with gastroliths. (Sauropods had no molars.) This adaptation would have made it possible for sauropods to eat almost continuously and thus generate enough energy to sustain their huge bodies.

Gastroliths have also been found in the fossilized stomachs of PLESIOSAURS.

genera (JEN-er-ah)
Plural of GENUS.

genus (JEE-nus) (Latin meaning "race" or "kind")
A unit of classification for plants and animals; a group of similar and closely related species. Some species within a genus can interbreed to produce hybrids (like the mule). Species of different genera cannot. Canis (the group to which dogs belong) is a genus. There are many species of Canis— dogs, wolves, foxes, coyotes, jackals. The same is true of dinosaurs. *Triceratops* is a genus name. There were many species of *Triceratops*. Dinosaurs are known by their genera names. As a rule, only scientists are familiar with the species names of the different dinosaur genera. *Tyrannosaurus rex* is one of the few that is well known by its full species name. *Tyrannosaurus* is the genus name and *rex* is the species name.

GENYODECTES (jen-ee-o-DEK-teez) "Biting Jaw" (Greek *genyos* = jaw + *dektes* = biting, because they were the jaws of a meat eater)
A Late Cretaceous CARNOSAUR. A partial skull including the jaws is all that is known of this dinosaur. The skull is similar to that of TYRANNOSAURUS, and *Genyodectes* may be a member of the TYRANNOSAURIDS. The FOSSILS of this large two-legged meat eater were found in Argentina.
Classification: Carnosauria, Theropoda, Saurischia

GEOSAURUS (JEE-o-sawr-us) "Earth Lizard" (Greek *ge-* =

earth + *sauros* = lizard. It is no longer known why this animal was given this name.)

Not a DINOSAUR, but an ocean-dwelling Early Jurassic crocodile. It had a long snout and paddlelike arms and legs. It was 15 feet (4.5 m) long, and its tail was broad and flat. *Geosaurus* went ashore only to lay EGGS. Its FOSSILS have been found in Belgium and Argentina.

GERANOSAURUS (jer-AN-o-sawr-us) "Crane Lizard" (Greek *geranos* = crane + *sauros* = lizard, referring to its long, slender legs)

The first Triassic ORNITHISCHIAN ever discovered and one of the three earliest known. Only PISANOSAURUS and HETERODONTOSAURUS are older in age. *Geranosaurus* was an ORNITHOPOD —a two-legged plant eater. It resembled *Heterodontosaurus* and had long, slender legs, a horny, beaklike snout, and canine TEETH. It is known only from a broken skull, lower jaws, a couple of leg bones, and part of a FOOT. These were found in Late Triassic deposits in South Africa.

Classification: Heterodontosauridae, Ornithopoda, Ornithischia

GIGANDIPUS (jih-GAN-dih-pus) "Giant Biped" (Greek *gigantos* = giant + *dipous* = two-footed, because only large hind footprints are known)

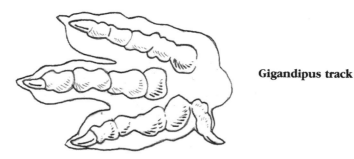

Gigandipus track

151

Name given to TRACKS made by a large, three-toed BIPEDAL dinosaur in Late Triassic or very early Jurassic mud in what is now the Connecticut River Valley. Scientists believe these tracks were made by a large CARNOSAUR, possibly a North American species of the European carnosaur TERATOSAURUS. So far, no bones of the animal that made the tracks have been found.

GILMOREOSAURUS (gil-MOHR-o-sawr-us) "Gilmore's Lizard" (Named in honor of Charles W. Gilmore, American paleontologist, + Greek *sauros* = lizard) Formerly considered a species of MANDSCHUROSAURUS.

The earliest-known HADROSAURINE (flat-headed HADROSAUR). This primitive duckbill had many IGUANODONT features and was rather small for a hadrosaur. Like all hadrosaurs, it walked on two legs and ate plants. It is known from an incomplete skeleton found in Middle Cretaceous sediments in Asia.

Classification: Hadrosauridae, Ornithopoda, Ornithischia

Gondwanaland (gond-WAH-nah-land) (Named for the land of the Gonds, an ancient kingdom of central India)

The name given to the southern supercontinent that was formed when PANGAEA broke up about 180 million years ago. It was made up of what are now called South America, Africa, Arabia, India, Madagascar, Australia, New Zealand, and Antarctica.

GONGBUSAURUS (GONG-boo-sawr-us) "Gongbu Lizard" (Named for the Gongbu region, where it was found, + Greek *sauros* = lizard)

A small Late Jurassic ORNITHOPOD of the FABROSAUR family.

This 3-foot (91-cm)-long, two-legged plant eater had a horny beak. It is known from fragments found in China.

Classification: Fabrosauridae, Ornithopoda, Ornithischia

GORGOSAURUS (GOHR-go-sawr-us) "Terrible Lizard" (Greek *gorgos* = terrible + *sauros* = lizard, referring to its enormous mouth and TEETH)

See ALBERTOSAURUS. These two dinosaurs are now considered to be the same animal, though *Gorgosaurus* may be a somewhat smaller species. The name *Albertosaurus* is the older name and therefore is the preferred one, even though the name *Gorgosaurus* was given to a nearly complete skeleton found in Alberta, Canada, whereas the name *Albertosaurus* was given to very fragmentary remains. FOSSILS assigned to *Gorgosaurus* have also been found in Baja California.

Classification: Carnosauria, Theropoda, Saurischia

GOYOCEPHALE (go-yo-SEF-ah-lee) "Decorated Head" (Mongolian *goyo* = decorated, elegant + Greek *kephale* = head, because of the pits and grooves on the head)

A low-domed PACHYCEPHALOSAUR similar to HOMALOCEPHALE found in Late Cretaceous deposits of Mongolia. This BIPEDAL, dome-headed plant eater is known from a partial skull and skeletal remains including much of the TAIL, the face, and hind limbs. Its flat skull roof is rough and pitted. It is unusual in having a pair of large, stabbing TEETH in the upper and lower jaws.

Classification: Pachycephalosauridae, Ornithopoda or Pachycephalosauria, Ornithischia

GRALLATOR (grah-LAH-tor) "Stilt Walker" (Latin *grallator*

Grallator track

= one who walks on stilts, referring to the length of the stride)

Name given to three-toed dinosaur footprints that resemble those of long-legged wading birds. These TRACKS have been found in Late Triassic or Early Jurassic rock in the eastern and southwestern United States, and in Germany, France, and Africa. The animal that made them was a small, two-legged, birdlike dinosaur that probably resembled COELOPHYSIS. It is possible that they were made by that dinosaur or a very close relative. Similar but smaller prints have been found recently in Nova Scotia. It is unknown whether these 200-million-year-old dime-sized tracks were made by an adult or a baby.

GRAVITHOLUS (grav-ih-THOH-lus) "Heavy Dome" (Latin *gravis* = heavy + *tholus* = dome, referring to its thickened skull)

A new GENUS of PACHYCEPHALOSAUR (dome-headed dinosaur). This Late Cretaceous creature is known only from a skull found in Alberta, Canada. Its skull roof was very wide and was thicker than that of STEGOCERAS, though its BRAIN was about the same SIZE as that of *Stegoceras*. Instead of knobs and spikes such as are found on some pachycephalosaur skulls, the skull of *Gravitholus* had a large depression and many smaller pits.

Like all pachycephalosaurs, *Gravitholus* was a BIPEDAL plant eater. It was probably about the same size as *Stegoceras*.

Classification: Pachycephalosauridae, Ornithopoda or Pachycephalosauria, Ornithischia

H

HADROSAURICHNUS (had-ro-sawr-IK-nus) "Bulky Lizard Footprint" (Greek *hadros* = bulky + *sauros* = lizard + *ichnos* = footprint)

Name given to ORNITHOPOD footprints that were found in Late Cretaceous sediments in northern Argentina. These TRACKS resemble those of duck-billed dinosaurs (HADROSAURS) and are thought to have been made by one of them.

hadrosaurids or **Hadrosauridae** (had-ro-SAWR-ih-dee) "Duck-billed Lizards" (Named after HADROSAURUS) Commonly called hadrosaurs.

The family of ORNITHOPODS called "duckbills" because their long, flat snouts were covered by horny material like the beak of a duck. They walked on two legs with their bodies horizontal and their TAILS extended for balance. They may have browsed on all fours. Hadrosaurs had strong, heavy legs; three-toed FEET; medium-length arms; and webbed, four-fingered HANDS. The toes were hoofed. The SKIN had a pebbly surface, and some hadrosaurs were covered with small, scaly, knob-like bumps. There were no TEETH in the front of the jaws, but the sides of the jaws were lined with hundreds of teeth arranged in several very complicated rows. Hadrosaurs ranged in size from 10 to 40 feet (3 to 12.2 m) long.

Because of their webbed hands, it was once thought that hadrosaurs were water dwellers that ate soft water plants. Scientists now believe that hadrosaurs lived in upland regions. They probably went into water only to escape predators such as ALBERTOSAURUS or TYRANNOSAURUS. Fossilized stomach contents show that they ate leaves, twigs, pine needles, seed, and fruit—FOOD of land animals.

Hadrosaurs seem to have evolved from an Asian IGUANO-DONT, PROBACTROSAURUS. They have been found in Late Cretaceous sediments in North America, South America, Europe, and Asia. Remains recovered on the north shores of Alaska suggest seasonal migration for these dinosaurs. Two kinds of hadrosaurs are known: HADROSAURINES, which were crestless or had solid skull CRESTS—ANATOSAURUS, BRACHYLOPHOSAURUS, and SAUROLOPHUS belonged to this group; and LAMBEOSAURINES, which had hollow crests—CORYTHOSAURUS, LAMBEOSAURUS, and PARASAUROLOPHUS were members of this group. Because of differences in their body skeletons, scientists can tell which group a hadrosaur belongs to even if they have not found its skull.

hadrosaurines or **Hadrosaurinae** (had-ro-SAWR-ih-nee) "Bulky Lizards" (Named after HADROSAURUS)

One of the two groups or subfamilies of HADROSAURS (duck-billed dinosaurs). Members of this group had long, slender limbs and low SPINES on their pelvic vertebrae. Their duck-like bills flared only slightly at the end and, in some, curled up a little along the edges, making them rather spoon-shaped. Some had CRESTS of solid bone; others had no crests at all. These HERBIVORES lived in North America, Europe, and Asia during Late Cretaceous times. ANATOSAURUS, BRACHYLOPHOSAURUS, CLAOSAURUS, EDMONTOSAURUS, GILMOREOSAURUS, HADROSAURUS, LOPHORHOTHON, PROSAUROLOPHUS, and SAUROLOPHUS were hadrosaurines.

hadrosaurs (HAD-ro-sawrz)
See HADROSAURIDS.

HADROSAURUS (HAD-ro-sawr-us) "Bulky Lizard" (Greek *hadros* = bulky + *sauros* = lizard, because it was a large animal)

The first dinosaur discovered in North America that has been recorded. The FOSSILS of this Late Cretaceous HADROSAUR were first found in New Jersey, but remains have since been found in Montana and Alberta, Canada, as well. Although the top of its skull has not been found, *Hadrosaurus* is considered to be a HADROSAURINE because of its body structure. *Hadrosaurus* was 30 feet (9 m) long, 10 feet (3 m) tall at the hips, and weighed 3 tons (2.7 metric tons). It walked on two legs and ate plants.

Some scientists consider *Hadrosaurus* and KRITOSAURUS to

Hadrosaurus

be the same. Others think that although these two hadro-saurs were quite similar, they were different GENERA.

Classification: Hadrosauridae, Ornithopoda, Ornithischia

HALLOPUS (HAL-o-pus) "Different Foot" (Greek *allo-* = different + *pous* = foot, because its foot was unlike those of dinosaurs)

Not a DINOSAUR, although at first it was thought to be. Further study of additional remains of this creature has led some scientists to think it was a THECODONT. Others believe it was a CROCODILIAN. It was about the size of a rooster and had four fingers and three toes. Its FOSSILS have been found in Colorado. It lived during Late Triassic and very early Jurassic times. It is known from a partial skeleton and a few other fragmentary bits.

HALTICOSAURUS (hal-tik-o-SAWR-us) "Nimble Lizard" (Greek *haltikos* = nimble + *sauros* = lizard, because it appeared to be agile)

A very primitive Late Triassic COELUROSAUR. This meat-eating BIPED is one of the earliest-known THEROPODS. It was small, agile, and lightly built, with FEET similar to those of the PROSAUROPODS. It was probably an early ancestor of PROCOMPSOGNATHUS and COELOPHYSIS. It is known from a fragmentary skeleton found in Germany.

Classification: Coelurosauria, Theropoda, Saurischia

hands

The forefeet of BIPEDAL dinosaurs are frequently called "hands." Each dinosaur group had distinctive hands, and scientists can tell by looking at a FOSSIL hand which dinosaur group it belonged to. Five-fingered hands, arranged some-

Hands

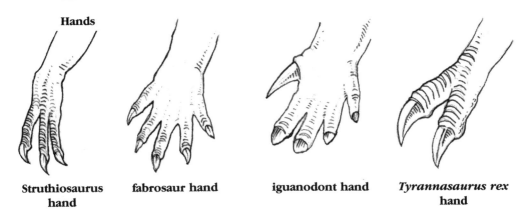

Struthiosaurus hand   fabrosaur hand   iguanodont hand   *Tyrannasaurus rex* hand

what like those of human hands with four short fingers and a shorter thumb, were the most common among the ORNITHOPODS. In all groups, the fingers were tipped with hooflike nails. The earliest ornithopod families—the FABROSAURS and the HYPSILOPHODONTS—had hands that appeared to be capable of grasping, quite similar to those of THEROPODS. However, the fingers were shorter. It is not known what they may have held. In some IGUANODONTS, the thumb was a bony spike that was probably used as a DEFENSE weapon. The HADROSAURS had only four fingers, which were connected with webbing.

The number of fingers on the hands of theropods ranged from two to five. Most COELUROSAURS had strong, three-fingered grasping hands. The fingers were long and could have been used to catch and hold large prey. Some CARNOSAURS may have had five-fingered hands, but most had only three, and the TYRANNOSAURS had only two. The fingers in both coelurosaurs and carnosaurs ended in long, sharp CLAWS—up to 12 inches (15 cm) long.

HAPLOCANTHOSAURUS (hap-lo-KANTH-o-sawr-us) "Single-spined Lizard" (Greek *haplo-* = single + *akantha* = spine, thorn + *sauros* = lizard, referring to its single-spined

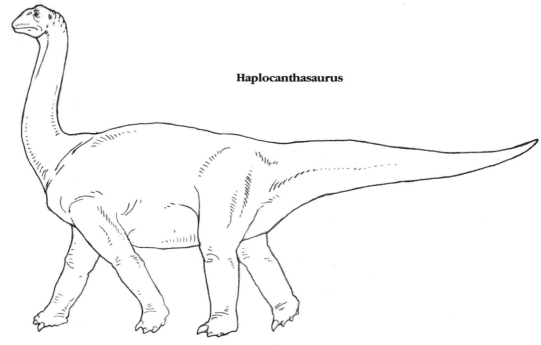

Haplocanthasaurus

vertebrae as opposed to the double SPINE on some SAUROPOD vertebrae)

An early North American sauropod—the most primitive known from this continent. This 72-foot (22-m) QUADRUPEDAL plant eater resembled CETIOSAURUS. It had long forelegs, a long body, and a relatively short neck and tail; the bones in its vertebrae were nearly solid instead of spongy. A nearly complete skeleton of *Haplocanthosaurus* was found in Late Jurassic deposits in Colorado.

Classification: Sauropoda, Sauropodomorpha, Saurischia

HARPYMIMUS (har-pee-MYM-us) "Harpy Mimic" (For the monster in Greek mythology + Greek *mimos* = mimic)

A Late Cretaceous ORNITHOMIMID found in Mongolia. This

ostrich dinosaur was about 10 feet (3 m) long. It is known from incomplete material.

Classification: Coelurosauria, Theropoda, Saurischia

hearing

See SENSORY PERCEPTION.

HELOPUS (he-LOP-us)

See EUHELOPUS.

herbivore (HER-bih-vohr) "Plant Eater" (Latin *herba* = plant + *vorare* = to devour)

Any animal that eats mainly plants, such as modern cows or horses. There were many more plant-eating (herbivorous) dinosaurs than meat eaters. All of the ORNITHISCHIAN dinosaurs and all of the SAUROPODOMORPHS were herbivores. Compare CARNIVORE; OMNIVORE.

herbivorous (her-BIV-or-us)

See HERBIVORE.

herding, herds

Many modern animals herd together for protection. Scientists think that many dinosaurs herded for the same reason. (See DEFENSE.) They have found evidence to support this theory. At Dinosaur State Park in Connecticut, thousands of dinosaur footprints have been uncovered. Some of these are parallel, suggesting herd movement. At Holyoke, Massachusetts, the TRACKWAYS of 19 BIPEDAL dinosaurs lead in a westerly direction. According to scientists, this is clearly evidence of herding. Near Glen Rose, Texas, a long line of huge tracks records the passage of a herd of SAUROPODS. These FOSSIL footprints seem to show an elephantlike herd structure, with YOUNG in the center surrounded by adults.

TRACKS are not the only evidence that dinosaurs herded. In Belgium, scientists discovered the skeletons of 31 adult IGUANODONS that had met simultaneous death. The bones of adult and juvenile ALLOSAURUS have been found together in Utah; entire families of COELOPHYSIS (from very young to adult) have been found in New Mexico; and great numbers of skeletons of PROTOCERATOPS (from hatchlings to adults) have been found together in Mongolia.

Herding is generally associated only with warm-blooded animals. Thus, herding behavior in dinosaurs is a strong argument for those scientists who believe dinosaurs were ENDOTHERMIC (warm-blooded).

herrerasaurids or **Herrerasauridae** (her-ray-rah-SAWR-ih-dee) "Herrera's Lizards" (Named after HERRERASAURUS)

The most primitive family of PROSAUROPODS. Some scien-

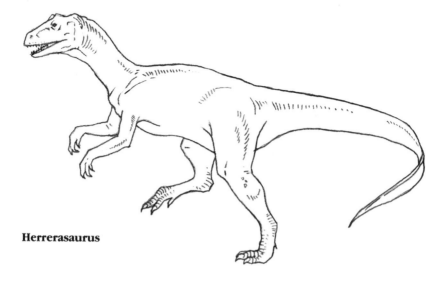

Herrerasaurus

tists think that this group may have included the ancestors of all the SAURISCHIAN dinosaurs. The herrerasaurids lived during Middle Triassic times and have been found in Argentina. They were smaller than later groups and were capable of walking on two or four legs. They had bladelike TEETH, perhaps for eating meat, as well as teeth adapted for eating plants. *Herrerasaurus* and ISCHISAURUS were members of this family. They are the oldest known saurischian dinosaurs.

Some scientists suggest that this family should be placed in a suborder called PALEOPODA.

HERRERASAURUS (her-RAY-rah-sawr-us) "Herrera's Lizard" (Named for an Argentine goatherd, a friend of the discoverer, + Greek *sauros* = lizard)

A primitive PROSAUROPOD, and one of the earliest-known dinosaurs. It was closely related to the ancestors of all SAURISCHIAN dinosaurs. *Herrerasaurus* resembled ANCHISAURUS but was smaller and more primitive. It probably walked on two legs. Its neck was short. *Herrerasaurus* is known from a nearly complete skeleton and remains of five individuals found in Argentina. This 230-million-year-old meat eater lived in Middle Triassic times. It was 6 to 8 feet (1.5 to 2 m) long and weighed 300 pounds (136 kg).

Classification: Prosauropoda, Sauropodomorpha, Saurischia

HESPERORNIS (hes-per-ORN-iss) "Western Bird" (Greek *hesperos* = western + *ornis* = bird, referring to the area where it was found)

Not a DINOSAUR, but a 4-foot (1.2-m) primitive, flightless bird resembling a modern loon or grebe. Although this bird could not fly, it was a good swimmer and diver. It lived on the surface of the NIOBRARA SEA. Sharp teeth lined the beak of this fish eater. Its FOSSILS were found in Late Cretaceous deposits in Kansas and Alberta, Canada.

HESPEROSUCHUS (hes-per-o-SOOK-us) "Western Crocodile" (Greek *hesperos* = western + *souchos* = crocodile, because it was discovered in western regions)

Not a DINOSAUR, but a small PSEUDOSUCHIAN of Late Triassic western North America. It had sharp teeth and grasping hands. This agile meat eater was 4 feet (1.2 m) long, about the size of a modern fox. It walked on four legs but probably ran on two. Dinosaurs are thought to have EVOLVED from a similar, but earlier, type of THECODONT.

heterodontosaurids or **Heterodontosauridae** (het-er-o-don-to-SAWR-ih-dee) "Different-toothed Lizards" (Named after HETERODONTOSAURUS) Also commonly called heterodontosaurs.

A family of primitive ORNITHOPODS. Members of this family had unusual TEETH for ORNITHISCHIANS. They had canine teeth in both upper and lower jaws; biting teeth in the front upper jaw that bit against a horny, toothless beak on the lower jaw; and flat-topped teeth in the back part of the jaws. These BIPEDAL plant eaters were quite small—about the size of a turkey. They have been found in Late Triassic sediments in South Africa. GERANOSAURUS, HETERODONTOSAURUS, and LYCORHINUS were members of this family.

HETERODONTOSAURUS (het-er-o-DON-to-sawr-us) "Different-toothed Lizard" (Greek *hetero-* = different + *odon-*

164

Heterodontosaurus

to- = tooth + *sauros* = lizard, referring to its three different kinds of TEETH)

A very primitive ORNITHOPOD; the first Triassic ORNITHISCHIAN known from a nearly complete skeleton. It was found in South Africa. The bones were fastened together, so scientists could tell exactly how they looked when the animal died. This BIPEDAL plant eater had a turkey-size body. It was built for SPEED and had grasping HANDS. Unlike most HERBIVOROUS dinosaurs, which had only one kind of teeth, *Heterodontosaurus* had three kinds. The front uppers, which were designed for biting and nipping, bit against a horny, toothless beak at the front of the lower jaw. There were broad, flat teeth in the back and sides of the jaws that acted like scissors to chop food, plus a pair of tusklike teeth called caniniforms in both the upper and lower jaws.

Classification: Heterodontosauridae, Ornithopoda, Ornithischia

HIEROSAURUS (hy-er-o-SAWR-us) "Powerful Lizard" (Greek *hieros* = powerful, holy + *sauros* = lizard. The reason for its name is unknown.)

A Late Cretaceous ANKYLOSAUR found in the NIOBRARA SEA formation in Kansas. *Hierosaurus* was probably washed into the sea by a flood. It is believed by some authorities that this dinosaur is the same as NODOSAURUS.

Classification: Nodosauridae, Ankylosauria, Ornithischia

HOMALOCEPHALE (ho-mah-lo-SEF-ah-lee) "Level Head" (Greek *homalos* = level + *kephale* = head, referring to its dome)

A Late Cretaceous PACHYCEPHALOSAUR (dome-headed dinosaur). It is known from a partial skull and parts of the skeleton found in Mongolia. Its head was large and flat. The dome was only slightly developed and was decorated with nodes along the back like the dome of PACHYCEPHALOSAURUS. It has been suggested that *Homalocephale* might have been a female pachycephalosaur, but others doubt this. Like all pachycephalosaurs, *Homalocephale* was BIPEDAL and ate plants. It had short forelegs and was probably about the size of a goat.

Classification: Pachycephalosauridae, Ornithopoda or Pachycephalosauria, Ornithischia

Homalocephale

homoiotherm (HO-moy-o-therm) "Uniform Heat" (Greek *homoios* = uniform + *therme* = heat)

An animal whose body temperature remains very nearly the same all the time. Usually homoiotherms are ENDOTHERMIC (warm-blooded), but large-bodied ECTOTHERMS (cold-blooded animals) may also achieve a uniform temperature. The larger an ectotherm's body, the slower the rate of heat absorption and heat loss.

Some scientists suggest that the very large dinosaurs, such as the SAUROPODS, were homoiotherms (but not necessarily endotherms). They believe that these dinosaurs could have maintained a nearly uniform body temperature in the mild Mesozoic climate without being warm-blooded, simply because they were so large.

homoiothermic

See HOMOIOTHERM.

HOPLITOSAURUS (hop-LITE-o-sawr-us) "Hoplite Lizard" (Greek *hoplites* = a heavily armed foot soldier + *sauros* = lizard, referring to the plates on its back)

An ANKYLOSAUR of Early Cretaceous South Dakota. This armored dinosaur was similar to SAUROPELTA, and some think it may be the same as that dinosaur. Its back was covered with rows of flattened, horny plates like those of an armadillo. *Hoplitosaurus* walked on four legs and ate plants. It is known only from incomplete material.

Classification: Nodosauridae, Ankylosauria, Ornithischia

horned dinosaurs

See CERATOPSIANS.

horns

The best-known of the horned dinosaurs are the CERATOP-SIANS. Their horns were used as DEFENSE weapons, and male ceratopsians may have used their horns as dueling weapons in fighting for mates or territories, as modern-day mountain goats do. Both male and female ceratopsians had horns; babies, however, were hornless until they were half grown. Some ceratopsians had small, stubby horns on their brows and a long nose horn—STYRACOSAURUS had a nose horn 2 feet (60 cm) long! Others had a short nose horn and very long brow horns.

CERATOSAURUS had a hornlike growth on its nose. It is the only known THEROPOD with such a growth. MAIASAURA, a HAD-ROSAUR, had a hornlike CREST, but this was not a true horn.

HUAYANGOSAURUS (hwah-YAHNG-o-sawr-us) "Huayang Lizard" (Named for the town of Huayang in Shanxi, China, where it was found, + Greek *sauros* = lizard)

A primitive STEGOSAUR from Middle Jurassic deposits of China. It is one of the oldest stegosaurs known. This 13.5-foot (4-m) dinosaur resembled STEGOSAURUS in many ways, but its plates and tail spikes were different. Its skull is deeper and more square than that of *Stegosaurus* and there are TEETH in the upper jaw. This four-legged plant eater is known from a nearly complete skeleton.

Classification: Stegosauridae, Stegosauria, Ornithischia

HULSANPES (HOOL-san-peez) "Foot from Khulsan" (Named for Khulsan, the place in Mongolia where it was found, + Latin *pes* = foot)

A very small DROMAEOSAUR found in Late Cretaceous deposits of Mongolia. This BIPEDAL meat eater is known only from an incomplete foot that resembles the feet of DEINONYCHUS.

Classification: Dromaeosauridae, Theropoda, Saurischia

HYLAEOSAURUS (hy-LEE-o-sawr-us) "Wood Lizard" (Greek *hyle* = wood + *sauros* = lizard, referring to the place it was found)

A primitive ANKYLOSAUR whose FOSSILS were found in England. It was one of the first three dinosaurs to be named. *Hylaeosaurus* was similar to ACANTHOPHOLIS. Two rows of SPINES protected its hips and clubless TAIL, and spikes protected each side. This 15-foot (4.5-m)-long NODOSAUR, like all ankylosaurs, was a QUADRUPEDAL plant eater. It lived during Early Cretaceous times and is known from part of a skull base and other skeletal parts. It has been suggested that POLACANTHUS is the same as this dinosaur, but not everyone agrees.

Classification: Nodosauridae, Ankylosauria, Ornithischia

Hylaeosaurus

HYPACROSAURUS (hi-PAK-ro-sawr-us) "Nearly the Highest Lizard" (Greek *'ypakros* = nearly the highest + *sauros* = lizard, referring to the high spines on its vertebrae)

A large, hollow-crested HADROSAUR. This duck-billed dinosaur resembled CORYTHOSAURUS but had a larger and less rounded CREST. Long SPINES on its vertebrae gave it a high ridge down its back. This 30-foot (9-m) LAMBEOSAURINE was a fast-running BIPEDAL plant eater and was one of the most abundant animals of Late Cretaceous Baja California. Its FOSSILS have also been found in Alberta, Canada.

Classification: Hadrosauridae, Ornithopoda, Ornithischia

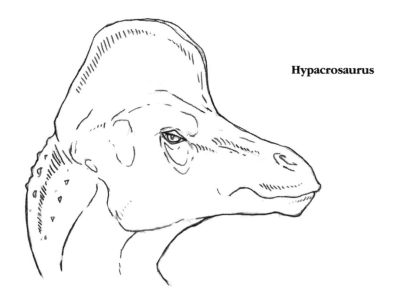

Hypacrosaurus

HYPSELOSAURUS (HIP-sih-lo-sawr-us) "High Lizard" (Greek *hypselos* = high + *sauros* = lizard, referring to its high back)

A small SAUROPOD of Late Cretaceous Europe. This four-legged plant eater resembled TITANOSAURUS. It was only 35 feet (10.7 m) long and weighed about 10 tons (9 metric tons).

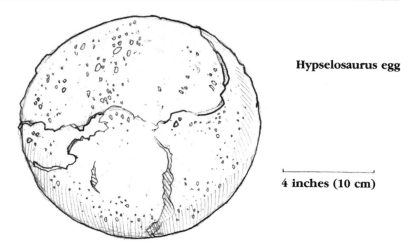

Hypselosaurus egg

4 inches (10 cm)

Hypselosaurus is best known for EGGS found in France, which scientists think were laid by this dinosaur. These FOSSIL eggs are twice the size of ostrich eggs and are nearly round; they have rough, sandpapery surfaces. They had been laid in craterlike NESTS in clutches of five and are the largest dinosaur eggs ever found.

Classification: Sauropoda, Sauropodomorpha, Saurischia

HYPSILOPHODON (hip-sih-LOHF-o-don) "High-crested Tooth" (Greek *hypselos* = high + *lophos* = crest + *odon-* = tooth, referring to the high, crestlike growths on the teeth)

A small, primitive ORNITHOPOD whose FOSSILS were first found on the Isle of Wight. This agile, long-legged, plant-eating BIPED was probably the swiftest of the ORNITHISCHIANS.

Hypsilophodon was 5 feet (1.5 m) long, 2 feet (60 cm) tall, and weighed about 140 pounds (63.5 kg). Half of its length was a rigid TAIL that it used for balancing. A few TEETH lined the front of its beaklike jaws. Although *Hypsilophodon* was once thought to be a tree climber, it is now known that it could not have been. It had grasping HANDS, but the fingers were too short to hold tree branches, and the FEET were not

171

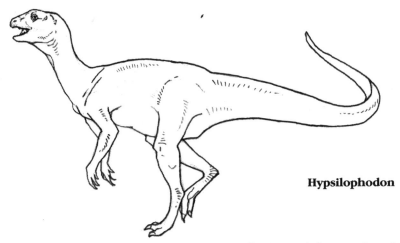

Hypsilophodon

equipped for climbing. The four toes all pointed forward and could not have gripped branches.

Hypsilophodon lived from Early to Late Cretaceous times. It is known from 20 complete or partial skeletons.

Classification: Hypsilophodontidae, Ornithopoda, Ornithischia

hypsilophodonts or **Hypsilophodontidae** (hip-sih-lohf-o-DON-tih-dee) "High-crested Tooths" (Named after HYPSILOPHODON)

A family of small- to medium-size ORNITHOPODS ranging from 2.5 to 10 feet (75 to 300 cm) long. All were BIPEDAL plant eaters with small heads, short beaklike snouts, large eyes, long legs, and medium-length arms. The TEETH were set in a single row, and there were no large canines. Hypsilophodonts had five fingers and four toes. They lived from Late Triassic through Cretaceous times and have been found in North America, South America, Europe, and Africa. Some scientists suggest that hypsilophodonts were the ancestors of the PACHYCEPHALOSAURS. DRYOSAURUS, HYPSILOPHODON, ORODROMEUS, OTHNIELIA, PARKSOSAURUS, and PISANOSAURUS were hypsilophodonts. A new species, as yet unnamed, was recently found in Early Cretaceous deposits in the Lake Proctor region of Texas. It is known from six nearly complete skeletons of 10-foot (3-m) long adults and ten chicken-size juveniles, which were found in a nestlike depression.

I

ICHTHYORNIS (ik-thee-ORN-iss) "Fish Bird" (Greek *ichthys* = fish + *ornis* = bird, referring to its diet)

Not a DINOSAUR, but a primitive bird similar to a sea gull. This bird was 8 inches (20 cm) tall. It had long wings, a flat beak, and teeth. It is the oldest known bird that could fly well. *Ichthyornis* was a fish eater. Its FOSSILS have been found in Kansas. It lived during Late Cretaceous times.

ichthyosaurs or **Ichthyosauria** (ik-thee-o-SAWR-ee-ah) "Fish Lizards" (Greek *ichthys* = *fish* + *sauros* = lizard, because they resembled fish)

Not DINOSAURS, but Mesozoic marine REPTILES with vertical tail fins and long, streamlined heads. These 7- to 30-foot (4.5- to 9-m)-long flesh eaters gave birth to live YOUNG. We know this because scientists have found skeletons of adult ichthyosaurs that contained baby ichthyosaurs within the abdominal cavity. These animals could not leave the water to lay their EGGS as sea turtles do. Scientists think that ichthyosaurs retained the eggs in their body cavities until they hatched. Ichthyosaurs appeared in the middle of the TRIASSIC PERIOD and lived to Cretaceous times. They have been found in North America, South America, and Europe.

IGUANODON (ig-WAHN-o-don) "Iguana Tooth" (Iguana + Greek *odon-* = tooth, because its TEETH resembled those of the modern iguana lizard)

Iguanodon

An Early Cretaceous ORNITHOPOD. The largest known specimens were 25 feet (7.5 m) long, 15 feet (4.5 m) tall, and weighed 5 tons (4.5 metric tons). This BIPEDAL, plant-eating dinosaur had three-toed FEET; its five-fingered HANDS had unique spikelike thumbs that grew at right angles to the other four fingers.

Traces of *Iguanodon* have been found on every continent except Antarctica. It was the second dinosaur named, and perhaps the first ever found. Several dozen adult specimens were found buried together in Belgium, which suggests that these animals traveled in HERDS.

Classification: Iguanodontidae, Ornithopoda, Ornithischia

iguanodont or **Iguanodontidae** (ig-wahn-o-DON-tih-dee) "Iguana-toothed" (Named after IGUANODON)

A family of large ORNITHOPODS with medium- to large-sized

heads, long toes, and TEETH arranged in a single row. These BIPEDAL plant eaters ranged in SIZE from 15 to 25 feet (4.5 to 7.5 m) long. They probably lived all over the world from Late Jurassic through Late Cretaceous times. IGUANODON, OURANOSAURUS, PROBACTROSAURUS, and TENONTOSAURUS were iguanodonts. (*Probactrosaurus* is thought to be the ancestor of the HADROSAURS.)

ILIOSUCHUS (il-ee-o-SOOK-us) "Crocodile Pelvis" (Latin *ilium* = pelvis + Greek *souchos* = crocodile)

A Middle Jurassic THEROPOD from Great Britain and possibly North America. It is known only from two pelvises. The classification of this dinosaur is uncertain. It may be a relative of ORNITHOLESTES. STOKESOSAURUS, which was found in Utah, may be the same as this dinosaur.

Classification: Coeluridae?, Theropoda, Saurischia

INDOSAURUS (in-doh-SAWR-us) "Indian Lizard" (Named for India, where it was found, + Greek *sauros* = lizard)

A Late Cretaceous CARNOSAUR, it was probably similar to ALLOSAURUS but more specialized. It had a broad head, and like all carnosaurs, it walked on two legs and ate meat. *Indosaurus* belonged to the family MEGALOSAURIDAE. It is known only from a partial skull found in India.

Classification: Carnosauria, Theropoda, Saurischia

INDOSUCHUS (in-doh-SOOK-us) "Indian Crocodile" (Named for India, where it was found, + Greek *souchos* = crocodile. The reason for this name is unknown. Perhaps it was first thought to be a crocodile.)

A CARNOSAUR of Late Cretaceous India. The head of this BIPEDAL meat eater resembled that of TYRANNOSAURUS but was smaller and less advanced. Its TEETH were sharply tapered and serrated. *Indosuchus* is known only from a partial skull.

Classification: Carnosauria, Theropoda, Saurischia

INGENIA (in-JEN-ee-ah) (Named for Ingeni, the place where it was found)

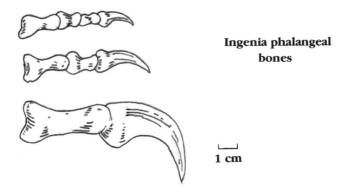

Ingenia phalangeal bones

1 cm

An OVIRAPTORID THEROPOD from Late Cretaceous deposits in southwest Mongolia. This little BIPED was closely related to OVIRAPTOR but was smaller. From the end of its toothless snout to the tip of its long TAIL, it was perhaps 4.5 feet (1.4 m) long. Like *Oviraptor,* it probably ate EGGS of other dinosaurs, insects, and possibly dead animals.

Classification: Coelurosauria, Theropoda, Saurischia

intelligence

Dinosaurs are usually considered to have been dim-witted, because most of them had very small BRAINS in proportion to the SIZE of their bodies. However, recent studies have caused scientists to think that perhaps dinosaurs were not as stupid as was formerly thought. They have discovered evidence that many kinds of dinosaurs—COELUROSAURS, ORNITHOPODS, CERATOPSIANS, PROSAUROPODS, and even SAUROPODS (which had tiny brains in comparison to their body size)—HERDED together and apparently protected their YOUNG. These are considered rather intelligent things to do. Also, most THEROPODS had relatively large brains. Those of CARNOSAURS were huge; the brain of TYRANNOSAURUS was even larger than human brains. Of course, carnosaurs were much larger than humans, but even so, their brains were a quite respectable size. Having a large brain in comparison to body size is associated with superior intelligence in modern animals. ANKYLOSAURS and STEGOSAURS had very small brains, but if nothing else, they managed to live 50 million years or more, and that is not bad for an animal such as STEGOSAURUS with a golf-ball-size brain. The most intelligent of all the dinosaurs probably was TROÖDON. It probably was at least as smart as an ostrich, which is smarter than any REPTILE living today.

ISCHISAURUS (ISS-chee-sawr-us) "Ischigualasto Lizard" (Named for the Ischigualasto rock formation, where it was found, + Greek *sauros* = lizard)

A PROSAUROPOD of Middle Triassic Argentina—one of the earliest known dinosaurs. This plant eater was related to PLATEOSAURUS but was much more primitive than that dinosaur. Like all prosauropods, it had a long neck and TAIL, and its head was small. It probably walked on all fours but could run on two. It is known only from skull fragments, parts of legs and pelvises, and some vertebrae.

Classification: Prosauropoda, Sauropodomorpha, Saurischia

ITEMIRUS (ee-TEM-ih-rus) "Itemir Lizard" (Named for the Itemir site in Russia, where it was found)

A small CARNOSAUR unlike any other known. It is known

from an extremely well preserved braincase recently found in Russia. This meat eater was somewhat similar to the TYR-ANNOSAURIDAE but was much smaller and lived earlier in the Late CRETACEOUS PERIOD. It probably shared a close ancestor with TYRANNOSAURUS. The earliest known of the Cretaceous carnosaurs, it has been placed in a family of its own—the Itemiridae.

Classification: Carnosauria, Theropoda, Saurischia

J

JAXARTOSAURUS (jak-SAR-to-sawr-us) "Jaxartes Lizard" (Named for the Jaxartes River in the U.S.S.R., near which it was found, + Greek *sauros* = lizard)

A primitive LAMBEOSAURINE HADROSAUR. This BIPEDAL plant eater is known only from fragments and a partial skull found in Late Cretaceous rock in China. The skull had a domelike CREST. Its discovery was important because it showed that hadrosaurs lived in many areas of Asia.

Classification: Hadrosauridae, Ornithopoda, Ornithischia

JIANGJUNMIAOSAURUS (jyahng-joon-MEEYOW-sawr-us) "Jiangjunmiao Lizard" (Named for the place where it was found, in Xinjiang Province, + Greek *sauros* = lizard)

A newly discovered large meat eater found in Cretaceous deposits of China. This CARNOSAUR was a close relative of AL-LOSAURUS and probably resembled that dinosaur.

Classification: Carnosauria, Theropoda, Saurischia

Jurassic (jer-ASS-ik) **Period** (Named for the Jura Mountains of France and Switzerland, because the rocks of those mountains are of that age)

The middle period of the MESOZOIC ERA. This geological period began 190 million years ago and ended 135 million years ago.

Very little is known about the dinosaurs of Early Jurassic times because most rock formations of that age (that we know about) are marine sediments, and dinosaurs were land animals. However, exciting new dinosaur discoveries that are of Early Jurassic age have been made in India. We may soon know much more about the dinosaurs of this age.

Many FOSSILS of Late Jurassic dinosaurs have been found. The largest of the dinosaurs (and the largest known land animals) lived during this period.

K

KELMAYISAURUS (KEL-my-sawr-us) "Kelmay Lizard" (Named for the city in Xinjiang Province near which it was found + Greek *sauros* = lizard)

A large, two-legged meat eater that lived in China during the Early CRETACEOUS PERIOD. This close relative of MEGALO-SAURUS is known only from the lower jaw.

Classification: Carnosauria, Theropoda, Saurischia

KENTROSAURUS (KEN-tro-sawr-us) "Spiked Lizard" (Greek *kentro-* = spike + *sauros* = lizard, referring to the spikes on its back)

A Late Jurassic STEGOSAUR. A double row of plates ran down the neck of this dinosaur and halfway down its back; from

Kentrosaurus

there, pairs of spikes ran to the tip of the TAIL. Another pair of spikes projected from the hips. The tail ended in double spikes. This plant eater was 16 feet (4.9 m) long and weighed 2 tons (1.8 metric tons) or more. It walked on four legs and had hooflike CLAWS on its toes. A nearly complete skeleton was found in Tanzania.

Classification: Stegosauridae, Stegosauria, Ornithischia

KRITOSAURUS (KRIT-o-sawr-us) "Noble Lizard" (Greek *kritos* = excellent, noble + *sauros* = lizard, because of its "Roman nose")

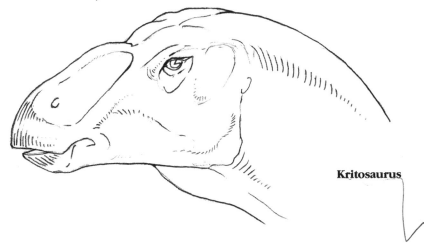

Kritosaurus

A Late Cretaceous HADROSAUR with a flat, broad head and a low ridge of bone in front of its eyes, giving it a humped nose. Some scientists think this duckbill was identical to HADROSAURUS, but others think they are different GENERA. *Kritosaurus* was a BIPEDAL plant eater. Its remains have been found in New Mexico and Baja California, and it is known from a nearly complete skeleton. It was about 30 feet (9.1 m) long and 15 feet (4.6 m) tall, and probably weighed about 3 tons (2.7 metric tons).

Classification: Hadrosauridae, Ornithopoda, Ornithischia

KRONOSAURUS (KROH-no-sawr-us) "Saturn's Lizard" (Greek Kronos = god of time [Roman Saturn] + *sauros* = lizard)

Not a DINOSAUR, but a short-necked, large-headed PLESIOSAUR. This marine REPTILE was 40 feet (12 m) long, and its head was 12 feet (3 m) long, the largest-known reptile skull. It propelled itself through Early Cretaceous oceans with long flippers. FOSSILS of this fish eater have been found in Australia.

"KUMMING-LONG" (KOOM-MING-long) "Kumming Dragon" (Unofficially named for Kumming City, Yünnan Province, China, where it was found, + Chinese *long* = dragon)

A newly discovered crested meat eater found in Early Jurassic deposits in China. It was similar to DILOPHOSAURUS except it had only 32 TEETH and its head was smaller and had a single CREST instead of a double one. This dinosaur was 17 feet (5.2 m) long. Its skull was 15 inches (40 cm) long. "Kumming-Long" is known from a nearly complete skeleton.

Classification: Carnosauria, Theropoda, Saurischia

L

LABOCANIA (lah-boh-KAHN-ee-ah) (Named for the La Bocana Roja rock formation, where it was found)

A large CARNOSAUR whose FOSSILS were found in Baja California. *Labocania* was related to TYRANNOSAURUS, but it was only two-thirds as large as TYRANNOSAURUS and had a larger head and a more massive body. Only a few bones of this BIPEDAL meat eater have been found. It lived during very early Late Cretaceous times.

Classification: Carnosauria, Theropoda, Saurischia

LAELAPS (LEE-laps) "Terrible Leaper" (Named for a hunting dog in Greek mythology)

Same as DRYPTOSAURUS. *Laelaps* was the first name given to this large CARNOSAUR, but the name was changed because another FOSSIL animal had already been named *Laelaps*.

Classification: Carnosauria, Theropoda, Saurischia

LAGOSUCHUS (lah-go-SOOK-us) "Rabbit Crocodile" (Greek *lagos* = hare + *souchos* = crocodile, referring to its SIZE)

Not a DINOSAUR, but a primitive PSEUDOSUCHIAN THECODONT. This rabbit-size creature was lightly built and had a small head. Like all early pseudosuchians, it probably held its body partially upright rather than sprawling. Its hind legs were strong, and its HANDS could grasp small prey. Scientists think that one of its relatives may have been an ancestor of the

THEROPOD dinosaurs. *Lagosuchus* lived during Late Triassic times. Its FOSSILS have been found in Argentina.

lambeosaurine or **Lambeosaurinae** (lam-bee-o-SAWR-ih-nee) "Lambe's Lizards" (Named after LAMBEOSAURUS)

One of the two groups of HADROSAURS; these were the hollow-crested duck-billed dinosaurs. Members of this group had robust limbs, high SPINES on their pelvic vertebrae, and broad, blunt beaks. The lower jaws curved downward. These HERBIVORES ranged in size from 13 to 40 feet (4 to 12 m) long. They lived during Late Cretaceous times and have been found in North America from Mexico to the north shores of Alaska, and in Asia. CORYTHOSAURUS, HYPACROSAURUS, LAMBEOSAURUS, PARASAUROLOPHUS, and TSINTAOSAURUS were lambeosaurines. Compare HADROSAURINES.

LAMBEOSAURUS (LAM-bee-o-sawr-us) "Lambe's Lizard" (Named in honor of Lawrence Lambe, Canadian vertebrate PALEONTOLOGIST, + Greek *sauros* = lizard)

Lambeosaurus

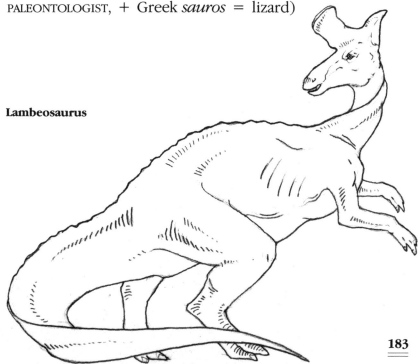

A Late Cretaceous, hollow-crested HADROSAUR (a LAMBEO-SAURINE). This duck-billed dinosaur may have been the long-est ORNITHISCHIAN dinosaur. The largest-known specimen was 40 feet (12 m) or more in length.

Lambeosaurus had a large, hatchet-shaped CREST with a backward-pointing spike. Its nose was narrow and ended in a broad, blunt beak. Its SKIN was pebbly, like that of CORYTHO-SAURUS, but lacked the bumps on the stomach. Pine needles and twigs or leaves of flowering trees were its favorite FOOD. This BIPED lived in upland regions. It is known from com-plete skeletons found in Alberta, Canada, and Baja California. It was almost as abundant as HYPACROSAURUS.

Classification: Hadrosauridae, Ornithopoda, Ornithischia

LANASAURUS (LAN-ah-sawr-us) "Woolly Lizard" (Latin *lana* = wool + Greek *sauros* = lizard)

A small, Late Triassic ORNITHOPOD found in South Africa. It was closely related to HETERODONTOSAURUS. It is known only from an upper jaw and some TEETH.

Classification: Heterodontosauridae, Ornithopoda, Ornith-ischia

LAOSAURUS (LAY-o-sawr-us) "Fossil Lizard" (Greek *laos* = stone, fossil + *sauros* = lizard, because the bones had turned to stone)

Name given to several Late Jurassic FOSSILS found in the western United States. They were long-legged ORNITHOPODS of the HYPSILOPHODONT line. The name *Laosaurus* has also been given to an ornithopod found in Late Cretaceous rock in Wyoming. The Cretaceous animal was medium size—pos-sibly 7.5 feet (2.3 m) long—and was very similar to HYP-SILOPHODON. The Jurassic specimens varied greatly in size. A turkey-size specimen has been reclassified and named *Othnielia rex* (see OTHNIELIA). Other Jurassic FOSSILS called *Laosaurus* need further study.

Classification: Hypsilophodontidae, Ornithopoda, Ornithischia

LAPLATASAURUS (lah-PLAH-tah-sawr-us) "La Plata Lizard" (Named for La Plata, Argentina, where it was found, + Greek *sauros* = lizard)

A medium-sized Late Cretaceous SAUROPOD similar in appearance to DIPLODOCUS but more closely related to TITANOSAURUS. *Laplatasaurus* was a slender-limbed sauropod about 70 feet (21.3 m) long and, like *Titanosaurus,* may have had bony plates, or scutes, embedded in its SKIN. This long-necked, four-legged HERBIVORE is known only from incomplete skeletons. Its FOSSILS have been found in Argentina, Uruguay, India, Madagascar, and Nigeria. Some scientists think that its discovery in so many different regions might indicate that there was a land connection between South America and Africa during the Late CRETACEOUS PERIOD. Others think that some of the fossil remains now thought to be those of *Laplatasaurus* may actually belong to a different sauropod. Some of the specimens are so fragmentary that it is difficult to make a positive identification at this time.

Classification: Sauropoda, Sauropodomorpha, Saurischia

Laurasia (lor-AY-shah) (Named for the Laurentian Mountains of Quebec, Canada, and for Asia)

Name given to the northern supercontinent that was formed when PANGAEA broke apart about 180 million years ago. It was made up of what is now North America, Greenland, Iceland, Europe, and Asia.

LEAELLYNASAURA (lee-el-in-ah-SAWR-ah) "Leaellyn's Lizard" (Named in honor of the finder's daughter, Leaellyn Rich, who helped discover it, + Greek *sauros* = lizard)

A small, Early Cretaceous HYPSILOPHODONT. It is known from several FOSSIL bones, including a partial skull with TEETH, partial skeleton, parts of the limbs, and a partial BRAIN endocast found in Australia. This two-legged plant eater was probably 6.5 to 10 feet (2 to 3 m) long. It had well-developed optic lobes, which indicates excellent EYESIGHT. It could probably see well in the dark, which was very useful since the area of Australia where it lived was below the Antarctic Circle at that time.

Classification: Hypsilophodontidae, Ornithopoda, Ornithischia

LEPTOCERATOPS (lep-toh-SAYR-uh-tops) "Slender Horned Face" (Greek *leptos* = slender + *keratops* = horned face, referring to its slender build)

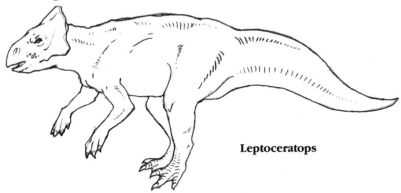

Leptoceratops

A small, primitive CERATOPSIAN. It had a large head with a short, solid FRILL and a parrotlike beak, but no HORNS. This plant eater was only 6 feet (1.8 m) long and 2.5 feet (76 cm) tall at the hips. It was basically QUADRUPEDAL but may have been capable of walking on two legs. Its forelegs were shorter than its hind legs. *Leptoceratops* is known from very complete material found in Alberta, Canada, and sediments that were formed during the late part of the Late CRETACEOUS PERIOD.

Classification: Protoceratopsidae, Ceratopsia, Ornithischia

LESOTHOSAURUS (leh-SOH-toh-sawr-us) "Lesotho Lizard" (Named for Lesotho, the country in Africa where it was found, + Greek *sauros* = lizard)

A primitive ORNITHOPOD of the FABROSAURID family. This BIPEDAL plant eater was only 3 feet (90 cm) long and was similar in build to HETERODONTOSAURUS, but it had a flatter, more primitive skull and no canine TEETH. Its small head had a horny, beaklike jaw lined with small, serrated teeth. *Lesothosaurus* had short front legs and five-fingered HANDS. The hind legs were long and slender; the FEET were also long and had hooflike CLAWS. *Lesothosaurus* probably grazed on all fours but ran on two legs. This Late Triassic dinosaur is one of the earliest known ORNITHISCHIANS. It is known from most of the skeleton and a skull found in southern Africa. It was originally considered a species of FABROSAURUS, and most descriptions of that dinosaur were based on the FOSSILS that are now known as *Lesothosaurus*.

Classification: Fabrosauridae, Ornithopoda, Ornithischia

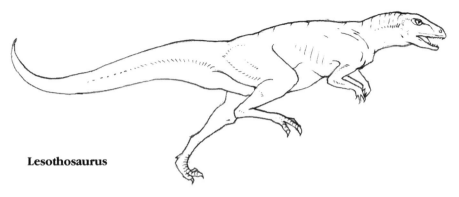

Lesothosaurus

LEXOVISAURUS (lex-OH-vih-sawr-us) "Lexovian Lizard" (Named for an ancient Gallic people who lived in the area near Lyons, France, + Greek *sauros* = lizard)

A STEGOSAUR of Middle Jurassic England and France. This four-legged plant eater was related to KENTROSAURUS but lived earlier. It is known only from incomplete material, but we do know that its plates and spikes were more varied than those of *Kentrosaurus*.

Classification: Stegosauridae, Stegosauria, Ornithischia

lizard-hipped dinosaurs
See SAURISCHIANS.

long-frilled ceratopsians
See CERATOPSIANS.

LONGOSAURUS (LONG-o-sawr-us) "Long's Lizard" (Named in honor of Robert Long, a North American PALEONTOLOGIST)

A large Late Triassic COELUROSAUR. It was 20 feet (6 m) long and had a long neck and TAIL. Its poorly preserved FOSSILS were found in New Mexico in the same deposits as COELOPHYSIS and was once thought to be a species of that dinosaur. It was a meat eater and walked on two legs.

Classification: Coelurosauria, Theropoda, Saurischia

LOPHORHOTHON (lo-fo-ROH-thon) "Crested Nose" (Greek *lophos* = crest + *rhothon* = nose, because it had a CREST on its nose)

A Late Cretaceous, solid-crested HADROSAUR whose FOSSILS have been found in Alabama and North Carolina. This duck-billed dinosaur was a member of the HADROSAURINE group and, like KRITOSAURUS, it had a solid bony hump on its nose.

It is known only from a partial skeleton, which appears to be that of a juvenile. It is estimated that this specimen was 12 to 15 feet (3.5 to 4.5 m) long. If the animal had lived to be adult, it would have grown to be much larger. Like all hadrosaurs, *Lophorhothon* was a BIPEDAL plant eater.

Classification: Hadrosauridae, Ornithopoda, Ornithischia

LUFENGOSAURUS (loo-FUNG-o-sawr-us) "Lu-Feng Lizard" (Named for the Lu-Feng rock formation, where it was found, + Greek *sauros* = lizard)

Lufengosaurus

A Late Triassic PROSAUROPOD similar to PLATEOSAURUS and about the same SIZE as that dinosaur. *Lufengosaurus* was basically QUADRUPEDAL but could stand on two legs. It had a small head and a long neck and TAIL. A nearly complete skeleton of this plant eater was found in western China. This dinosaur may be the same as MASSOSPONDYLUS.

Classification: Prosauropoda, Sauropodomorpha, Saurischia

LUKOUSAURUS (loo-ko-SAWR-us) "Lu-Kou Lizard" (Named for the place in Yünnan, China, where it was found, + Greek *sauros* = lizard)

Name given to a partial skull and jaws of a small COELUROSAUR found in Late Triassic deposits in China. This little BIPEDAL meat eater was probably closely related to PROCOMPSOGNATHUS.

Classification: Coelurosauria, Theropoda, Saurischia

LYCORHINUS (ly-ko-RY-nus) "Wolf Nose" (Greek *lykos* = wolf + *rhinos* = nose, referring to its mammallike snout)

A small Late Triassic ORNITHOPOD. It was closely related to HETERODONTOSAURUS but was somewhat more primitive. This plant eater had large canines in both its upper and lower jaws and had cheek TEETH, but no teeth in the front of its jaws. Its canines may have been used for DEFENSE. Like *Heterdontosaurus, Lycorhinus* was probably BIPEDAL. It is known only from a jaw and several teeth found in South Africa.

Classification: Heterodontosauridae, Ornithopoda, Ornithischia

M

MACROPHALANGIA (mak-ro-fah-LAN-jee-ah) "Long Toes" (Greek *makros* = long + *phalanges* = toe bones, because the toes were very long)

This dinosaur is now known to be the same as CHIROSTEN-
OTES.

MACRUROSAURUS (mak-ROO-ro-sawr-us) "Long-Tailed
Lizard" (Greek *makros* = long + *oura* = tail + *sauros* =
lizard, because of the great length of the TAIL)

Name given to 40 tail vertebrae of an Early Cretaceous SAU-
ROPOD. This four-legged plant eater was closely related to TI-
TANOSAURUS but probably resembled DIPLODOCUS. The vertebrae
were found in England. No other fossils of this dinosaur are
known.

Classification: Sauropoda, Sauropodomorpha, Saurischia

MAIASAURA (mah-ee-ah-SAWR-ah) "Good Mother Lizard"
(Greek *maia* = good mother + *saura* = lizard, feminine—
because it was found near a NEST of YOUNG)

A primitive Late Cretaceous HADROSAUR. This two-legged
duck-billed dinosaur was found in Montana near a nest of 15

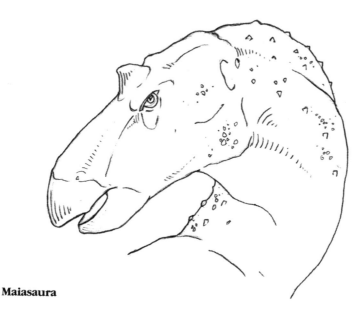

Maiasaura

babies. It is estimated that the adult, which is known only from a skull, was 30 feet (9 m) long and 15 feet (4.5 m) tall. It had a tiny, solid, horn-shaped CREST above and between its eyes. The jaws were shallow like those of the HADROSAURINES, and it belonged to that group; however, its bill was short and wide, similar to those of LAMBEOSAURINES.

The babies were a little over 3 feet (1 m) long and 12 inches (30 cm) tall. They were perhaps about a month old. Apparently they had either been taken to graze on coarse plant FOOD, or food had been brought to them in the nest, because their TEETH show considerable wear. FOSSILS of hatchlings and "adolescent" *Maiasaura* have also been found. The hatchlings were 18 inches (46 cm) long, and the half-grown juveniles were about 15 feet (4.6 m) long.

The nest found in Montana was a hollowed-out, bowl-shaped structure that had been dug on a small mud mound. It was about 7 feet (2 m) in diameter and 30 inches (76 cm) deep. There were many other such nests in the same area, suggesting a dinosaur "nursery" (or crèche). The discovery of this hadrosaur family provides some evidence that hadrosaurs cared for their young.

Classification: Hadrosauridae, Ornithopoda, Ornithischia

MAJUNGASAURUS (mah-JOONG-ah-sawr-us) "Majunga Lizard" (Named for the Majunga District of Madagascar, where it was found, + Greek *sauros* = lizard)

A medium-size CARNOSAUR of Late Cretaceous Madagascar. This BIPEDAL meat eater was a member of the MEGALOSAUR family. It is known from an incomplete jaw, some TEETH, and numerous other skeletal remains.

Classification: Carnosauria, Theropoda, Saurischia

MAJUNGATHOLUS (mah-JOONG-ah-tho-lus) "Majunga Dome" (Named for the Majunga District of Madagascar, where it was found, + Latin *tholus* = dome, because it had a domed skull)

The first PACHYCEPHALOSAUR to be found in GONDWANALAND sediments. It is known only from a partial skull found in Madagascar. Unlike the skulls of most pachycephalosaurs, which have divided domes on the back of the skull and small fenestrae (holes) in the temples, the skull of *Majungatholus* has a single dome on the front portion and large fenestrae at the temples. The sides of the skull are decorated with nodes, or small bumps, and grooves. This Late Cretaceous dinosaur was larger than most pachycephalosaurs. The only larger "dome-head" was PACHYCEPHALOSAURUS. Like other pachycephalosaurs, *Majungatholus* was BIPEDAL and ate plants.

Classification: Pachycephalosauridae, Ornithopoda or Pachycephalosauria, Ornithischia

MAMENCHISAURUS (mah-MUN-chee-sawr-us) "Mamenchi

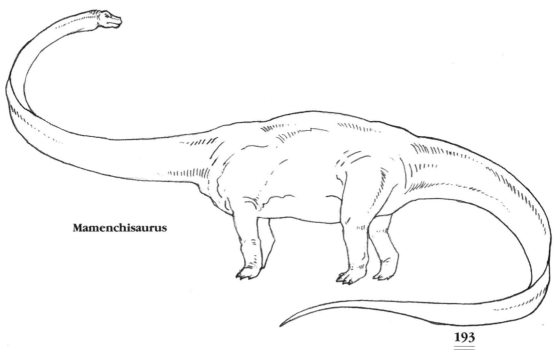

Mamenchisaurus

Lizard" (Named for Mamenchi, the area of China where it was found, + Greek *sauros* = lizard)

A Late Jurassic or Early Cretaceous SAUROPOD. This huge four-legged plant eater resembled DIPLODOCUS. It had short legs and a very long, 36-foot (11-m) neck that had 19 vertebrae—longer than the neck of any other dinosaur known. *Mamenchisaurus* was about 72 feet (22 m) long and weighed approximately 30 tons (27.2 metric tons). It is known from a skeleton that is complete except for the end of the TAIL.

Classification: Sauropoda, Sauropodomorpha, Saurischia

MANDASUCHUS (man-dah-SOOK-us) "Manda Crocodile" (Named for Manda, Tanzania, where it was found, + Greek *souchos* = crocodile)

Not a DINOSAUR, but a PSEUDOSUCHIAN THECODONTIAN. Some scientists think it may have been an ancestor of the PROSAUROPODS. This four-legged REPTILE looked like a crocodile. It was about the same size as a crocodile—8 feet (2.4 m) in length—but it had a shorter snout, and it probably lived only on dry land. Its FOSSILS have been found in Triassic rock in Tanzania; they are over 200 million years old.

MANDSCHUROSAURUS (mand-CHOOR-o-sawr-us) "Manchurian Lizard" (Named for Manchuria, where it was found, + Greek *sauros* = lizard)

A flat-headed HADROSAUR found in Late Cretaceous rock in Manchuria. This HADROSAURINE is known from a nearly complete skeleton. It seems to be closely related to NIPPONOSAURUS. *Mandschurosaurus* was a BIPEDAL plant eater. It is one of the largest hadrosaurs.

Classification: Hadrosauridae, Ornithopoda, Ornithischia

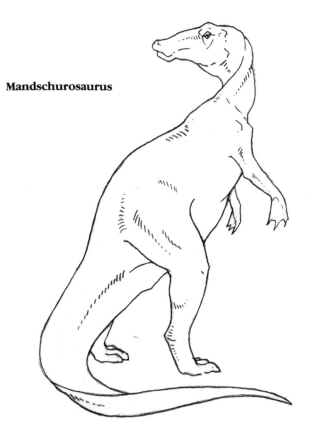

Mandschurosaurus

MARSHOSAURUS (MAHRSH-o-sawr-us) "Marsh's Lizard" (Named in honor of Othniel Charles Marsh, North American PALEONTOLOGIST, + Greek *sauros* = lizard)

A medium-size Late Jurassic CARNOSAUR. It is estimated that this BIPEDAL meat eater was 6 feet (1.8 m) tall, 17 feet (5.2 m) long, and weighed about 1,000 pounds (453.6 kg). It had long, heavy legs, a large head, and serrated TEETH. It is known from an incomplete skeleton found in Utah.

Classification: Carnosauria, Theropoda, Saurischia

MASSOSPONDYLUS (mass-o-SPON-dih-lus) "Bulky Verte-

Massospondylus

brae" (Latin *massa* = bulk, mass + Greek *spondylos* = vertebra, because its vertebrae were large)

A lightly built, 13.5- to 20-foot (4- to 6-m) PROSAUROPOD. It was a close relative of THECODONTOSAURUS and resembled that dinosaur. *Massospondylus* was probably at least partially BIPEDAL. It may have eaten both meat and plants. (See OMNIVORE.) Its jaws were lined with both powerful serrated TEETH suitable for tearing meat, and weak flat teeth suitable only for eating plants. This dinosaur was a slender animal with a long neck and TAIL. It is known from an incomplete skeleton found in Late Triassic rock in South Africa. It has also been found in North America.

Classification: Prosauropoda, Sauropodomorpha, Saurischia

MASTODONSAURUS (MAS-to-don-sawr-us) "Mast-toothed Lizard" (Greek *mastos* = breast + *odon-* = tooth + *sauros*

= lizard, referring to the nipple-shaped projections on its molars)

Not a DINOSAUR, but the largest amphibian that ever lived. This contemporary of the dinosaur is known from 15 complete and very well preserved skulls and a skeleton recently discovered in Middle Triassic rock in Germany. The skulls are about 4.5 feet (1.4 m) long. The skeleton has not yet been assembled. These animals apparently were frequent prey of CARNIVOROUS THECODONTS. Many of their bones bear thecodont tooth marks. *Mastodonsaurus* in turn preyed on smaller amphibians. Many small amphibian bones have been found with mastodonsaur tooth marks on them.

megalosaurids or **Megalosauridae** (meg-ah-lo-SAWR-ih-dee) "Big Lizards" (named after MEGALOSAURUS) Also commonly called megalosaurs.

A family of THEROPODS. This family includes a large number of dinosaurs that are so poorly known that they cannot be specifically placed in one of the other family groups. Megalosaurs probably averaged 20 to 30 feet (6 to 9 m) in length. They had massive skulls; long jaws; sharp, serrated TEETH; medium-length arms; three or more fingers; powerful hind legs; and large, sharp, curved CLAWS. Some had elongated SPINES on their neck vertebrae to help support the heavy muscles needed to hold up their enormous heads. These BIPEDAL meat eaters lived in Europe, Asia, Africa, North America, South America, Australia, and Madagascar. They flourished from Early Jurassic through Cretaceous times. ALTISPINAX, DRYPTOSAURUS, MEGALOSAURUS, and TORVOSAURUS were megalosaurs.

megalosaurs (MEG-ah-lo-sawrz)
See MEGALOSAURIDS.

MEGALOSAURUS (MEG-ah-lo-sawr-us) "Big Lizard" (Greek *megalo-* = big + *sauros* = lizard, because it was such a large animal)

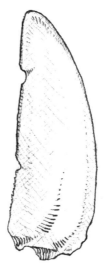

Megalosaurus tooth

A large CARNOSAUR closely related to ALLOSAURUS. This meat eater had a large head, knifelike TEETH, short arms, and strong hind legs. It was 30 feet (9 m) long and 10 feet (3 m) tall when standing erect, and weighed 2 tons (1.8 metric tons). It was BIPEDAL; it probably walked with its body held horizontally and its TAIL outstretched, to balance its huge head.

Megalosaurus was the first dinosaur on record to be discovered and named. An IGUANODON bone had been found earlier, but it was not identified or named. *Megalosaurus* lived throughout Jurassic and Early Cretaceous times. FOSSIL bones have been found in England and France, but a complete skeleton of this predator has never been discovered. However, many of its TRACKS have been found. Scientists have learned nearly as much from the tracks as they have from the fossil bones.

Classification: Carnosauria, Theropoda, Saurischia

melanorosaurids or **Melanorosauridae** (mel-ahn-or-o-SAWR-ih-dee) "Black Mountain Lizards" (Named for MELANO-ROSAURUS)

A family of PROSAUROPODS. Members of this family were the largest and latest of the prosauropods. They ranged from 20 to 40 feet (6 to 12 m) in length, and they lived in Africa and Argentina during Late Triassic times. The melanorosaurids were completely QUADRUPEDAL. They had massive limbs and heavy bodies. Unlike earlier prosauropods, their bones were long and solid. Their heads were small, and their legs were elephantlike. In general, they looked very much like small sauropods. They ate only plants. MELANOROSAURUS and RIOJASAURUS were melanorosaurids. VULCANODON is also sometimes classed as a melanorosaurid. It lived during Early Jurassic times, but some authorities think *Vulcanodon* was a primitive SAURO-POD rather than a prosauropod.

MELANOROSAURUS (mel-AN-or-o-sawr-us) "Black Mountain Lizard" (Greek *melan- = black* + *oros* = mountain + *sauros* = lizard)

The largest of the PROSAUROPODS. It was about 40 feet (12 m) long. In general, it resembled the later SAUROPODS. It had a small head, massive legs, elephantlike feet, a long neck and TAIL, and solid bones to support its great body weight. An incomplete skeleton of this four-legged plant eater was found in South Africa.

Classification: Prosauropoda, Sauropodomorpha, Saurischia

Mesozoic (mez-o-ZO-ik) **Era** "Middle Life" (Greek *mesos* = middle + *zoikos* = life)

The "age of REPTILES"—the geological period that followed

the Paleozoic Era and came before the Cenozoic Era. The Mesozoic began 225 million years ago and ended 65 million years ago. This was the era when the dinosaurs ruled the earth. The Mesozoic is divided into three periods: the Triassic, the Jurassic, and the Cretaceous.

METRIACANTHOSAURUS (met-ree-ah-KANTH-o-sawr-us) "Moderate-spined Lizard" (Greek *metrios* = moderate + *akantha* = spine + *sauros* = lizard, referring to the vertebral spines)

A large carnosaur of Late Jurassic England. It had 10-inch (25-cm) spines on its vertebrae but otherwise was similar to megalosaurus and was a member of the Megalosauridae. *Metriacanthosaurus* was a bipedal meat eater. It is known from a pelvis, right femur, and vertebral column.

Classification: Carnosauria, Theropoda, Saurischia

MICROCERATOPS (my-kro-SAYR-ah-tops) "Tiny Horned Face" (Greek *mikros* = tiny, small + *keratops* = horned face, referring to its overall size)

A primitive protoceratopsian of Late Cretaceous Mongolia. This tiny plant eater was only 30 inches (76 cm) long. It was closely related to Protoceratops and had a horny beak and a small frill. It may have run on its two long, slender hind

Microceratops

legs but probably grazed on all fours. It is known from moderately well preserved remains.

Classification: Protoceratopsidae, Ceratopsia, Ornithischia

MICROHADROSAURUS (my-kro-HAD-ro-sawr-us) "Small Hadrosaur" (Greek *mikros* = small + *hadrosaurus* = bulky lizard, because it was a small duckbill)

A small, 9-foot (2.6-m)-long duckbill that was found in Cretaceous deposits in China. This BIPEDAL plant eater is known only from the lower jaw.

Classification: Hadrosauridae, Ornithopoda, Ornithischia

MICROPACHYCEPHALOSAURUS (my-kro-pak-ee-SEF-ah-lo-sawr-us) "Small Thick-headed Lizard" (Greek *mikros* = small + *pachys* = thick + *kephale* = head + *sauros* = lizard, because it was a small dome-headed dinosaur)

A small PACHYCEPHALOSAUR. *Micropachycephalosaurus* was closely related to HOMALOCEPHALE and resembled that dinosaur. It had a flat dome. This BIPEDAL plant eater is known only from a partial skull recently discovered in Late Cretaceous rocks in China.

Classification: Pachycephalosauridae, Ornithopoda or Pachycephalosauria, Ornithischia

MICROVENATOR (my-kro-ven-AY-tor) "Small Hunter" (Greek *mikros* = small + *venator* = hunter, because it was a small predator)

A turkey-size Early Cretaceous COELUROSAUR of western North America. This hollow-boned dinosaur was a BIPEDAL meat eater. Counting the TAIL, it was 4 feet (1.2 m) long. It was 30 inches (76 cm) tall and weighed about 14 pounds (6.4 kg). It was very birdlike and had a small head, a long neck, short arms

Microvenator

with three long fingers, strong hind legs, and a long tail. It probably was a swift runner. It is known from a partial skeleton found in Montana.

Classification: Coelurosauria, Theropoda, Saurischia

migration

Recent recovery of skeletal remains of HADROSAURS, TYRANNOSAURS, and TROÖDONTS from the north shore of Alaska suggests that some Late Cretaceous dinosaurs migrated great distances with the seasons. Plants recovered in the area indicate that that region had a mild to cold temperate climate during the Late CRETACEOUS PERIOD.

MINMI (MIN-my) (Named for the Minmi rock formation in which it was discovered)

A peculiar ANKYLOSAUR recently found in Queensland, Australia. This armored dinosaur was a NODOSAUR about the SIZE of STRUTHIOSAURUS—5 to 6 feet (1.5 to 1.8 m) long. This dinosaur is different from all other known ankylosaurs. It had a unique spinal structure called paravertebrae. These were little horizontal plates of bone that ran along each side of the spine on its back vertebrae. The purpose of these little plates is not known. Paravertebrae are not found in any other known vertebrate animal. Because of its paravertebrae, this dinosaur's species name is "paravertebra"; its full name is *Minmi paravertebra*. *Minmi paravertebra* was discovered in Cretaceous marine deposits. It had apparently drifted out to sea, sunk to the bottom upside down, and been buried in that position, preserving the paravertebrae in place.

Minmi was a four-legged plant eater. It is known only from the trunk portion immediately in front of the pelvis, one foot, a fragment of the pelvis, and some armor.

Classification: Nodosauridae, Ankylosauria, Ornithischia

MONGOLOSAURUS (mon-go-lo-SAWR-us) "Mongolian Lizard" (Named for Mongolia, where it was found, + Greek *sauros* = lizard)

One of the last of the SAUROPODS. This four-legged plant eater lived in Mongolia during Late Cretaceous times. It was related to TITANOSAURUS and probably resembled that dinosaur. It is known only from very fragmentary material.

Classification: Sauropoda, Sauropodomorpha, Saurischia

MONOCLONIUS (mon-oh-KLOH-nee-us) "Single Stem"

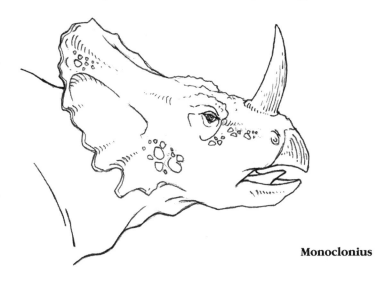

Monoclonius

(Greek *mono* = single + *klon* = stem, twig, referring to the single horn on its nose)

One of the first true CERATOPSIANS of western North America. Its FRILL was short, but its huge head was 6 feet (1.8 m) long from the tip of its beaklike snout to the end of its frill. A single, long HORN grew on its nose, but only knobs appeared on the brow. The nose horn curved slightly upward. *Monoclonius* was QUADRUPEDAL and had hoofed toes. It carried its huge head close to the ground and fed on low ground plants. *Monoclonius* was 20 feet (6 m) long. Its FOSSILS have been found in Late Cretaceous deposits in Alberta, Canada, and it is known from several complete skulls and other skeletal material.

Classification: Ceratopsidae, Ceratopsia, Ornithischia

MONTANACERATOPS (mon-TAN-ah-sayr-ah-tops) "Montana Horned Face" (Named for the state where it was found + Greek *keratops* = horned face)

A very early PROTOCERATOPSIAN. It was a close relative of both PROTOCERATOPS and LEPTOCERATOPS but was more advanced than either. The bony FRILL was longer than that of *Protoceratops,* and a small HORN grew on its nose. Its head was smaller than that of *Leptoceratops,* and its forelegs were

Montanaceratops

longer. This small dinosaur is known from a nearly complete skeleton found in Late Cretaceous rocks in Montana.

Classification: Protoceratopsidae, Ceratopsia, Ornithischia

MOROSAURUS (MOHR-o-sawr-us) "Foolish Lizard" (Greek *moros* = foolish + *sauros* = lizard, because it had a small head and was presumed to be stupid)

Name given to a small SAUROPOD found in Wyoming. This dinosaur is now considered to be a young CAMARASAURUS.

Classification: Sauropoda, Sauropodomorpha, Saurischia

mosasaurs or **Mosasauridae** (mo-zah-SAWR-ih-dee) "Meuse Lizards" (Named after MOSASAURUS)

Not DINOSAURS, but a group of large Late Cretaceous marine lizards related to modern monitor lizards. Mosasaurs were 50 feet (15 m) or more long. They had large heads, short legs with flipperlike hands and feet, and long, slim bodies. The nostrils were rather far back on the top of the skull. Mosasaurs were meat eaters. They probably hunted various kinds of sea animals. AMMONITE shells have been found that clearly show mosasaur tooth marks. Mosasaurs swam close to the surface of oceans all over the world and have been found in marine deposits in many places. MOSASAURUS and TYLOSAURUS were mosasaurs.

MOSASAURUS (MOH-zah-sawr-us) "Meuse Lizard" (Named after the Meuse River in Holland, where it was first found, + Greek *sauros* = lizard)

Not a DINOSAUR, a Late Cretaceous MOSASAUR—the first of its kind found. It is known only from a huge head with enormous 4-foot (1.2-m)-long jaws filled with sharp teeth. This giant marine lizard is estimated to have been 20 to 26 feet (6 to 8 m) long. It was found in Holland and was one of the very first Mesozoic FOSSILS ever discovered.

MOSCHOPS (MOSS-kops) "Calf Face" (Greek *moschos* = calf + *ops* = face, because its skull resembled that of a calf)

Not a DINOSAUR, but a THERAPSID. (Therapsids were the mammallike REPTILES from which mammals arose). *Moschops* lived during the PERMIAN PERIOD; it was already extinct by the beginning of the MESOZOIC ERA. It was 8 feet (2.5 m) long and 5 feet (1.5 m) tall at the shoulders. The shoulders of this QUADRUPED were much higher than the hips, so that the back sloped sharply downward. Its bulky body, heavy limbs, and broad feet gave *Moschops* a rather clumsy look. Its weak jaws and peglike teeth indicate that it was a plant eater. Its remains have been found in South Africa and Russia.

MUSSAURUS (moos-SAWR-us) "Mouse Lizard" (Latin *mus* = mouse + Greek *sauros* = lizard, referring to the very small size of the specimen)

The smallest dinosaur ever found. It appears to be a newly hatched baby PROSAUROPOD but was very close to being a

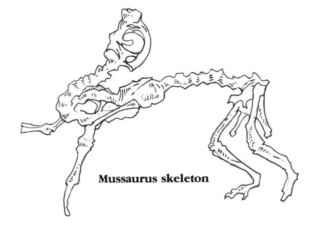

Mussaurus skeleton

primitive SAUROPOD. *Mussaurus* was about 8 inches (20 cm) long. The skull of this tiny four-legged SAURISCHIAN was only 1.25 inches (3.2 cm) long. It was very much like the skulls of sauropods. A nearly complete *Mussaurus* skeleton (lacking only the TAIL and rib cage) was found in a NEST that contained remains of four more individuals and several large eggshell fragments. *Mussaurus* and the nest were found in Argentina. The rock in which it was found is either very late Triassic or very early Jurassic. This dinosaur may have been a hatchling of the prosauropod COLORADIA found in the same formation.

Classification: Prosauropoda, Sauropodomorpha, Saurischia

MUTTABURRASAURUS (moot-tah-BUR-rah-sawr-us) "Mut-

Muttaburrasaurus

taburrra Lizard" (Named for Muttaburra, Queensland, Australia, the locality where it was found, + Greek *sauros* = lizard)

An Early Cretaceous IGUANODONTID ORNITHOPOD from Australia. This animal is known from a nearly complete skeleton and several partial skeletons. It is one of the best-known of all Australian dinosaurs. *Muttaburrasaurus* was a BIPEDAL plant eater that probably foraged on low shrubs. It closely resembled IGUANODON and was about the same SIZE. It even had the same kind of spiked thumbs that *Iguanodon* had.

Classification: Iguanodontidae, Ornithopoda, Ornithischia

N

naming dinosaurs

Dinosaur names may seem strange and hard to say, but each dinosaur's name has a meaning. The person who first discovers the dinosaur's FOSSILS gets to name it. Dinosaurs are usually given a Latin or Greek name that describes the dinosaur or its bones in some way. For example, TYRANNOSAURUS's name is from the Greek words meaning "tyrant lizard" because it was the largest known predator that ever lived. DIPLODOCUS is from the Greek words meaning "double-beamed" because part of its TAIL bones have two beams instead of one.

Sometimes a dinosaur will be named for the place where it is found. ALBERTOSAURUS was found in Alberta, Canada. Occasionally a dinosaur will be named for a PALEONTOLOGIST or for a friend of the finder. MARSHOSAURUS was named for Othniel Charles Marsh, one of the great early dinosaur hunters of North America. AVACERATOPS was named for the wife of the discoverer.

NANOSAURUS (NAN-o-sawr-us) "Dwarf Lizard" (Greek *nanos* = dwarf + *sauros* = lizard, referring to its overall SIZE)

A very small Jurassic ORNITHOPOD of the FABROSAUR family. It closely resembled HYPSILOPHODON. It ranged from 2 to 4 feet (60 to 120 cm) long and 12 to 18 inches (30 to 46 cm) tall at the hips. This little BIPEDAL plant eater is known from most of a skeleton (minus the skull) recently found in Utah and from fragments found in Colorado.

Classification: Fabrosauridae, Ornithopoda, Ornithischia

Nanosaurus

NANOTYRANNUS (nan-o-ty-RAN-us) "Pygmy Tyrant" (Greek *nanus* = small, dwarf + *tyrannos* = tyrant, because it was a small meat eater resembling TYRANNOSAURUS)

This Late Cretaceous CARNOSAUR lived in Montana and South Dakota. It is estimated that this THEROPOD was one-third as large as *Tyrannosaurus.* It may have been 17 feet (5.2 m) long, 10 feet (3 m) tall, and weighed about 1,000 pounds (453.6 kg). It is known only from one 2-foot (60-cm)-long skull and several thin, serrated TEETH that were shaped like carving knives.

Classification: Segnosauridae, Segnosauria, Ornithischia

NANSHIUNGOSAURUS (nan-SHOONG-o-sawr-us) "Nanh-siung Lizard" (Named for Nanhsiung, China, where it was found, + Greek *sauros* = lizard)

An unusual dinosaur recently found in China. Although originally classed as a TITANOSAURID, it is now believed to be related to the SEGNOSAURIDS. It lived during the CRETACEOUS PERIOD. It is known from a partial spinal column and pelvis. *Nanshiungosaurus*'s name was misspelled when it was originally written up; that is why the spelling differs from that of the city.

Classification: Carnosauria?, Theropoda?, Saurischia?

NAVAHOPUS (NAH-vah-hoh-pus) "Navaho Foot" (Named for the formation in which it was discovered and the Navaho Indian Reservation + Greek *pous* = foot)

Name given to a TRACKWAY made in Arizona by an Early Jurassic PROSAUROPOD. The trackway consists of a trail of six prints of the hind FEET and six prints of the forefeet. The hind feet had four toes with strong CLAWS on the middle toes—they were quite similar to the hind feet of AMMOSAURUS. The forefeet are unique. They were small and rather hooflike, with two short, clawed fingers and a sicklelike claw on the thumb. The dinosaur that made the tracks was basically QUADRUPEDAL but was able to walk on two legs. It was about four-fifths the SIZE of a specimen of *Ammosaurus* found in the same area.

NEMEGTOSAURUS (NEH-meg-to-sawr-us) "Nemegt Lizard" (Named for the Nemegt rock beds, where it was found, + Greek *sauros* = lizard)

A Late Cretaceous SAUROPOD related to DIPLODOCUS; it probably resembled that dinosaur. This four-legged plant eater

Nemegtosaurus skull

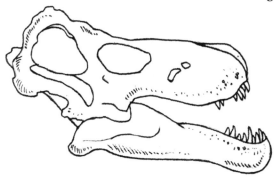

lived later than most DIPLODOCIDAE. It was a long-necked beast and probably cropped the tops of tall trees. It is known from a skull and much of a skeleton found in Mongolia.

Classification: Sauropoda, Sauropodomorpha, Saurischia

nests

We know that at least some dinosaurs laid EGGS in nests. Dinosaur nests are quite similar to those of modern crocodiles and marine turtles. They were craterlike pits dug in sand or mud. The eggs were usually laid in concentric circles arranged in tiers, the smallest circle being at the bottom of the pit, the next larger circle a tier above it, and the largest at the top. The eggs were separated by and covered with sand.

The first dinosaur nests discovered were those of PROTO-CERATOPS and were found in Mongolia. Since then nests of at least four other kinds of dinosaurs have been found. In most cases, many nests belonging to the same kind of dinosaur seem to be grouped together in a single area. Such a grouping is called a crèche. In one site in Montana, more than 30 ORODROMEUS nests were found. However, at a site in Argentina, only a single nest has been found to date. This nest contained five tiny PROSAUROPOD hatchlings, which have been named MUSSAURUS.

The size and shape of dinosaurs' nests varied according to the SIZE of the dinosaur that made them. A nest found in France is 15 feet (4.5 m) in diameter. Scientists believe this nest was made by the SAUROPOD HYPSELOSAURUS. The bowl-shaped nest of MAIASAURA (a HADROSAUR) is 7 feet (2 m) in diameter and 2.5 feet (76 cm) deep; it was found in Montana. A 6-foot (1.8-m) HYPSILOPHODONT'S nest found in the same area was only 3.5 feet (1 m) in diameter. The nests of TROÖDONS were paired, linear rows rather than circular. Dinosaur nests have been found in Mongolia, China, Canada, Montana, and Texas.

Some scientists think that, at least in the case of *Protoceratops,* more than one female may have shared a single nest. They think it unlikely that one could have laid as many eggs as have been found in some nests.

Niobrara (ny-o-BRAHR-ah) **Sea** (Named for the Niobrara River in northern Nebraska and Wyoming)

Name given to the shallow sea that extended across central North America from the Gulf of Mexico to the Arctic Ocean, splitting the continent in half, during Late Cretaceous times. The Niobrara Sea was 1,000 miles (1,600 km) wide. Inhabitants of this sea tended to be large. Even oysters were huge, some as much as 18 inches (46 cm) in diameter, and some PLESIOSAURS were 43 feet (13.1 m) long.

NIPPONOSAURUS (nip-on-o-SAWR-us) "Japanese Lizard" (Japanese *Nippon* = Japan, where it was found, + Greek *sauros* = lizard)

A small, Late Cretaceous HADROSAUR with a small, domelike

CREST on its skull. This HADROSAURINE is known from an incomplete skeleton found in Japan. It may be the same as GILMOREOSAURUS.

Classification: Hadrosauridae, Ornithopoda, Ornithischia

NOASAURUS (NOH-ah-sawr-us) "Northwestern Argentina Lizard" (NOA = Spanish abbreviation for Northwestern Argentina + Greek *sauros* = lizard)

A Late Cretaceous COELUROSAUR found in Argentina. It resembled the DROMAEOSAURIDS, but the sicklelike CLAW on its foot was of a different shape, and *Noasaurus* was probably smaller. This small THEROPOD may have been 6 feet (1.8 m) long. It is known from a jaw, limb bones, a few pieces of skull, and vertebrae.

Classification: Coelurosauria, Theropoda, Saurischia

nodosaurids or **Nodosauridae** (no-do-SAWR-ih-dee) "Knobby Lizards" (Named after NODOSAURUS)

One of the two families of ANKYLOSAURS. These were the most primitive of the armored dinosaurs. They had clubless TAILS, large spikes on their sides, pear-shaped heads, and thick bony plates, or scutes, on their backs, heads, and tails. Their legs were more slender than and not as massive as those of the ANKYLOSAURIDAE. The smallest nodosaurid was 5 feet (1.5 m) long; the largest was 19 feet (5.8 m) long. These four-legged plant eaters lived in Europe and North America throughout the CRETACEOUS PERIOD. HYLAEOSAURUS, NODOSAURUS, PANOPLOSAURUS, SAUROPELTA, and STRUTHIOSAURUS were Nodosauridae.

NODOSAURUS (no-do-SAWR-us) "Knobby Lizard" (Latin *nodus* = knot, knob + Greek *sauros* = lizard, because of

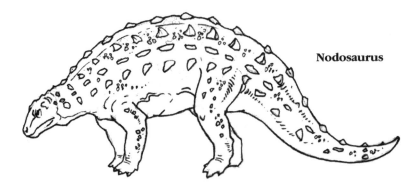

Nodosaurus

its knobby SKIN)

One of the earliest known ANKYLOSAURS (armored dinosaurs). This four-legged plant eater was 17.5 feet (5.3 m) long
and 6 feet (1.8 m) tall. It was a NODOSAURID. Shell-like, knobby
plates covered its head, body, and clubless TAIL, and there
were spikes on its sides. It is known from incomplete skeletal material. FOSSILS of *Nodosaurus* have been found in Early
Cretaceous deposits in New Jersey, Alabama, Kansas, and Wyoming. STEGOPELTA is the same as this dinosaur, and some
authorities think HIEROSAURUS is also the same animal.

Classification: Nodosauridae, Ankylosauria, Ornithischia

nothosaurs or **Nothosauria** (no-tho-SAWR-ee-ah) "Spurious Lizards" (Greek *nothos* = spurious, false + *sauros* =
lizard, because they no longer lived on land)

Not DINOSAURS, nor even related to dinosaurs, but Triassic
REPTILES that had returned to a life in the sea. These small,
rather long-necked and long-tailed animals had small skulls
and sharp teeth. They preyed on fish and other sea animals.
They had paddlelike arms and legs with webbed hands and
feet, only moderately changed for a life in the sea. They
probably lived near shores and may have been able to move
about on land like the seals and walruses of today. Nothosaurs were the ancestors of PLESIOSAURS. The best-known no-

thosaur is NOTHOSAURUS, which was 10 feet (3 m) long. Its FOSSILS have been found in Europe and Israel.

NOTHOSAURUS (no-tho-SAWR-us)
See NOTHOSAURS.

O

OHMDENOSAURUS (OHM-den-o-sawr-us) "Ohmden's Lizard" (Named in honor of a German scientist + Greek *sauros* = lizard)

An Early Jurassic SAUROPOD—one of the earliest known. The dinosaur was related to CETIOSAURUS and probably resembled that dinosaur. It is known from very fragmentary material found in the Holzmaden Beds in southern West Germany. The discovery of this large four-legged plant eater is important because the study of its remains will help to fill in some of the gaps in our understanding of the EVOLUTION of all sauropods.

Classification: Sauropoda, Sauropodomorpha, Saurischia

OMEISAURUS (o-may-yee-SAWR-us) "Omei Lizard" (Named for Omei, a city in China near where it was found, + Greek *sauros* = lizard)

A large Late Jurassic SAUROPOD. It was similar to EUHELOPUS and, like that dinosaur, had forelegs and hind legs of nearly equal length. *Omeisaurus,* like all sauropods, was huge, had a very long neck and TAIL, and walked on four legs. It was a plant eater and probably browsed on treetops. It is known from a skeleton found in central China.

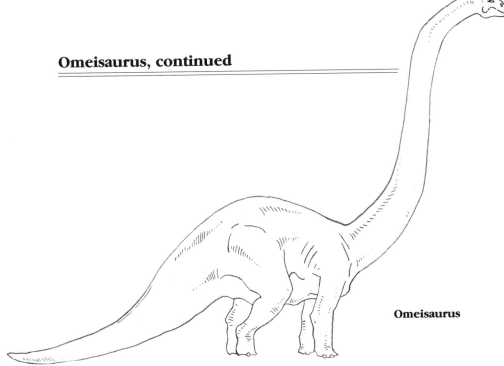

Omeisaurus

Classification: Sauropoda, Sauropodomorpha, Saurischia

omnivore (AHM-nih-vor) "All Eater" (Latin *omnis* = all + *vorare* = to devour)

Any animal that eats both plants and other animals. The "ostrich dinosaurs" and the early PROSAUROPODS may have been omnivores. Coyotes and raccoons are modern omnivorous animals. Compare CARNIVORE; HERBIVORE.

omnivorous (ahm-NIV-or-us)

See OMNIVORE.

OMOSAURUS (OH-mo-sawr-us) "Rough Lizard" (Greek *omos* = rough + *sauros* = lizard, referring to its spiny back)

Same as DACENTRURUS. The name was changed because another animal had already been named *Omosaurus*.

Classification: Stegosauridae, Stegosauria, Ornithischia

OPISTHOCOELICAUDIA (o-piss-tho-SEE-lih-caw-dee-ah)

"Posterior Hollow Tail" (Greek *opisthe* = backward + *ko-ilos* = hollow + Latin *cauda* = tail, referring to its TAIL vertebrae)

A recently discovered Late Cretaceous SAUROPOD similar to EUHELOPUS. This ponderous QUADRUPED had forelegs and hind legs of nearly equal length. It had a short tail, which it held far off the ground. *Opisthocoelicaudia* was a plant eater and probably ate almost continuously, nipping off the top branches of trees and swallowing them whole. It is known from a nearly complete skeleton (minus the neck and skull) that was found in Mongolia.

Classification: Sauropoda, Sauropodomorpha, Saurischia

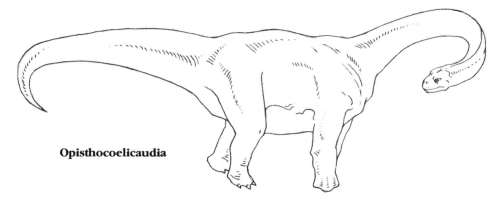

Opisthocoelicaudia

opisthopubic (o-PISS-tho-pyu-bic) **pelvis** "Backward Pubis" (Greek *opisthe* = backward + Latin *pubis* = pubic bone)

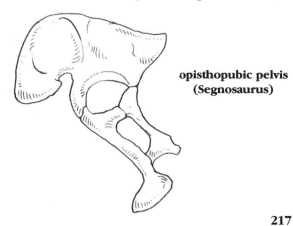

opisthopubic pelvis
(Segnosaurus)

A type of pelvis with a backwardly directed pubis as in those of ORNITHISCHIANS and birds. The ilium is broad and deep, more like those of SAURISCHIANS.

ORNATOTHOLUS (or-nay-to-THOH-lus) "Ornate Dome" (Latin *ornatus* = ornate + Greek *tholos* = dome)

A Late Cretaceous PACHYCEPHALOSAUR found in Alberta, Canada. Its rather low-domed skull roof is rough and pitted. This dome-headed dinosaur was originally believed to be a female STEGOCERAS but now is considered to be sufficiently different to be a separate GENUS. It is known only from the skull roof. Pachycephalosaurs were BIPEDAL plant eaters.

Classification: Pachycephalosauridae, Ornithopoda or Pachycephalosauria, Ornithischia

ornithischians or **Ornithischia** (or-nih-THISS-kee-ah) "Bird-hipped" (Greek *ornitho-* = bird + *ischion* = hip, because their pelvises resembled those of modern birds)

One of the two orders of animals called DINOSAURS. All ornithischians had birdlike pelvises and hoofed toes, and all were plant eaters. All except the PACHYCEPHALOSAURS had beaked mouths. Both two- and four-legged kinds lived worldwide from Middle TRIASSIC times to the end of the CRETACEOUS PE-

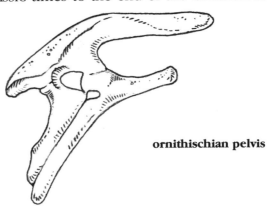

ornithischian pelvis

RIOD. Some were no larger than a cat, while others were 40 feet (12 m) long. Ornithischians are generally divided into four suborders: the ORNITHOPODA, the STEGOSAURIA, the ANKYLOSAURIA, and the CERATOPSIA. Some scientists add a fifth: the PACHYCEPHALOSAURIA.

ORNITHOLESTES (or-nith-o-LESS-teez) "Bird Robber" (Greek *ornitho-* = bird + *lestes* = robber, because it was imagined catching ARCHAEOPTERYX)

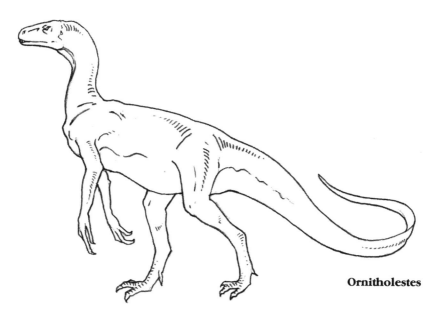

Ornitholestes

A 6-foot (1.8-m), lightly-built COELUROSAUR of Late Jurassic North America. This small-headed, long-tailed, BIPEDAL dinosaur ate lizards and other small game that it caught with its long-fingered, three-clawed HANDS. It is known from incomplete skeletal material found in Wyoming. *Ornitholestes* has been considered to be the same as COELURUS, but new studies indicate that they were different GENERA.

Classification: Coelurosauria, Theropoda, Saurischia

ornithomimids or **Ornithomimidae** (or-nith-o-MY-mih-dee) "Ostrich Dinosaurs" (Named after ORNITHOMIMUS)

A family of COELUROSAURS resembling modern ostriches in SIZE and shape. Ornithomimids had small heads, toothless beaks, enormous eyes, large BRAINS, long necks, and long legs. Unlike ostriches, however, these dinosaurs had long TAILS and three-toed FEET (ostriches have only two toes), and instead of wings they had medium-length arms with three-fingered HANDS. These swift little THEROPODS lived in Late Cretaceous North America, Africa, Israel, and Asia. They probably were OMNIVORES—that is, they may have eaten both meat and plants. DROMICEIOMIMUS, ELAPHROSAURUS, GALLIMIMUS, ORNITHOMIMUS, and STRUTHIOMIMUS were ornithomimids.

ORNITHOMIMUS (or-nith-o-MY-mus) "Bird Imitator" (Greek *ornitho-* = bird + *mimos* = imitator, mimic, because it resembled an ostrich)

A Late Cretaceous ORNITHOMIMID ("ostrich dinosaur") that lived in Colorado, Wyoming, Montana, Mongolia, and Alberta, Canada. It is known from the incomplete skeletons of several different individuals. This BIPEDAL dinosaur so closely resembled STRUTHIOMIMUS that some scientists consider them to be the same. However, others are convinced that the two were different dinosaurs.

Ornithomimus was probably about 8 feet (2.5 m) tall and 15 feet (4.5 m) long. Most of its length was neck and TAIL. A horny beak covered its toothless jaws. Its diet may have consisted of fruit, small REPTILES, insects, and the EGGS of other dinosaurs. *Ornithomimus* may have been ENDOTHERMIC (warm-blooded). It probably could run as swiftly as an ostrich—few other dinosaurs would have been faster. Although its head was small, it had a quite large braincase, and it is considered

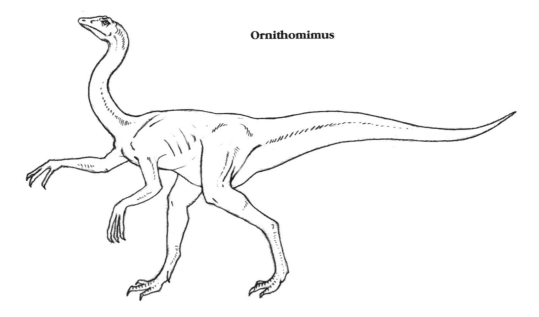

Ornithomimus

to be one of the most intelligent of the dinosaurs. Its INTEL-
LIGENCE and its SPEED were its best DEFENSES against larger
predators.

Classification: Coelurosauria, Theropoda, Saurischia

ornithopods or **Ornithopoda** (or-nih-THOP-o-dah) "Bird-
footed" (Greek *ornitho- = bird + pod-* = foot, because the
feet were thought to resemble those of birds, though they
actually do not)

One of the suborders of ORNITHISCHIAN dinosaurs. Ornithopods first appeared in Late Triassic times, and, as a group,
they lasted through Late Cretaceous times. All were plant eaters with horned beaks and were basically BIPEDAL (some may
have grazed on all fours). They walked or ran with their bodies parallel to the ground and their TAILS outstretched for
balance. Their FEET had three or four toes, with hooflike CLAWS

or nails. Ornithopod HANDS had either four or five fingers. The ornithopods included the HYPSILOPHODONTS, FABROSAURS, HETERODONTOSAURS, CAMPTOSAURS, IGUANODONTS, and HADROSAURS. The PACHYCEPHALOSAURS have always been included in this suborder until recently. Now some scientists think pachycephalosaurs belong in a suborder of their own because they were quite different from other ornithopods.

Ornithosuchidae (or-nith-o-SOOK-ih-dee) "Bird Crocodiles" (Named after ORNITHOSUCHUS)

A family of very advanced PSEUDOSUCHIANS. These THECODONTS were so advanced that some scientists think they may have been primitive dinosaurs. ORNITHOSUCHIANS lived in North America, South America, Europe, and Africa during Middle and Late Triassic times. These four-legged meat eaters were 4 to 6 feet (1.2 to 1.8 m) long. They had sharp, daggerlike TEETH and five-fingered HANDS. HESPEROSUCHUS, ORNITHOSUCHUS, RIOJASUCHUS, and SALTOPOSUCHUS were members of this family.

ORNITHOSUCHUS (or-nith-o-SOOK-us) "Bird Crocodile" (Greek *ornitho-* = bird + *souchos* = crocodile, because it was lightly built and BIPEDAL, like a bird)

Not a DINOSAUR, but possibly an ancestor of the THEROPODS. A few think that *Ornithosuchus* was a very primitive dinosaur, but most scientists think it was an advanced PSEUDOSUCHIAN THECODONT. This meat eater was 6 feet (1.8 m) long, weighed 110 pounds (50 kg), and had sharp, daggerlike teeth. Its skull was large and narrow, and its hands had five fingers. The remains of this creature were found in Middle and Late Triassic rocks in Scotland. Similar animals have been found in North America, Europe, Africa, and South America.

ORODROMEUS (or-oh-DROHM-ee-us) "Mountain Runner" (Greek *oros* = mountain + *dromeus* = runner, because it was found on a mountain and was a swift runner)

A Late Cretaceous HYSILOPHODONT found in Montana. This two-legged plant eater was 8 feet (2.5 m) long. It is known from NESTS, EGGS, and about 25 skeletons of all ages—embryos to adults.

Clutches of 24 eggs were laid in circular nests 3.5 feet (1 m) in diameter and then covered with vegetation. Hatchlings apparently left the nest as soon as they hatched but remained in the nesting area.

Classification: Hypsilophodontidae, Ornithopoda, Ornithischia

"ostrich dinosaurs"
See ORNITHOMIMIDS.

OTHNIELIA (oth-NEEL-ee-ah) (Named in honor of Othniel Charles Marsh, American PALEONTOLOGIST)

A small ORNITHOPOD of Late Jurassic North America. It was only 2.5 feet (80 cm) long. It had a small head and large eyes; its beaklike jaws were lined with TEETH; and its HANDS had five fingers. This turkey-size, BIPEDAL plant eater was found in

Othnielia

Utah, Wyoming, and Colorado. It was once thought to be a species of LAOSAURUS but is now considered a separate GENUS.

Classification: Hypsilophodontidae, Ornithopoda, Ornithischia

OURANOSAURUS (oo-RAHN-o-sawr-us) "Valiant Lizard" (Touareg, a dialect of Niger, *ourane* = valiant, fearless + Greek *sauros* = lizard, because the natives use this word to describe fearless animals)

An Early Cretaceous ORNITHOPOD. This BIPEDAL plant eater was related to IGUANODON and was about the same size—it measured 23 feet (7 m) long and 16.5 feet (5 m) tall. But unlike *Iguanodon, Ouranosaurus* had very high SPINES on

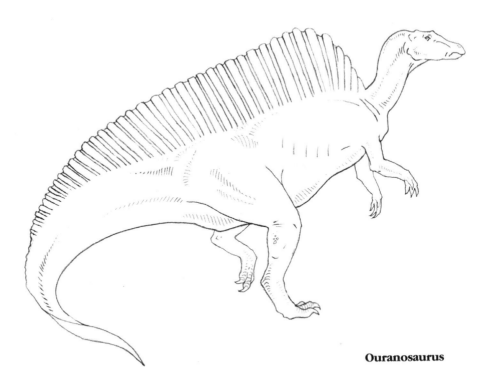

Ouranosaurus

224

its vertebrae that ran down the middle of its back and TAIL. These spines may have supported a sail or fin that helped keep *Ouranosaurus* from overheating. Two complete specimens of this animal were found in the Sahara Desert of Niger, Africa. *Ouranosaurus* is the only known ORNITHISCHIAN with a sail.

Although *Ouranosaurus* is classed as an IGUANODONT, it had several features like those of HADROSAURS. Its head was long and flat, and it had a ducklike bill. This dinosaur was probably related to the ancestors of the hadrosaurs.

Classification: Iguanodontidae, Ornithopoda, Ornithischia

OVIRAPTOR (oh-vih-RAP-tor) "Egg Stealer" (Latin *ovum* = egg + *raptor* = robber, because it was found near a NEST OF EGGS)

A small Late Cretaceous COELUROSAUR. This dinosaur was similar to ORNITHOMIMUS but was much smaller—it was only 5 feet (1.5 m) long. With its lightly-built skull, large BRAIN,

Oviraptor

and powerful, toothless beak, *Oviraptor* resembled birds even more closely than *Ornithomimus*. Its body may even have been insulated by feathers or something similar.

Oviraptor had huge HANDS with three long, slender fingers that were capable of holding prey. It walked on two long, slender legs. Part of several skeletons of this little THEROPOD were found in Mongolia. One specimen was found near a nest of PROTOCERATOPS eggs. This has led scientists to assume that *Oviraptor* ate eggs. Its diet probably also included insects and berries, and it may have scavenged on carcasses of dead animals like crows of today.

Classification: Coelurosauria, Theropoda, Saurischia

oviraptorid or **Oviraptoridae** (oh-vih-rap-TOR-ih-dee) "Egg Stealers" (Named after OVIRAPTOR)

A family of small Late Cretaceous COELUROSAURS whose FOSSILS were found in Mongolia. They had toothless beaks and were BIPEDAL, lightly-built animals with hollow bones. Their skulls were unusually short and deep, with large BRAIN cavities. Oviraptorids were about five feet long, but their bodies were only about the SIZE of a large turkey. Oviraptorids closely resembled birds. OVIRAPTOR is the best known of this family.

P

Pachycephalosauria (pak-ee-sef-ah-lo-SAWR-ee-ah) "Dome-headed Lizards" (Named after PACHYCEPHALOSAURUS)

A proposed new suborder of ORNITHISCHIA. (See PACHYCEPHALOSAURS.)

pachycephalosaurs or **Pachycephalosauridae** (pak-ee-sef-ah-lo-SAWR-ih-dee) "Dome-headed Lizards" (Named after PACHYCEPHALOSAURUS)

A specialized branch of small ORNITHISCHIAN dinosaurs that is usually included in the ORNITHOPODA suborder. However, some scientists now think this group should be in a separate suborder called the PACHYCEPHALOSAURIA because they are different from other ornithopods. The pachycephalosaurs had very thick skulls, or "domes." The purpose of these domes is unknown, but males had thicker skulls than females. Perhaps pachycephalosaurs lived in HERDS and the males competed for mates or territories by butting their heads together, like mountain goats. The domes might have been used as a means of DEFENSE, too. Perhaps males warded off attackers while the females and YOUNG fled. However, pachycephalosaurs seem to have had a very good sense of smell, which would have been their best defense against large CARNOSAURS.

Pachycephalosaurs probably descended from a line of HYPSILOPHODONTS. They were BIPEDAL plant eaters. They walked with their bodies held horizontally, like birds, with their TAILS extended for balance. Unlike other ornithopods, pachycephalosaurs had no beaks. Their jaws were lined with short, sharp TEETH.

Pachycephalosaurs ranged from turkey size to 15 feet (4.6 m) long. Their FOSSILS have been found in Late Cretaceous deposits in North America, England, China, Madagascar, and Mongolia. GRAVITHOLUS, PACHYCEPHALOSAURUS, STEGOCERAS, TYLOCEPHALE, and YAVERLANDIA are pachycephalosaurs.

The GENERA in this family varied a great deal. Some had very thick, high-rising domes, while others had rather flat domes. In some, the dome was divided; in others, it was a single mass.

PACHYCEPHALOSAURUS (pak-ee-SEF-ah-lo-sawr-us) "Thick-headed Lizard" (Greek *pachys* = thick + *kephale* = head + *sauros* = lizard, because of its thick skull)

A large Late Cretaceous PACHYCEPHALOSAUR. This dinosaur had a plate of bone 9 inches (23 cm) thick covering its BRAIN. Wartlike knobs and 5-inch (13-cm) spikes fringed this dome and decorated the dinosaur's small nose. This BIPEDAL plant eater is known only from skulls found in Wyoming and Alberta, Canada. These skulls were 26 inches (66 cm) long—three times as large as the skull of STEGOCERAS. If the rest of *Pachycephalosaurus*'s body was in proportion to its skull, it was 15 feet (4.6 m) long—the largest of the pachycephalosaurs.

Pachycephalosaurus

Classification: Pachycephalosauridae, Ornithopoda or Pachycephalosauria, Ornithischia

PACHYRHINOSAURUS (PAK-ee-ry-no-sawr-us) "Thick-nosed Lizard" (Greek *pachys* = thick + *rhino-* = nose + *sauros* = lizard, referring to the thick plate on its nose)

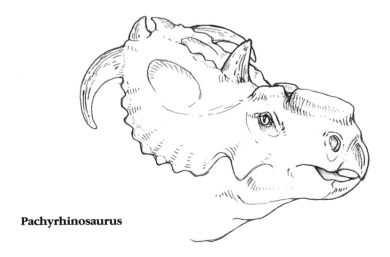

Pachyrhinosaurus

A Late Cretaceous CERATOPSIAN. This unusual horned dinosaur had a large oval plate of bone on its nose instead of a
HORN. This plate measured 14 inches by 22 inches (36 cm by
56 cm), and was 5 inches (13 cm) thick. It was slightly cra-
tered, like a volcano. Similar fist-size knobs grew above the
eyes. Spikes edged the short, wide FRILL, and one unicornlike
horn was positioned in the center of the frill. *Pachyrhinosaurus*
had strong TEETH and a beaklike snout. It was 20 feet (6 m)
long and weighed 4 tons (3.6 metric tons). It walked on four
strong legs; it carried its head near the ground, because its
hind legs were longer than the forelegs. *Pachyrhinosaurus*
probably ate very coarse ground plants. Remains of about a
thousand have been found in Alberta, Canada.

Classification: Ceratopsidae, Ceratopsia, Ornithischia

PALAEOSCINCUS (pay-lee-o-SKINK-us) "Ancient Lizard"
(Greek *palaios* = ancient + *scincus* = genus name of modern lizards called skinks, because its tooth resembled that of
a skink)

An ANKYLOSAUR (armored dinosaur) of Late Cretaceous North America. It was once thought to be the same as PANOPLO-SAURUS or EDMONTONIA; however, recent authorities believe that *Palaeoscincus,* which is known only from a single tooth found in Montana, is a different ankylosaur.

Classification: Nodosauridae, Ankylosauria, Ornithischia

paleontologist (pay-lee-on-TOL-o-jist) (From PALEONTOL-OGY)

A person who learns about ancient life by studying FOSSILS; a specialist in paleontology.

paleontology (pay-lee-on-TOL-o-jee) (From Greek *palaios* = ancient + *onta* = beings, living things)

The science of studying ancient life as it is revealed by FOSSILS; a branch of biology and geology.

Paleontology is an exciting field of study. One branch deals only with fossil animals without backbones. This is called invertebrate paleontology. Vertebrate paleontology deals only with fossil animals that had backbones. Some paleontologists specialize in studying DINOSAURS. This is a branch of vertebrate paleontology. Some of them go all over the world looking for new fossils. Others spend their lives studying fossils that have already been collected; still others do a little of both. Many thousands of tons of fossils are stored in museums around the world, waiting to be studied and identified. From these fossils, scientists will gather many pieces of evidence that will tell them what life on earth was like many millions of years ago.

Paleopoda (pay-lee-OP-o-dah) "Ancient Feet" (Greek *palaios* = ancient + *pod-* = foot)

A name given to a suborder sometimes used for the very early SAURISCHIANS. This suborder includes the STAURIKOSAURIDS, the HERRERASAURIDS, the ANCHISAURIDS, and the PLATEOSAURIDS. Some scientists think the SEGNOSAURS belong to this suborder, too.

Paleozoic (pay-lee-o-ZOH-ik) **Era** "Ancient Life" (Greek *palaios* = ancient + *zoikos* = life)

The geological age preceding the MESOZOIC ERA. It began 600 million years ago and ended 225 million years ago. This is the period during which fish, sea plants, amphibians, land plants, and REPTILES developed.

Pangaea (pan-JEE-ah) "All Earth" (Greek *pan* = all + *gaia* = earth)

Name given to the huge "supercontinent" that probably existed on earth during the PERMIAN and TRIASSIC PERIODS. Scientists believe that at that time, all of earth's land mass was clumped together into one single continent. According to the theory, Pangaea began to break up during the Late Triassic Period, forming two supercontinents, which are called LAURASIA and GONDWANALAND. Then, during Late Cretaceous times, these supercontinents also broke up and drifted apart, finally forming the continents as we know them today.

PANOPLOSAURUS (pan-OP-lo-sawr-us) "Armored Lizard"

Panoplosaurus

Panoplosaurus, continued

(Greek *panoplo-* = armored + *sauros* = lizard, referring to the plates on its back)

A Late Cretaceous ANKYLOSAUR of western North America. This four-legged plant eater was the last of the North American NODOSAURIDS. Rows of thick bony plates covered its pear-shaped head and its neck, back, and TAIL. Long spikes protected its sides and shoulders, but its tail was clubless. *Panoplosaurus* grew to be at least 18 feet (5.5 m) long and weighed about 3 tons (2.7 metric tons). It has been found in Alberta, Canada; Montana; and Texas. Although not everyone agrees, it is now generally believed that EDMONTONIA was a species of *Panoplosaurus*.

Classification: Nodosauridae, Ankylosauria, Ornithischia

PARASAUROLOPHUS (par-ah-sawr-OL-o-fus) "Similar Crested Lizard" (Greek *para* = similar + SAUROLOPHUS, because this dinosaur also had a CREST)

A Late Cretaceous LAMBEOSAURINE HADROSAUR of western North America. The remarkable crest of this duck-billed dinosaur

Parasaurolophus

was a hollow tube 5 feet (1.5 m) long that extended back over the animal's shoulders. The purpose of this tube is not known. It was once thought to be a snorkel, but it has no opening at the end. It may have improved the dinosaur's sense of smell. All of the air *Parasaurolophus* breathed traveled from the nostrils at the tip of the snout, up to the tip of the crest, and then back down the crest before it went down the windpipe to the lungs.

Parasaurolophus was 30 feet (9 m) long and 16 feet (4.9 m) tall, and weighed 3 to 4 tons (2.7 to 3.6 metric tons). It was a BIPEDAL land dweller and ate pine needles and oak or poplar leaves. Its HANDS were webbed, and its ducklike beak was spoon-shaped. It is known from a nearly complete skeleton found in Alberta, Canada. Its FOSSILS have also been found in New Mexico.

Classification: Hadrosauridae, Ornithopoda, Ornithischia

parental care

For a long time scientists assumed that dinosaurs laid their EGGS and then left the babies to fend for themselves when they hatched (as most modern REPTILES do). But now scientists believe that at least some dinosaurs gave care of some kind to their YOUNG. This theory is supported by several pieces of evidence.

Many families of COELOPHYSIS (both juveniles and adults) have been found together in New Mexico, and two young DROMICEIOMIMUS were found with an adult in Alberta, Canada. Five young BRACHYCERATOPS were found near an adult in Montana, and many hatchling and juvenile HADROSAURS have been found with only one or two adults in several areas of Montana. More recently, the skull of an adult hadrosaur was found near a NEST of month-old babies in Montana. The teeth of the 15 MAIASAURA babies were worn, indicating that the babies had been eating coarse food. Scientists think this indicates that one or both parents were taking care of the young. The adults may have taken the young from the nest to graze during the day and returned them at night, or the adults could have brought food to the nest. Either way, the babies surely must have had some kind of adult supervision.

Perhaps the most convincing evidence of adult care of the young is supplied by a SAUROPOD TRACKWAY discovered in Texas. This trackway seems to show that sauropods traveled in HERDS with a ring of adults surrounding and protecting the young in the same way that modern elephants do.

Scientists suggest that some dinosaurs may have watched and protected the nests until the young hatched. Then, the babies that were too small to travel with the adults may have been placed in "nurseries" with one or more adults protecting them until they were large enough to join the herd. Modern giraffes care for their young in this way.

PARKSOSAURUS (PARKS-o-sawr-us) "Parks's Lizard" (Named in honor of W. A. Parks, Canadian dinosaur collector and researcher, + Greek *sauros* = lizard)

A small Late Cretaceous ORNITHOPOD of western North America. It was 7 feet (2 m) long and weighed 150 pounds (68 kg). This dinosaur belonged to the HYPSILOPHODONT fam-

Parksosaurus

ily and resembled HYPSILOPHODON. It had a long neck and a small head with a horny beak. Its forelimbs were short and strong; it ran on its long hind legs but may have grazed on all fours in the bushy undergrowth of evergreen forests. *Parksosaurus* FOSSILS have been found in Alberta, Canada, and in Montana.

Classification: Hypsilophodontidae, Ornithopoda, Ornithischia

PARROSAURUS (PAYR-o-sawr-us) "Parr's Lizard" (Named in honor of Albert Parr, American zoologist, + Greek *sauros* = lizard)

Name given to 13 vertebrae of a Late Cretaceous SAUROPOD found in southeastern Missouri. This four-legged plant eater is believed to be a descendant of CAMARASAURUS; however, it probably resembled TITANOSAURUS. Like all sauropods, it had a small head and a long neck. Not enough material has been found to determine its SIZE.

Classification: Sauropoda, Sauropodomorpha, Saurischia

PATAGOSAURUS (PAT-ah-go-sawr-us) "Patagonian Lizard" (Named for the area of Argentina where it was found + Greek *sauros* = lizard)

A SAUROPOD found in Middle Jurassic rock in Patagonia, Argentina. It is known from FOSSILS of seven individuals, including one nearly complete skeleton (minus the skull). At one site a "family" of four specimens of various SIZES was found. This huge, four-legged plant eater was a CETIOSAURID and was about the same size and shape as CETIOSAURUS, but more primitive. It was also more primitive than HAPLOCANTHOSAURUS, but was more advanced than AMYGDALODON.

Classification: Sauropoda, Sauropodomorpha, Saurischia

pelycosaurs or **Pelycosauria** (pel-ee-ko-SAWR-ee-ah) "Basin Lizards" (Greek *pelyko* = basin + *sauros* = lizard, referring to the shape of their hips)

Not DINOSAURS, nor even distant relatives of dinosaurs, but an order of primitive mammallike REPTILES. They lived during the PERMIAN PERIOD and were extinct before the beginning of the TRIASSIC, millions of years before the dinosaurs lived. They were probably the ancestors of the THERAPSIDS, which in turn were the ancestors of mammals.

Some pelycosaurs were meat eaters; others were plant eaters. Some grew to be 10 feet (3 m) long. Many were semiaquatic. All were QUADRUPEDAL. Some had sails on their backs, which may have helped regulate their body temperature. DIMETRODON was a pelycosaur.

PENTACERATOPS (PEN-tah-sayr-ah-tops) "Five-horned Face" (Greek *pente* = five + *keratops* = horned face, because it had five HORNS)

A long-frilled CERATOPSIAN related to CHASMOSAURUS. It had two long brow horns, a shorter nose horn, and two addi-

Pentaceratops

tional hornlike growths, one on each cheek. This four-legged plant eater had an enormous neck shield, or FRILL. Its head (including the frill) was 7.5 feet (2.3 m) long—more than one-third as long as its 20-foot (6-m) body.

Pentaceratops FOSSILS have been found in Late Cretaceous rock in New Mexico and Alberta, Canada; it is known from a nearly complete skeleton.

Classification: Ceratopsidae, Ceratopsia, Ornithischia

Permian (PUR-mee-en) **Period** (Named for the old province of Perm in northeastern Russia, where rocks of this age were first described)

The last period of the PALEOZOIC ERA; the geological time period that came just before the TRIASSIC PERIOD (the first period of the MESOZOIC ERA). The Permian Period began 290 million years ago and ended 225 million years ago.

PHOBOSUCHUS (foh-bo-SOOK-us) "Fear Crocodile" (Greek *phobos* = fear + *souchos* = crocodile, because it was the most fearsome of all CROCODILIANS)

Not a DINOSAUR, but the largest crocodile that ever lived. This 50-foot (15-m) REPTILE lived in swamps in Late Cretaceous Texas and Montana. The skull of this meat eater was 6 feet (1.8 m) long. *Phobosuchus* probably preyed on dinosaurs as well as anything else it could catch.

phytosaurs or **Phytosauria** (fy-to-SAWR-ee-ah) "Plant Lizards" (Greek *phyton* = plant + *sauros* = lizard, because it was first thought that they were plant eaters)

Not DINOSAURS, but a suborder of THECODONTS. They looked very much like crocodiles but were not closely related to them. These REPTILES grew to be 10 to 30 feet (3 to 9 m) long.

They were the dominant animals of the Late Triassic Period. Phytosaurs lived in freshwater marshes, lakes, and streams, and ate fish, small amphibians, dinosaurs, or any other small animal they could catch. Their bodies were protected by heavy bony plates, or scutes. Rutiodon is the best-known phytosaur.

PIATNITZKYSAURUS (pyaht-NITS-kee-sawr-us) "Piatnitzky Lizard" (Named in honor of a friend of the finder + Greek *sauros* = lizard)

A middle-size carnosaur. *Piatnitzkysaurus* was related to Allosaurus but was smaller and more primitive, and it had longer arms. It lived 15 million years earlier than *Allosaurus*. This bipedal meat eater is known from most of a skeleton

Piatnitzkysaurus

(minus FEET and HANDS) that were found in Middle Jurassic rock in Patagonia, Argentina.

Classification: Carnosauria, Theropoda, Saurischia

PINACOSAURUS (PIHN-ah-ko-sawr-us) "Board Lizard" (Greek *pinako-* = board + *sauros* = lizard, referring to its hard armored back)

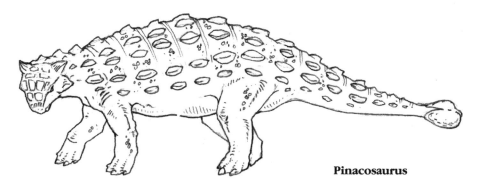

Pinacosaurus

One of the earliest known ANKYLOSAURIDS. This armored dinosaur was related to ANKYLOSAURUS. It had sharp spikes along its back and sides; its TAIL ended in a flat bone with sharp edges (it looked somewhat like a double-edged stone ax). *Pinacosaurus* was lightly built and had short legs and slender FEET. It grew to be about 12 feet (3 m) long. This QUADRUPED traveled arid uplands during Late Cretaceous times, seeking low ground plants to eat. Almost complete skeletons of a young adult and five sheep-size juveniles were found in Mongolia. Its FOSSILS have also been found in China. SYRMO-SAURUS is now known to be the same as this dinosaur.

Classification: Ankylosauridae, Ankylosauria, Ornithischia

PISANOSAURUS (pee-SAN-o-sawr-us) "Pisano's Lizard" (Named for a friend of the finder + Greek *sauros* = lizard)

One of the earliest ORNITHISCHIANS known. This primitive ORNITHOPOD may have been an ancestor of HYPSILOPHODON. This small dinosaur had long, slender FEET and is believed to be a bipedal plant eater. Its skull and TEETH resembled those of the PROSAUROPODS. *Pisanosaurus* is known from very incomplete material found in Argentina. It lived about the middle of the TRIASSIC PERIOD.

Classification: Hypsilophodontidae, Ornithopoda, Ornithischia

PIVETEAUSAURUS (peev-TOH-sawr-us) "Piveteau's Lizard" (Named in honor of Jean Piveteau, French paleontologist, + Greek *sauros* = lizard)

Name given to the skull of a Middle Jurassic CARNOSAUR that was found in Normandy, France. The cranium closely resembles that of ALLOSAURUS. This BIPEDAL meat eater is classed in the MEGALOSAURIDAE. It was once considered to be a species of EUSTREPTOSPONDYLUS.

Classification: Carnosauria, Theropoda, Saurischia

plated dinosaurs
See STEGOSAURS.

plateosaurids or **Plateosauridae** (play-tee-o-SAWR-ih-dee) "Flat Lizards" (Named after PLATEOSAURUS)

An advanced family of PROSAUROPODS. They had larger and heavier bodies than earlier prosauropods. Their HANDS were fairly short and the fingers spread outward, indicating that they were used to support weight much of the time. Plateosaurids were probably more QUADRUPEDAL than BIPEDAL and probably ate only plants. They did not have bladelike TEETH such as ANCHISAURIDS had. Plateosaurids have been found on almost every continent. They lived during Late Triassic times. They ranged from 9 to 26 feet (3 to 8 m) long. AMMOSAURUS, LUFENGOSAURUS, and PLATEOSAURUS were plateosaurids.

PLATEOSAURUS (PLAY-tee-o-sawr-us) "Flat Lizard" (Greek *plateo-* = flat + *sauros* = lizard, referring to its flat, plate-like TEETH)

One of the earliest and one of the largest SAURISCHIAN dinosaurs of the TRIASSIC PERIOD. *Plateosaurus* was a 26-foot (8-m) PROSAUROPOD that lived in Europe, South Africa, and Nova Scotia. It had a small head and a long neck and TAIL. This plant eater was basically QUADRUPEDAL but could stand on its hind legs to eat from the tops of trees. It probably lived in

Plateosaurus

HERDS. A number of complete *Plateosaurus* skeletons have been found.

Classification: Prosauropoda, Sauropodomorpha, Saurischia

plesiosauroids or **Plesiosauroidea** (plee-zee-o-sawr-OY-dee-ah) "Near Lizards" (Named after PLESIOSAURUS)

Not DINOSAURS, but a suborder of PLESIOSAURS. They had small heads at the end of very long, snaky necks. Their bodies were barrel-shaped. These sea-going REPTILES probably swam close to the surface of the oceans, using their long necks to catch fish below the surface. They ranged in size from 7 to 45 feet (2 to 13.5 m) long. They lived during the Late Jurassic to the Late Cretaceous times and have been found in North America, Europe, and Australia. ELASMOSAURUS and *Plesiosaurus* were plesiosauroids.

plesiosaurs or **Plesiosauria** (plee-zee-o-SAWR-ee-ah) "Near Lizards" (Named after PLESIOSAURUS)

Not DINOSAURS, but an order of marine REPTILES that lived in the open oceans of Mesozoic times. Plesiosaurs were not related to dinosaurs in any way, but they lived during the same time period. Some plesiosaurs swallowed small stones, either for ballast so that they could dive or to grind their food. Plesiosaurs were fish eaters that propelled themselves through the water with flippers much the same way that modern marine turtles do. They may have been able to move about on land like modern walruses.

There were two kinds of plesiosaurs, the PLIOSAUROIDS and the PLESIOSAUROIDS. Plesiosauroids had long, snaky necks, small heads, and barrel-shaped bodies. ELASMOSAURUS and *Plesiosaurus* belonged to this group. Pliosauroids were large animals and probably were comparable to modern whales. They were quite streamlined, with large heads and short necks. KRONOSAURUS was a pliosauroid.

Plesiosaurs have been found in Cretaceous sediments on every continent, including Antarctica. They also lived in Jurassic times. They were the largest of the marine reptiles—some were only 8 feet (2.5 m) long, but the largest were 40 feet (12.2 m) long.

PLESIOSAURUS (PLEE-zee-o-sawr-us) "Near Lizard" (Greek *plesios* = near + *sauros* = lizard, because it was once thought to be related to lizards)

Not a DINOSAUR, but a long-necked PLESIOSAUR. This marine REPTILE was 10 feet (3 m) long. It had a long, snaky neck, a barrel-shaped body, and a small head. *Plesiosaurus* swam close to the surface of oceans during Jurassic times, propelling itself along with its long, paddlelike legs. It used its long neck to search for food below the surface. It ate small fish and other sea animals. *Plesiosaurus* remains have been found in England.

PLEUROCOELUS (ploor-o-SEE-lus) "Hollow Side" (Greek

Pleurocoelus

pleura = rib, side + *coelis* = hollow, referring to the hollows in the sides of its vertebrae) Also called Astrodon.

An Early Cretaceous sauropod that lived in the eastern and western part of the United States and in Portugal and England. This four-legged plant eater had long, narrow teeth and probably resembled Apatosaurus in size and shape. Its hind feet had three claws, but its forefeet had no inner claw like those of *Apatosaurus* or Diplodocus. A long line of huge sauropod tracks found in Texas near the Paluxy River may have been made by *Pleurocoelus*. The dinosaur that made the tracks also had three claws on its hind feet and none on its front feet.

An incomplete skeleton of a very young *Pleurocoelus,* estimated to have been 13.5 feet (4 m) long, was found in Maryland and the District of Columbia. Fossil bones found in Texas and Montana were much larger. These animals were probably adult *Pleurocoelus.*

The dinosaur named *Astrodon* turned out to be the same as the one named *Pleurocoelus.* Since the name *Pleurocoelus* was given first, it is the name used.

Classification: Sauropoda, Sauropodomorpha, Saurischia

pliosauroids or **Pliosauroidea** (ply-o-sawr-OY-dee-ah) "More Lizards" (Greek *pleion* = more + *sauros* = lizard) Also called pliosaurs.

Not dinosaurs, but a suborder of short-necked, large-headed plesiosaurs. The smallest pliosauroids were about 10 feet (3 m) long, and the largest was 40 feet (12 m) long. It had a 12-foot (3.5-m) head. Pliosauroids had a small vertical tail fin. They cruised the oceans in Mesozoic times, like sperm whales do today. They caught fish and other sea animals in their

large mouths and dived for marine mollusks. KRONOSAURUS
was a pliosauroid.

pliosaurs
See PLIOSAUROIDS.

podokesaurids or **Podokesauridae** (po-doh-kee-SAWR-ih-
dee) "Swift-footed Lizards" (Named after PODOKESAURUS)

A primitive family of COELUROSAURS. This group had small
heads; hollow bones; relatively short necks; very short, slender forelimbs; five fingers; and very long hind legs. They
ranged from 2 feet (60 cm) to 10 feet (3 m) long. Podokesaurids lived during Late Triassic and possibly into the Early
Jurassic times. They have been found in North America, South
America, Europe, Africa, and Asia. COELOPHYSIS, HALTICOSAU-
RUS, PODOKESAURUS, SALTOPUS, and TRIASSOLESTES were members of this family. Some scientists include DILOPHOSAURUS in
this family instead of with the CARNOSAURS.

PODOKESAURUS (po-DOH-kee-sawr-us) "Swift-footed Lizard" (Greek *podokes* swift-footed + *sauros* = lizard, because its long legs indicated it was a fast runner)

A small Late Triassic or Early Jurassic COELUROSAUR of eastern North America. This BIPEDAL meat eater was 5 feet (1.5
m) long and 2 feet (60 cm) tall. It was closely related to (or
may even have been the same as) COELOPHYSIS. *Podokesaurus* was lightly built and had a long TAIL, long hind legs, and
a long, flexible neck. The only known specimen was found
in Massachusetts.

Classification: Coelurosauria, Theropoda, Saurischia

POEKILOPLEURON (po-kih-LOP-loor-on) "Varied Side"

(Greek *poikilos* = varied + *pleura* = side, because many bones from one side of the animal were found)

A large, Middle Jurassic CARNOSAUR closely related to MEGALOSAURUS. This BIPEDAL meat eater had short, stout arms and five short fingers on its HANDS. It is known from a shoulder blade, an arm, some hand and finger bones, a leg, a nearly complete FOOT, and 21 TAIL vertebrae. Its FOSSILS have been found in France and Russia.

Classification: Carnosauria, Theropoda, Saurischia.

POLACANTHUS (po-lah-KANTH-us) "Many Spines" (Greek *polys* = many + *akantha* = spine, referring to the SPINES on its back)

A primitive ANKYLOSAUR of the NODOSAUR family. A nearly complete skeleton of this 15-foot (4.6-m) dinosaur was found in England. It had two rows of spines down its back and two rows of triangular bony plates on its clubless TAIL. A shield of bone covered the hips. This QUADRUPEDAL plant eater lived in Early Cretaceous times. It has been suggested that *Polacanthus* is the same as HYLAEOSAURUS, but that cannot be proved either way at this time.

Classification: Nodosauridae, Ankylosauria, Ornithischia

PRENOCEPHALE (preen-o-SEF-ah-lee) "Forward-bent Head" (Greek *prenes* = forward-bent + *kephale* = head, because it probably walked with its head bent forward)

A small PACHYCEPHALOSAUR from Cretaceous Mongolia. This 7-foot (2-m) "dome-head" was related to STEGOCERAS. Its head was 10 inches (25 cm) long and had a high, well-developed, solid dome. Nodes, or small bony knobs, decorated the back of the skull. The front TEETH were long and sharp. *Preno-*

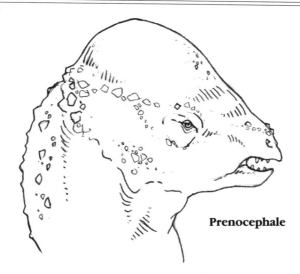

Prenocephale

cephale was a BIPEDAL plant eater and is known from a complete skeleton and most of another skeleton.

Classification: Pachycephalosauridae, Ornithopoda or Pachycephalosauria, Ornithischia

PROBACTROSAURUS (proh-BAK-tro-sawr-us) "Before Staff Lizard" (Greek *pro* = before + *bactros* = staff + *sauros* = lizard, because it was an earlier form than BACTROSAURUS)

An IGUANODONT of Late Cretaceous times. This dinosaur was similar to *Bactrosaurus,* and scientists think it might be an ancestor of the HADROSAURS. Like all ORNITHOPODS, it was BIPEDAL and ate plants. It is known from a nearly complete skeleton found in Mongolia.

Classification: Iguanodontidae, Ornithopoda, Ornithischia

PROCERATOSAURUS (proh-sayr-AT-ah-sawr-us) "Before Ceratosaurus" (Greek *pro* = before + *Ceratosaurus* = horned lizard, because it is believed to be an earlier form than CERATOSAURUS)

A Late Jurassic CARNOSAUR that is known from a skull found in Gloucester, England. The skull has an open framework and a small bump on the snout similar to that of *Ceratosaurus*. This suggests that it was a close relative of that BIPEDAL meat eater.

Classification: Carnosauria, Theropoda, Saurischia

PROCHENEOSAURUS (proh-KEEN-ee-o-sawr-us) "First Goose Lizard" (Greek *pro* = before + *cheneo-* = goose + *sauros* = lizard, because it lived earlier than CHENEOSAURUS)

A small Late Cretaceous HADROSAUR (duck-billed dinosaur). This BIPED was 15 feet (4.5 m) long and had a small, bump-like CREST on its head. It is considered by some to be the first hollow-crested hadrosaur, or LAMBEOSAURINE. Others believe it is a juvenile form of CORYTHOSAURUS or LAMBEOSAURUS. Two nearly complete skeletons of this plant eater have been found, one in Alberta, Canada, and one in Asia.

Classification: Hadrosauridae, Ornithopoda, Ornithischia

procompsognathids or **Procompsognathidae** (proh-komp-sog-NATH-ih-dee) "Before Elegant Jaws" (Named after PROCOMPSOGNATHUS)

The most primitive of the COELUROSAUR families. These little BIPEDAL meat eaters were no more than 4 feet (1.2 m) long. They had very long necks and TAILS. Their HANDS had four fingers. They lived during the Late TRIASSIC PERIOD and have been found in Germany and China. LUKOUSAURUS and *Procompsognathus* were members of this family.

PROCOMPSOGNATHUS (proh-komp-SOG-nath-us) "Before Elegant Jaw" (Greek *pro* = before + *kompos* = elegant +

Procompsognathus

gnathos = jaw, because it was an earlier COELUROSAUR than COMPSOGNATHUS)

A swift little coelurosaur of Early Jurassic Germany. It is one of the most primitive coelurosaurs that is known. It was 11.5 inches (29 cm) tall at the hips and 4 feet (1.2 m) long. It had hollow bones; a long, flexible neck; long hind legs; and a long TAIL. The HANDS had four fingers, and the FEET had three forward-pointing toes and a dewclaw. *Procompsognathus* ate insects and small animals. It is known from an incomplete skeleton.

Classification: Coelurosauria, Theropoda, Saurischia

PROSAUROLOPHUS (proh-sawr-OL-o-fus) "First Crested Lizard" (Greek *pro* = before + *sauros* = lizard + *lophos* = crest, because it was an earlier form than SAUROLOPHUS)

The earliest known solid-crested HADROSAUR. This duckbill was similar to ANATOSAURUS, but unlike *Anatosaurus*, *Prosaurolophus* had a miniature CREST that rose like small knobs above the eyes and ended in a short, backward-pointing spike. Its bill was smaller and shorter and less widely flared than that of *Anatosaurus*. Like all duckbills, this BIPEDAL plant eater

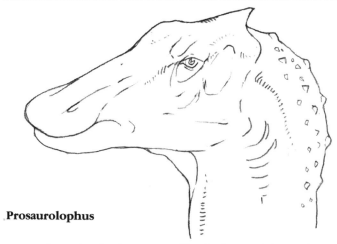

Prosaurolophus

carried its body horizontally, balanced by a long crocodile-like TAIL. It probably lived in plains regions. It is known from two skulls and a partial skeleton found in Late Cretaceous sediments of Alberta, Canada.

Classification: Hadrosauridae, Ornithopoda, Ornithischia

prosauropods or **Prosauropoda** (proh-sawr-OP-o-dah) "Before Sauropods" (Greek *pro* = before + SAUROPODS, because they were thought to be the forerunners of sauropods)

An infraorder of the SAUROPODOMORPHA. Most scientists think that the ancestors of the sauropods may have come from this suborder. However, not everyone agrees. A few scientists think that the prosauropods are related to the sauropods only through a common ancestor.

Early prosauropods were semi-QUADRUPEDAL. That is, they were able to walk on either two or four legs. All prosauropods were plant eaters, but the earliest forms probably also included meat (small ORNITHISCHIANS or mammals) in their DIET. These early groups had bladelike TEETH, as well as teeth suited for plant eating. They also had very lightweight bones. Later prosauropods were entirely quadrupedal, had solid bones, and ate only plants. All prosauropods had rather long necks and small heads. They ranged in size from 8 to 40 feet (2.4 to 12 m) long. They have been found almost everywhere in the world and lived from Middle Triassic to possibly very early Jurassic times.

Prosauropods have been divided into four families: The HERRERASAURIDAE were the smallest and most primitive. Some scientists think that the ancestors of all SAURISCHIANS came from this family. HERRERASAURIDS walked on either two or four legs and ate both plants and meat. They lived during Middle Triassic times and have been found in Argentina. HERRERASAURUS and ISCHISAURUS were members of this family. Some scientists think that this family should be placed in the suborder PALEOPODA.

The ANCHISAURIDAE were somewhat more advanced than the Herrerasauridae but were still quite primitive. They, too, were relatively small—8 to 10 feet (2.4 to 3 m) long. They were lightly built and had some hollow bones. They had long necks, long TAILS, and long slender fingers and toes. ANCHISAURIDS walked on either two or four legs and may have eaten both meat and plants. They lived from the Middle to the Late Triassic and have been found almost all over the world. ANCHISAURUS, EFRAASIA, and THECODONTOSAURUS were members of this family.

The PLATEOSAURIDAE were more advanced than the anchisaurids, and were much larger; however, their heads were comparatively smaller. This group was also more quadrupedal. Their HANDS were fairly short; the fingers spread outward, indicating that they were used to support the weight much of the time. PLATEOSAURIDS had thicker and stronger bones than the earlier families. This group ate only plants; they did not have bladelike teeth. Plateosaurids were from 7 to 26 feet (2 to 8 m) long. They have been found in Late Triassic sediments on every continent except Australia and

Antarctica. LUFENGOSAURUS, AMMOSAURUS, and PLATEOSAURUS were members of this family.

The MELANOROSAURIDAE were the largest and latest members of the prosauropods. They were from 20 to 40 feet (6 to 12 m) long. Their bodies were heavy and, unlike the earlier prosauropods, their bones were solid. These prosauropods were never BIPEDAL; their legs were massive like those of an elephant. The heads were very small, and the necks and tails quite long. Members of this family have been found in Late Triassic sediments in Africa and South America. MELANOROSAURUS and RIOJASAURUS were melanorosaurids. VULCANODON, which was found in Early Jurassic sediments in Zimbabwe, is sometimes placed in this family, but some scientists think it may be a very primitive sauropod rather than a prosauropod.

Proterosuchia (proh-tayr-o-SOOK-ee-ah) "Earlier Crocodiles" (Greek *proteros* = earlier + *souchos* = crocodile, because they were an earlier form than CROCODILES)

Not DINOSAURS, but a suborder of primitive THECODONTS that first appeared in the Late PERMIAN PERIOD. They became the largest Early Triassic creatures and may have included the ancestors of the crocodiles. Many of this group lived in lakes and rivers in South Africa, but some were also land dwellers. Proterosuchia were CARNIVORES and closely resembled crocodiles. They had a sprawling posture and bony plates on their backs. Some grew to be 13 feet (4 m) long.

PROTIGUANODON (proh-tih-GWAHN-o-don) "First Iguanatooth" (Greek *protos* = first + *odon-* = tooth, because its finder thought it was an early IGUANODONT)

This dinosaur has now been identified as a PSITTACOSAURUS.

PROTOAVIS (PROH-toh-ay-viss) "Ancestral Bird" (Greek *protos* = first + Latin *avis* = bird, because it is the earliest known bird)

Not a DINOSAUR, but a bird that was about 75 million years older than the oldest-known ARCHAEOPTERYX. Two partial skeletons of this crow-sized bird were discovered in 1986 in Triassic deposits in Texas. It had many dinosaurian features, such as clawed fingers, a tail, and teeth, but it was more bird-like than *Archaeopteryx. Protoavis* had no teeth in the back of its jaws; it possessed a wishbone and had a skull like those of modern birds. This 225-million-year-old bird could probably fly. It possessed a keellike chest (similar to those of modern birds) to which strong, wing-flapping muscles were likely attached.

PROTOCERATOPS (proh-toh-SAYR-ah-tops) "First Horned Face" (Greek *protos* = first + *keratops* = horned face, because it is the earliest known true CERATOPSIAN)

A pig-size, four-legged, plant-eating dinosaur with a turtle-like beak and a small FRILL—the first of the true ceratopsians. Some had small bumps on their noses; others did not. It is

Protoceratops

possible they represent males and females. Both were about the same SIZE, weighing about 900 pounds (410 kg) and measuring about 6 feet (1.8 m) from the tips of their snouts to the ends of their TAILS.

This forerunner of the horned dinosaurs was the first dinosaur known from every stage of life—potato-shaped EGGS to full grown. Its eggs were the first dinosaur eggs ever found. Several of the NESTS contained hatchlings, and some of the eggs contained fragments of unhatched babies. Skulls and skeletons of adults were found nearby. Scientists had always assumed that dinosaurs were egg-laying REPTILES. This discovery proved, for the first time, that this was true. The rough-shelled eggs were found in bowl-shaped nests that had been dug in sand. The eggs were 6 inches (15 cm) long and had been placed in rows around the sides of the bowl, then covered and separated by sand.

Protoceratops FOSSILS have been found in Late Cretaceous deposits in Mongolia.

Classification: Protoceratopsidae, Ceratopsia, Ornithischia

protoceratopsians or **Protoceratopsidae** (proh-toh-sayr-uh-TOPS-ih-dee) "First Horned Faces" (Named after PROTOCERATOPS)

A family of CERATOPSIA. These were the most primitive of the true CERATOPSIANS. They were mainly QUADRUPEDAL plant eaters, although some may have been partially BIPEDAL. They had relatively enormous heads with parrotlike beaks, well-developed FRILLS (except for LEPTOCERATOPS), and very small HORNS or none at all. Protoceratopsians ranged in size from 30 inches (76 cm) to 7 feet (2 m) long. They lived during Late Cretaceous times in North America and Asia. BAGACERA-

TOPS, Leptoceratops, MICROCERATOPS, MONTANACERATOPS, and PROTOCERATOPS were protoceratopsians.

protorosaurs or **Protorosauria** (proh-toh-roh-SAWR-ee-ah) "First Lizards" (Greek *protos* = first + *sauros* = lizards, because they were the first known lizardlike REPTILES)

Not dinosaurs, but lizardlike reptiles. They preceded lizards and filled the same ecological niches that lizards do today. Small protorosaurs probably lived in the undergrowth, eating insects and small reptiles, but larger ones ate fish and lived near the sea. They, in turn, probably served as food for Triassic COELUROSAURS. Protorosaurs have been found in Europe. They lived during the PERMIAN and TRIASSIC PERIODS. They ranged from 2 to 20 feet (60 cm to 6 m) in length. TANYSTROPHEUS was a protorosaur.

Protosuchia (proh-toh-SOOK-ee-ah) "First Crocodiles" (Named for PROTOSUCHUS)

Not DINOSAURS, but the earliest true crocodiles. They were relatively small—about 3 feet (90 cm) long—and had rather short heads, but their arms and legs were like those of modern CROCODILIANS, and both their backs and bellies were covered with rows of bony plates. Animals belonging to this group have been found in Late Triassic or Early Jurassic deposits in North America, South America, and Africa. *Protosuchus* was a member of this group.

PROTOSUCHUS (proh-toh-SOOK-us) "First Crocodile" (Greek *protos* = first + *souchos* = crocodile)

Not a DINOSAUR, but the very first known crocodile. Except for its shorter head, it looked almost exactly like modern crocodiles and probably lived like them. It had short legs and rows of bony plates protecting both the back and belly. Its FOSSILS were found in Arizona, where it lived from Late Triassic to Early Jurassic times.

pseudosuchians or **Pseudosuchia** (soo-doh-SOOK-ee-ah)
"False Crocodiles" (Greek *pseudo-* = false + *souchos* = crocodile, because they resembled crocodiles, but were not)

Not DINOSAURS, but a suborder of THECODONTS. Pseudosuchians lived during the TRIASSIC PERIOD in North America, South America, Europe, and Africa. Scientists think that the ancestors of dinosaurs were pseudosuchian thecodonts. In body build, most pseudosuchians resembled crocodiles but were less sprawl-legged, and some were capable of running on two legs. They were probably OMNIVORES, eating both plants and meat. Their jaws were lined with sharp teeth. They ranged anywhere from rabbit-size to 10 feet (3 m) long. EUPARKERIA, ORNITHOSUCHUS, RIOJASUCHUS, and SCLEROMOCHLUS were pseudosuchians.

psittacosaurs or **Psittacosauridae** (sit-ah-ko-SAWR-ih-dee)
"Parrot Lizard" (Named for PSITTACOSAURUS)

A family of ORNITHISCHIAN dinosaurs that are believed to be the ancestors of the CERATOPSIANS. These dinosaurs were mainly BIPEDAL and are usually classed as ORNITHOPODS. However, some scientists now consider them to be the most primitive family of the CERATOPSIA. These plant eaters probably grazed on all fours. They had large heads with parrotlike beaks. They were about 6 feet (1.8 m) long. Psittacosaurs lived during the CRETACEOUS PERIOD and have been found in Mongolia. *Psittacosaurus* was a member of this family.

Psittacosaurus

PSITTACOSAURUS (SIT-ah-ko-sawr-us) "Parrot Lizard" (Greek *psittako-* = parrot + *sauros* = lizard, because its skull was shaped like a parrot's)

An ancestor of the CERATOPSIANS. *Psittacosaurus* had parrot-like jaws and the faintest hint of a bony FRILL. This 6.5-foot (2-m) plant eater lived in early Late Cretaceous Mongolia and China. Unlike later ceratopsians, *Psittacosaurus* was mainly BIPEDAL but probably walked on all fours when grazing. It is known from many complete skeletons in excellent condition.

A baby *Psittacosaurus,* about half the size of a pigeon, is one of the smallest dinosaurs found to date.

Classification: Psittacosauridae, Ornithopoda or Ceratopsia, Ornithischia

PTERANODON (tayr-AN-o-don) "Winged and Toothless" (Greek *pteron* = wing + *anodontos* = toothless, because it could fly and was toothless)

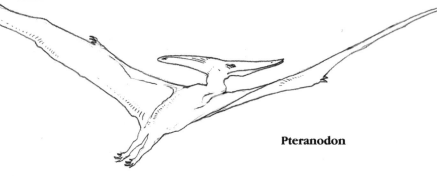

Pteranodon

Not a DINOSAUR, but a tailless Late Cretaceous PTEROSAUR. It weighed 33 pounds (15 kg). It had a turkey-size body, and a head that was 6 feet (1.8 m) long from the tip of its long, toothless beak to the end of a long, bony crest on the back of the head. In some, this crest doubled the length of the head. The purpose of the crest is unknown. Some specimens of *Pteranodon* had no crest, so perhaps it was a sex characteristic. It may have been used as a brake for landing, or it could have been a rudder, since the creature had no tail. Or it may simply have acted as a balance for the very long beak. Although *Pteranodon* had a 27-foot (8.2-m) wingspread, it could have flown only in a light or moderate wind. It may have been a glider rather than a true flyer. This flying fish eater may have fished on the wing. It was probably ENDO-THERMIC (warm-blooded) and may have had fur. Its FOSSILS have been found in Kansas.

pterodactyls or **Pterodactyloidea** (tayr-o-dak-til-OY-dee-ah) "Wing Fingers" (Named after PTERODACTYLUS)

Not a DINOSAUR, a suborder of PTEROSAURS that developed in Late Jurassic times, 50 million years after the RHAMPHO-RHYNCHOIDEA. Early forms were small, no larger than a sparrow, but Cretaceous pterodactyls were huge, with up to 40-foot (12-m) wingspreads. All had long, curved necks and long

Pterodactylus

faces. Some had few or no teeth, while others had closely spaced, bristlelike teeth in their long jaws. They may have caught insects in flight or snatched fish from the water. They had either very short tails or none at all. Some had impressive crests. Pterodactyls have been found in North America, Europe, Africa, and Australia. PTERANODON, *Pterodactylus,* and QUETZALCOATLUS were pterodactyls.

PTERODACTYLUS (tayr-o-DAK-til-us) "Wing Finger" (Greek *pteron* = wing + *daktylos* = finger, because the fourth finger supported the wing)

Not a DINOSAUR, but a tailless PTEROSAUR. Some were as small as a sparrow; others were as large as a hawk. Their wingspread ranged from 12 to 30 inches (30 to 76 cm). These flying creatures were common along Later Jurassic shorelines in Europe and Africa. They probably caught insects in the air. Some authorities believe their legs were poorly adapted for land travel.

pterosaurs or **Pterosauria** (tayr-o-SAWR-ee-ah) "Winged Lizards" (Greek *pteron* = wing + *sauros* = lizard, referring to its leathery wings)

Not DINOSAURS, but the order of winged ARCHOSAURS capable of flying or gliding. They are classed as FLYING REPTILES because of their very reptilian heads, teeth, and pelvises. Their hind feet were similar to those of dinosaurs or birds. Pterosaurs were lightly built, with hollow bones and small bodies. They had large brains, which suggests that they had good maneuverability when flying. They probably could flap their wings slowly but may have relied upon thermal updrafts (up-rising columns of warm air) or light breezes to get off the ground. The smallest pterosaurs were the size of sparrows; the largest were giants with 40-foot (12-m) wingspreads.

A pterosaur's wing was formed by a leathery membrane that stretched from the side of its body to the tip of its fourth finger. This fourth finger was very long and supported the front edge of the wing. The other fingers were short and were equipped with sharp claws.

Pterosaurs probably had a poor sense of smell, and no doubt they relied on keen eyesight for hunting. Their eyes were very large. Most were fish eaters, and they may have fished on the wing. Some had throat pouches similar to those of modern pelicans. These probably fished from the surface of the seas. Some may have eaten insects. Still others had elongated, bristlelike teeth, resembling the baleen that mod-ern whales use to strain plankton from seawater. These pter-osaurs may have eaten plankton.

Pterosaurs were probably ENDOTHERMIC (warm-blooded). At least some are known to have had long, dense fur. Many had ridges or crests on their skulls. Some had long tails; others were tailless. Pterosaurs probably lived all over the world from Late Triassic through Late Cretaceous times. Two kinds are known. The RHAMPHORHYNCHOIDEA lived during the TRIAS-SIC and JURASSIC PERIODS. They were small in size and had long tails. The PTERODACTYLOIDEA lived from Late Jurassic to Late Cretaceous times. They probably had no tails. Some had long bony crests. Some grew to be huge.

Q

quadruped (KWAHD-roo-ped) "Four-footed" (Latin *quadrupes* = four-footed)

Any animal that stands or walks on four legs. Quadrupedal means "four-footed." ANKYLOSAURS, CERATOPSIANS, SAUROPODS, and STEGOSAURS were quadrupeds. Compare BIPED.

quadrupedal (Kwahd-roo-PED-al)
See QUADRUPED.

QUAESITOSAURUS (kwy-see-to-SAWR-us) "Abnormal Lizard" (Latin *quaesitus* = abnormal, uncommon + Greek *sauros* = lizard, because this SAUROPOD's skull was unlike that of any other sauropod)

A Late Cretaceous sauropod found in the Gobi Desert of Mongolia. This dinosaur is known from an almost complete skull—one of the very few sauropod skulls known. The skull is massive and has a long face. The nostrils are near the top of the head. The skull closely resembles that of NEMEGTOSAURUS, but *Nemegtosaurus* has a much narrower snout and only eight TEETH in each jaw. *Quaesitosaurus* has nine teeth in each jaw. Its snout is wide and scooplike. The middle ear cavity is abnormally large, indicating very sensitive hearing. (See SENSORY PERCEPTION.) This huge, four-legged dinosaur probably ate large volumes of soft vegetation. It may have been semi-aquatic.

Classification: Sauropoda, Sauropodomorpha, Saurischia

Quetzalcoatlus

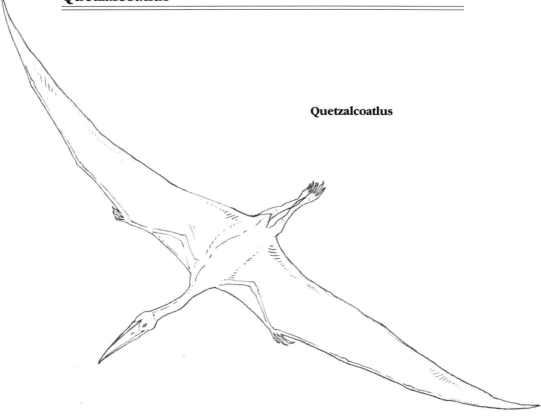

Quetzalcoatlus

QUETZALCOATLUS (ket-sol-ko-AT-lus) (Named after the Aztec feathered serpent god, Quetzalcoatl)

Not a DINOSAUR, but a giant PTEROSAUR. *Quetzalcoatlus* is the largest known flying creature. One found in late Late Cretaceous rock in Texas had a 40-foot (12-m) wingspread. It had a small head and a long neck. Together they measured 8 feet (2.5 m) long. *Quetzalcoatlus* had a long, slender beak, and it may have probed in the mud for mollusks, or it may have been vulturelike and fed on carcasses. It probably lived on flat, low-lying ground, and it may have used thermal updrafts (rising columns of warm air) to become airborne. This flying giant is known from parts of the wings of one individual and scattered bones of a dozen smaller ones.

R

RAPTOR (RAP-tor) "Plunderer" (Latin *raptor* = plunderer, because it was a predator)

This dinosaur is known only from a back vertebra of a CARNOSAUR. Although very poorly known, it is important because it was found in Early Cretaceous deposits in Australia and is the only large meat eater known from that continent.

Classification: Carnosauria, Theropoda, Saurischia

REBBACHISAURUS (reh-bash-ih-SAWR-us) "Rebbach Lizard" (Named for the territory of Rebbach, where the specimen was found, + Greek *sauros* = lizard)

A name given to a few SAUROPOD bones found in Morocco. These bones are similar to those of CAMARASAURUS, and this huge plant eater may have resembled that dinosaur. Its discovery was important because it showed that sauropods lived in GONDWANALAND during the Early CRETACEOUS PERIOD. Like all sauropods, *Rebbachisaurus* was QUADRUPEDAL.

Classification: Sauropoda, Sauropodomorpha, Saurischia

reproduction

See EGGS; YOUNG.

reptiles or **Reptilia** (rep-TIL-ee-ah) "Creeping Animals" (Latin *reptilis* = creeping)

A class of cold-blooded (ECTOTHERMIC), egg-laying, air-breathing animals with backbones. Most of these animals have a sprawling gait (or crawl on their bellies), three-chambered hearts, and bodies covered with horny plates or scales. Some reptiles live on land; others live in water. One class of reptiles (the DIAPSIDA) has two openings in the skull behind each eye socket. DINOSAURS, PTEROSAURS, and THECODONTS are placed in this class because they had diapsid-type skulls. Snakes, lizards, turtles, and crocodiles are living reptiles.

RHABDODON (RAB-do-don) "Rod Tooth" (Greek *rhabdos* = rod + *odon-* = tooth, referring to the shape of the TEETH)

Name given to jaw fragments and a few other bones of a Late Cretaceous ORNITHOPOD. *Rhabdodon* belonged to the IGUANODONT family but was similar in appearance to CAMPTOSAURUS. Scientists estimate that this BIPEDAL plant eater was 16 feet (5 m) long. Its FOSSILS were found in France.

Classification: Iguanodontidae, Ornithopoda, Ornithischia

rhamphorhynchoids or **Rhamphorhynchoidea** (ram-fo-rink-OY-dee-ah) "Prow Beaks" (Named after RHAMPHORHYNCHUS)

Not DINOSAURS, but the earliest of the PTEROSAURS. Some were no larger than sparrows; others were hawk size or larger. These animals were the first of the flying vertebrates. They lived from the Late Triassic through Jurassic times in Russia, Europe, Africa, and North America. They had short necks and long tails; some had small rudders on the tips of their tails. The wings were long and narrow. The jaws were well developed, with numerous teeth. Some rhamphorhynchoids were probably fish eaters; others may have been scavengers, eating carcasses. Some may have had fur. DIMORPHODON, RHAMPHORHYNCHUS, and SORDES are examples of this group.

RHAMPHORHYNCHUS (ram-fo-RINK-us) "Prow Beak" (Greek *rhamphos* = prow + *rhynchos* = beak, because its beak was curved)

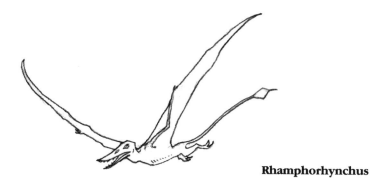

Rhamphorhynchus

Not a DINOSAUR, but a small, long-tailed PTEROSAUR of Late Jurassic Europe and Africa. This flying fish eater had a 4-foot (1.2-m) wingspan. Its body, including its tail, was only 18 inches (46 cm) long. The neck was short, but the head was long, and sharp teeth lined the long beak. *Rhamphorhynchus* had a small, flat membrane on the end of its very long, stiff tail. This membrane probably acted as a rudder.

RHOETOSAURUS (REE-toh-sawr-us) "Trojan Lizard" (Latin *rhoeteus* = Trojan + Greek *sauros* = lizard)

One of the earliest-known SAUROPODS. It was found in Early Jurassic rock in Australia. This huge four-legged plant eater belonged to the CETIOSAURINAE family. It had a long neck and TAIL, and was similar to CETIOSAURUS. Its skull was larger than that of DIPLODOCUS, and the nostrils were high on its head. It had peglike TEETH. It is known from an incomplete skeleton. Its discovery was important because it showed that sauropods lived in GONDWANALAND during Early Jurassic times.

Classification: Sauropoda, Sauropodomorpha, Saurischia

RIOJASAURUS (ree-OH-ha-sawr-us) "Rioja Lizard" (Named for La Rioja Province, Argentina, where it was found, + Greek *sauros* = lizard)

A 20-foot (6-m) Late Triassic PROSAUROPOD similar to MELAN-OROSAURUS. This dinosaur was a small-headed, long-necked HERBIVORE with a massive body and elephantlike legs. It was completely QUADRUPEDAL. A nearly complete skeleton of *Riojasaurus* was found in Argentina.

Classification: Prosauropoda, Sauropodomorpha, Saurischia

RIOJASUCHUS (ree-OH-ha-sook-us) "Rioja Crocodile" (Named for La Rioja Province, Argentina, where it was found, + Greek *souchos* = crocodile)

Not a DINOSAUR, but an advanced THECODONT; some scientists think it was the first meat-eating dinosaur, but most think it was a thecodont. This animal was probably one of the most dangerous of the thecodonts. Its short, strong jaws had only a few teeth, but those were daggerlike. *Riojasuchus* was a rather small QUADRUPED. It weighed less than 100 pounds (45 kg). Its FOSSILS have been found in Late Triassic Argentina.

Riojasaurus

RUTIODON (ROOT-ee-o-don) "Wrinkle Tooth" (Greek *rhytis* = wrinkle + Greek *odon-* = tooth)

Not a DINOSAUR, but a typical PHYTOSAUR. This 12-foot (3.5-

m) REPTILE has been found in Late Triassic deposits in North America, Europe, and Asia. It resembled a crocodile. It had a long skull and body, and bony plates, or scutes, covered its body. The nostrils were set far back—they were just in front of the eyes—and they were raised above the skull by cone-shape bumps. This aggressive animal lived in lakes and streams and preyed on small dinosaurs and any other animal it could catch. *Rutiodon* was the most dangerous animal of the Late TRIASSIC PERIOD.

S

SAICHANIA (SY-kahn-ee-ah) "Beautiful One" (Name derived from the Mongolian word *saikhan* = beautiful, nice looking, perhaps because it was such an unusually fine specimen)

A Late Cretaceous ANKYLOSAUR. This armored dinosaur is the best-known of the Asian ankylosaurs. Many specimens have been found. One found in Mongolia had many of its ARMOR PLATES in position, and the skull was very well preserved. Its neck, back, and stomach were covered by rows of spikes and knobs on bony plates. *Saichania* was an ANKYLOSAURID and

Saichania

had a heavy bony club on the end of its TAIL similar to that of ANKYLOSAURUS. Scientists estimate that this animal grew to be about 23 feet (7 m) long. Like all ankylosaurs, *Saichania* was QUADRUPEDAL and ate plants.

Classification: Ankylosauridae, Ankylosauria, Ornithischia

sails

See SPINES.

SALTASAURUS (sahlt-ah-SAWR-us) "Salta Lizard" (Named for Salta Province, Argentina, where it was found, + Greek *sauros* = lizard)

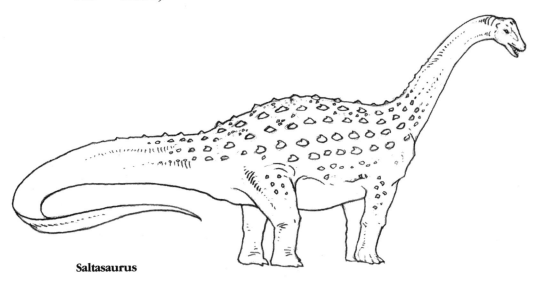

Saltasaurus

A Late Cretaceous SAUROPOD. This long-necked, long-tailed plant eater measured 40 feet (12.2 m) from the tip of its snout to the end of its TAIL. It had massive, elephantlike legs and walked on all fours. It may have been capable of rearing up on two legs to reach the highest branches of tall trees. *Saltasaurus* was a TITANOSAURID. It is the earliest sauropod known to have had armor plates, or scutes, attached to its SKIN. Remains of several individuals have been found in Argentina.

Classification: Sauropoda, Sauropodomorpha, Saurischia

SALTOPOSUCHUS (sahlt-o-po-SOOK-us) "Leaping Crocodile" (Latin *saltus* = leaping + Greek *pous* = foot + *souchos* = crocodile, though it was really more of a runner than a leaper)

Not a DINOSAUR, but a PSEUDOSUCHIAN THECODONT. It looked very much like a small THEROPOD and was very lightly built with hollow bones. SALTOPOSUCHUS was probably capable of running swiftly on two legs. Its hind legs were long, but its front legs were short. Its tail (which was longer than the body) counterbalanced its large head. From the tip of its snout to the end of its tail, *Saltoposuchus* was 4 feet (1.2 m) long. Its jaws were lined with sharp teeth, indicating that it was a meat eater. It lived in Europe during the TRIASSIC PERIOD.

SALTOPUS (SAHLT-o-pus) "Leaping Foot" (Latin *saltus* = leaping + Greek *pous* = foot, because the finder thought it was a leaper, but it was really a runner)

A small COELUROSAUR of Triassic Europe. This BIPEDAL dinosaur was similar to PODOKESAURUS but was smaller. It was an agile little meat eater about the SIZE of a house cat. It stood only 8 inches (20 cm) high at the hips and weighed about 2 pounds (1 kg). Its HANDS had five fingers and were capable of grasping prey. *Saltopus* was a swift runner with sharp TEETH, and it probably ate small lizards and other small animals. It had a long, swanlike neck and large eyes. It is known from partial skeletons found in Scotland.

Classification: Coelurosauria, Theropoda, Saurischia

SARCOLESTES (sar-ko-LESS-teez) "Flesh Robber" (Greek *sarko-* = flesh + *lestes* = robber; the reason for this name is unknown.)

Name given to a partial lower left jaw found in the Middle Jurassic of England. It was first thought to be a SCELIDOSAURID, but some authorities now think it might have been a NODO-SAURID ANKYLOSAUR. The jaw is quite similar to the jaw of the nodosaur SAUROPELTA. It contained TEETH and a large ARMOR PLATE that was fused to the side of the jaw. If this dinosaur proves to be an ankylosaur, it will be the oldest one known.

Classification: Nodosauridae?, Ankylosauria?, Ornithischia?

SARCOSAURUS (SAR-ko-sawr-us) "Flesh Lizard" (Greek *sarko-* = flesh + *sauros* = lizard, because it was a meat eater)

An Early Jurassic CARNOSAUR that was related to MEGALOSAU-RUS. It probably resembled that dinosaur. This big BIPEDAL meat eater is known only from vertebrae, a pelvis, and a hind leg found in England.

Classification: Carnosauria, Theropoda, Saurischia

SAURECHINODON (sawr-eh-KY-no-don) "Lizard with Spiny Teeth" (Greek *sauros* = lizard + *echinos* = spiny creature + *odon-* = tooth) A new name for ECHINODON.

A small Late Jurassic ORNITHOPOD whose fossils were found in England and North America. It is known only from fragments of the upper and lower jaws. The jaws were similar to those of an earlier ornithopod, FABROSAURUS. *Saurechinodon* had a small head and a horny, beaklike jaw lined with TEETH. Like all ornithopods, it walked on two legs and ate plants.

Classification: Fabrosauridae, Ornithopoda, Ornithischia

saurischians or **Saurischia** (sawr-ISS-kee-ah) "Lizard-hipped" (Greek *sauros* = lizard + *ischion* = hip, because their pelvises resembled those of lizards)

One of the two orders of animals called DINOSAURS. Saurischians had lizardlike pelvises and clawed FEET. Some were BIPEDAL, and others were QUADRUPEDAL. Some were meat eaters; some were plant eaters; others ate both meat and plants. Saurischians lived all over the world from Middle Triassic times to the end of the CRETACEOUS PERIOD. Some of them were no bigger than a chicken, while others were tall enough that they could have looked over a five-story building.

The saurischians have been divided into two suborders: The THEROPODA were bipedal meat eaters and included both COELUROSAURS and CARNOSAURS. (It is from Theropoda that birds probably EVOLVED.) The SAUROPODOMORPHA were basically or entirely quadrupedal. All ate plants; a few may have included meat in their DIET. This group included the PROSAUROPODS and the SAUROPODS. It is from this group that the largest and the smallest of the known dinosaurs have been found.

SAUROLOPHUS (sawr-OL-o-fus) "Crested Lizard" (Greek *sauros* = lizard + *lophus* = crest, referring to the hornlike growth on its head)

A solid-crested HADROSAUR of Late Cretaceous times. The CREST of this duck-billed dinosaur was a spikelike HORN that curved upward over the top of its skull. This BIPEDAL plant eater was about 22 feet (6.5 m) long and 17 feet (5.2 m) tall. It had a long, spoon-shaped bill, and its body resembled that

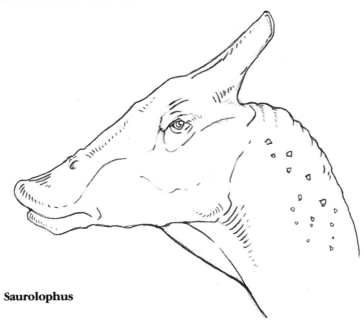

Saurolophus

of EDMONTOSAURUS. *Saurolophus* is known from complete skeletons found in western Canada and Mongolia.

   Classification: Hadrosauridae, Ornithopoda, Ornithischia

SAUROPELTA (sawr-o-PEL-tah) "Lizard with Shield" (Greek *sauros* = lizard + Latin *pelta* = shield, referring to its armor)

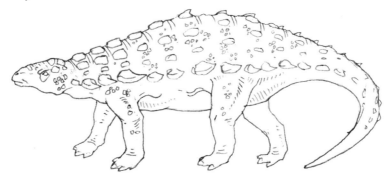

Sauropelta

The earliest known North American ANKYLOSAUR, and one of the largest of the *Nodosauridae*. It was 19 feet (5.8 m) long and weighed about 3 tons (2.7 metric tons). This Early Cretaceous plant eater was a ponderous animal that walked on four short, stubby legs. Its back and clubless TAIL were covered with rounded horny plates. Long spikes lined its sides. *Sauropelta* is known from many incomplete skeletons found in several western states.

HOPLITOSAURUS may be the same as this dinosaur.

Classification: Nodosauridae, Ankylosauria, Ornithischia

SAUROPLITES (sawr-OP-lih-teez) "Hoplites Lizard" (Greek *sauros* = lizard + *hoplites* = heavily armed foot soldier, referring to its armed back and tail)

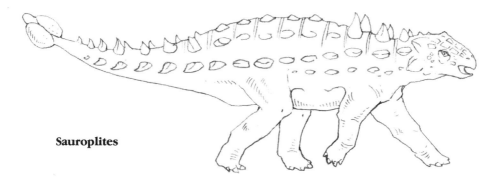

Sauroplites

The earliest known Asian ANKYLOSAUR and the oldest known ANKYLOSAURIDA. It was found in very early Early Cretaceous rock near the Chinese-Mongolian border. It had a clubbed TAIL, walked on four legs, and ate plants. It has been estimated that this ankylosaur was at least 18 feet (5.5 m) long. *Sauroplites* is known from very fragmentary material—a small piece of pelvis and several dermal plates.

Classification: Ankylosauridae, Ankylosauria, Ornithischia

sauropodomorphs or **Sauropodomorpha** (sawr-o-pod-ah-MORF-ah) "Lizard-footed Forms" (Greek *sauros* = lizard + *podo-* = foot + *morphe* = form)

A suborder of SAURISCHIAN dinosaurs. This group includes both the SAUROPODS and the PROSAUROPODS. Most were basically four-legged, and all ate plants, although some of the earlier prosauropods could also walk on two legs, and some probably ate meat as well as plants. Sauropodomorphs ranged in size from 7-foot (2-m) prosauropods to gigantic 100-foot (30.5-m) BRACHIOSAURS. They all had small heads, long necks, and long tails. Sauropodomorphs were very different from the other kind of saurischian dinosaurs, the THEROPODS. It is possible that sauropodomorphs and theropods EVOLVED from two different THECODONTS. Sauropodomorphs have been found on every continent except Antarctica. They lived from the Middle TRIASSIC PERIOD through the CRETACEOUS PERIOD.

There were two infraorders of sauropodomorphs. The PROSAUROPODA were the more primitive of the two and lived during the Triassic Period. They included both semi-QUADRUPEDAL and completely quadrupedal types, and both OMNIVORES and HERBIVORES. The SAUROPODA were all quadrupedal herbivores. They lived during Jurassic and Cretaceous times.

SAUROPODOPUS (sawr-o-POD-o-pus) "Sauropod Foot" (sauropod + Greek *pous* = foot)

Name given to footprints found in South Africa that were

Sauropodopus tracks

made by a very early SAUROPODOMORPH that had elephantlike feet. These TRACKS were made in early Late Triassic times. No bones of the animal that made them have been found.

sauropods or **Sauropoda** (sawr-OP-o-dah) "Lizard-footed" (Greek *sauros* = lizard + *podo-* = foot, because these animals had five toes like modern lizards)

The infraorder of giant, four-legged, plant-eating SAURIS-CHIAN dinosaurs. This group included the largest known land animals. Sauropods had huge bodies, long necks, whiplike TAILS, and elephantlike legs. Their long necks enabled them to reach vegetation other animals could not reach and gave them a good view of approaching danger, such as a pack of hungry CARNOSAURS. Sauropods had quite small BRAINS in comparison to their body SIZE, but an auxiliary nerve center in the hip region controlled the hind legs and tail.

The size of sauropods varied greatly. Small CAMARASAURS were only 30 feet (9 m) long, while giants like SEISMOSAURUS and an as-yet-unnamed species found at Dry Mesa, Colorado, may have been 130 feet (40 m) in length. It is a mystery how these huge animals with such tiny heads could have eaten enough to stay alive. Most scientists doubt that sauropods could have been ENDOTHERMIC, because warm-blooded animals require more food than cold-blooded animals. However, scientists think that sauropods may have been HOMOIOTHERMIC. (Their huge bodies may have held enough heat at night to keep their body temperature fairly even.)

Sauropods lived on dry land or in swampy areas. It was once thought that sauropods were lake dwellers, because scientists believed sauropods were too heavy to walk on land. But recent bone studies show that their legs were perfectly capable of supporting their weight on land. It is also now known that these animals would not have been able to breathe if they were completely submerged in water—the pressure of the water on their lungs would have been too great. However, sauropods probably enjoyed an occasional dip in the water, just as modern elephants do. It was also once thought that sauropods ate only soft water plants, because sauropods had weak teeth. We now know that sauropods ate twigs and needles from tall pines, firs, and sequoias.

Fossil footprints indicate that sauropods traveled in HERDS with the YOUNG protected by a ring of adults. They traveled slowly, perhaps no faster than 4 miles (6.4 km) per hour. A sauropod hatchling found in Oklahoma was 6 feet (1.8 m) long, 18 inches (45 cm) tall, and probably weighed 75 pounds (34 kg).

Sauropods hatched from EGGS about twice the size of ostrich eggs. They may have lived for more than 100 years, and they may have never stopped growing as long as they lived. As a group, they existed from Early Jurassic times to the end of the CRETACEOUS PERIOD. Sauropod fossils have been found on every continent except Antarctica. Some sauropods seem to have had bony plates embedded in their SKIN.

All scientists once thought that PROSAUROPODS were the ancestors of sauropods, because prosauropods were somewhat similar in body build to sauropods, and they lived at an earlier time period than did the sauropods. However, some scientists now consider it possible that these two groups of dinosaurs EVOLVED from a common ancestor.

There were two major groups, or families, of sauropods: those with peg-shaped TEETH and those with spatulate, or spoon-shaped, teeth. The spatulate group is called the BRACHIOSAURIDAE (a few call this family the CAMARASAURIDAE). The Brachiosauridae is divided into four subfamilies: the CETIO-

SAURINAE, the BRACHIOSAURINAE, the CAMARASAURINAE, and the EUHELOPODINAE.

The peg-toothed family is called the TITANOSAURIDAE (some call this family the ATLANTOSAURIDAE). This family is also divided into four subfamilies: the TITANOSAURINAE, the ATLANTOSAURINAE, the DIPLODOCINAE, and the DICRAEOSAURINAE.

Many recent discoveries have made it necessary to restudy the sauropods. When this study is completed, there may be some changes in the classification of sauropods. It is probable that some of the current subfamilies will be raised to family level. This has already been proposed for the DIPLODOCIDAE.

SAUROPUS (SAWR-o-pus) "Lizard Foot" (Greek *sauros* = lizard + *pous* = foot, because these prints resembled those of modern lizards)

Name given to long, slender footprints found in Late Triassic rock in the Connecticut Valley of the eastern United States. Scientists believe these TRACKS were made by a primitive ORNITHOPOD that was similar to PISANOSAURUS. The footprints resemble the foot of *Pisanosaurus* quite closely, but no FOSSILS of that dinosaur have been found in North America.

SAURORNITHOIDES (sawr-or-nith-OY-deez) "Birdlike Lizard" (Greek *sauros* = lizard + *ornithoides* = birdlike, because it had a birdlike build)

A Late Cretaceous COELUROSAUR. This lightly-built little BIPED was a close relative of DROMAEOSAURUS and TROÖDON. (It so closely resembled *Troödon* that some scientists think it was the same GENUS.) *Saurornithoides* was 6.5 feet (2 m) long and had long, grasping fingers, a small head with large eyes, powerful beaklike jaws, and a sicklelike CLAW on each foot. It

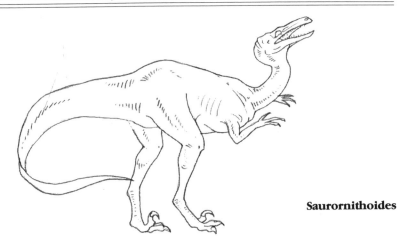

Saurornithoides

had a large BRAIN and was probably one of the most intelligent of the dinosaurs—it might have been as intelligent as modern birds. It probably ate lizards, small dinosaurs, and ratlike mammals. *Saurornithoides* is known from a skull and several other bones found in Mongolia.

Classification: Coelurosauria, Theropoda, Saurischia

SAURORNITHOLESTES (saur-or-NITH-o-les-teez) "Lizard Bird-robber" (Greek *sauros* = lizard + *ornithos* = bird + *lestes* = robber, because it resembled ORNITHOLESTES)

A small DROMAEOSAURID COELUROSAUR recently discovered in Alberta, Canada. It is based on very scanty material, but it is believed that, like DROMAEOSAURUS, this small BIPEDAL meat eater was a Late Cretaceous descendant of *Ornitholestes*.

Classification: Coelurosauria, Theropoda, Saurischia

scelidosaurid or **Scelidosauridae** (skel-yde-oh-SAWR-ih-dee) "Ribbed Lizards" (Named after SCELIDOSAURUS)

A primitive family of ORNITHISCHIANS. Scelidosaurids had small heads, weak jaws, and bony plates on their backs, necks, and TAILS. They were once considered ancestors of both the

STEGOSAURS and ANKYLOSAURS. Scelidosaurids lived in England during the Early JURASSIC PERIOD. *Scelidosaurus* is the only known member of this family.

SCELIDOSAURUS (skel-yde-oh-SAWR-us) "Ribbed Lizard" (Greek *skelido-* = rib + *sauros* = lizard, because a large number of ribs were recovered)

One of the earliest known armored ORNITHISCHIANS. This 12-foot (3.5-m) plant eater had rows of low bony plates on its back, neck, and TAIL similar to those of ANKYLOSAURS. The plates that ran down the center were solid and shaped like a cone. Its head was quite small, and its jaws were weak, indicating that it was a plant eater.

Some scientists consider this dinosaur to be an ancestor of STEGOSAURS; others suggest that it was a very early ankylosaur; still others suggest that it may have been an ORNITHOPOD (a

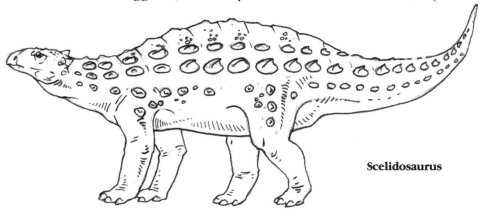

Scelidosaurus

BIPEDAL ornithischian) that somewhat resembled TENONTOSAU-RUS. It is known from three specimens found in Early Jurassic deposits in England. One is an almost complete skeleton.

Classification: Scelidosauridae, Ankylosauria?, Ornithischia

SCLEROMOCHLUS (sklayr-o-MOH-klus) "Hard Jumper"

(Greek *scleros* = hard + *mochleuo* = to heave up, because it was presumed that it jumped like a kangaroo)

Not a DINOSAUR, but a very advanced PSEUDOSUCHIAN. It was so advanced that a few consider it to be a primitive dinosaur. It was probably very closely related to the ancestor of the dinosaurs. *Scleromochlus* was 1 foot (30 cm) long, lightly built, and BIPEDAL. This little meat eater had a small head, a short neck, a slender body, a long, lizardlike tail, and hollow bones. Several portions of the skeleton have been found in Late Triassic deposits in Scotland.

SCOLOSAURUS (sko-lo-SAWR-us) "Thorn Lizard" (Greek *skolos* = thorn + *sauros* = lizard, referring to the long spikes on its body)

Name given to a nearly complete ANKYLOSAUR skeleton found in Late Cretaceous deposits in Alberta, Canada. This skeleton was 17 feet (5.2 m) long. The body—from the head to the tip of its short, clubbed TAIL—was covered with horny spikes. Two long spikes protruded from the tail. *Scolosaurus* is now considered to be the same as EUOPLOCEPHALUS. Since *Euoplocephalus* is the older name, it is the preferred name for this dinosaur.

Classification: Ankylosauridae, Ankylosauria, Ornithischia

SCUTELLOSAURUS (skoo-TEL-o-sawr-us) "Little Shield Lizard" (Latin *scutulum* = a little shield + Greek *sauros* = lizard, referring to the many small scutes, or bony plates, that covered this dinosaur)

A small and very primitive Late Triassic (or very early Jurassic) ORNITHOPOD. This FABROSAURID was recently found in Arizona and is one of the earliest known ORNITHISCHIANS of North America. It was not older but was more primitive than

Scutellosaurus

PISANOSAURUS. Its toes had CLAWS rather than the hooflike nails of later ornithischians. *Scutellosaurus* was closely related to LESOTHOSAURUS and was similar in SIZE—about 4 feet (1.2 m) long—but was different in several ways. It had a much longer TAIL—twice as long as the body and neck together. Its forelegs were longer and its hind legs were shorter than those of *Lesothosaurus*. *Scutellosaurus* was covered by tiny bony plates similar to those of EUOPLOCEPHALUS. Its FEET indicate that this dinosaur was basically BIPEDAL and lived on land. However, its HANDS were large, which indicates that the weight of the armor may have occasionally forced it to walk on all fours. *Scutellosaurus* was a plant eater; its TEETH were triangular, serrated, and arranged in a single row. This dinosaur is known from one nearly complete skeleton and a partial skeleton of another individual.

Classification: Fabrosauridae, Ornithopoda, Ornithischia

SECERNOSAURUS (see-KER-no-sawr-us) "Severed Lizard" (Latin *secerno* = sever + Greek *sauros* = lizard, referring to its non-LAURASIAN origin; it was "cut off" from other HADROSAURS.)

The second most primitive HADROSAUR known. *Secernosaurus* has the distinction of being one of only two hadrosaurs ever discovered in GONDWANALAND. (The other one has not yet been named.) This Late Cretaceous duckbill was found in Argentina. It was a HADROSAURINE and was crestless, but had some IGUANODONT features. This BIPEDAL plant eater is known from a partial braincase and a few other FOSSIL bones.

Classification: Hadrosauridae, Ornithopoda, Ornithischia

SEGISAURUS (SEE-gih-sawr-us) "Segi Lizard" (Named for Segi Canyon in Arizona, where it was found, + Greek *sauros* = lizard)

Segisaurus

A very late Late Triassic or Early Jurassic COELUROSAUR. Unlike other coelurosaurs, this rabbit-size SAURISCHIAN had a collarbone and solid leg bones. It was a speedy little BIPED, and this was probably its best DEFENSE against larger predators. Its HANDS resembled those of ORNITHOLESTES. It probably ate small lizards and insects. *Segisaurus* FOSSILS have been found in Arizona. A complete skeleton has not been found.

Classification: Coelurosauria, Theropoda, Saurischia

segnosaurids or **Segnosauridae** (seg-no-SAWR-ih-dee) "Slow Lizards" (Named after SEGNOSAURUS)

A new group of Late Cretaceous dinosaurs recently found in Mongolia. These dinosaurs are unlike any other known.

They seem to represent a unique line of EVOLUTION. Perhaps they evolved from an animal that was a link between the two major orders of dinosaurs, the SAURISCHIA and the ORNITHISCHIA. The pelvis (called OPISTHOPUBIC PELVIS) is very unusual. The pubis is backward-directed like those of ornithischians, but the ilium is broad and deep as in saurischians. These dinosaurs seem to have been meat eaters, possibly preying on fish, and appear to have been at least partially QUADRUPEDAL. Their rather small heads had narrow, toothless beaks and small "cheek" TEETH. Segnosaurids may be an evolutionary tie between saurischians and ornithischians. Two kinds of segnosaurids have been described—Segnosaurus and ERLIKOSAURUS. A third is known only from a pelvis.

SEGNOSAURUS (SEG-no-sawr-us) "Slow Lizard" (Latin *segnis* = slow + Greek *sauros* = lizard, possibly because it seems to be an evolutionary throwback)

A strange new type of dinosaur found in Late Cretaceous deposits in Mongolia. This dinosaur had an OPISTHOPUBIC PELVIS and a relatively small head; its snout ended in a narrow, toothless beak. Twenty-four small, pointed TEETH lined each side of the jaws. It probably ate fish. *Segnosaurus* had long arms and seems to have been at least partially QUADRUPEDAL. The short HANDS were three-fingered. The FEET had four toes with long, thick, curved CLAWS.

From the tip of its nose to the end of its TAIL, *Segnosaurus* was probably 23 feet (7 m) long and 6 feet (1.8 m) tall at the hips. Scientists think it was an ORNITHOPOD. *Segnosaurus* is known from a jaw, fore and hind limbs, pelvis, and several other bones.

Classification: Segnosauridae, Segnosauria, Ornithischia

SEISMOSAURUS (syz-mo-SAWR-us) "Earthshaker Lizard" (Greek *seismos* = earthquake + *sauros* = lizard, because of its presumed size)

A Late Jurassic SAUROPOD found in New Mexico in 1986. It is known from most of a skeleton. It is estimated that *Seismosaurus* may have weighed 80 to 100 tons (73 to 91 metric tons) and may have been 120 feet (36.5 m) long and stood 18 feet (5.5 m) tall at the shoulders. If correct, this was the longest dinosaur known. This four-legged plant eater may have been even larger than ULTRASAURUS and may have weighed twice as much as APATOSAURUS!

Classification: Sauropoda, Sauropodomorpha, Saurischia

sensory perception

Most dinosaurs had a well-developed sense of smell, good EYESIGHT, and good hearing. Their ability to see, hear, and smell was probably the best DEFENSE of unarmed dinosaurs. By getting early warnings of approaching enemies, they had ample time to escape.

Scientists can determine how good a dinosaur's vision was by the size of the eye sockets in the skull. The eyes of STENONYCHOSAURUS and DROMAEOSAURUS were very large, so these dinosaurs must have had extremely good vision. They should also have been able to judge distances quite accurately, because their eyes were spaced far apart and were on the front of their heads (rather than on the sides). They probably had good night vision, too.

There is evidence that HADROSAURS and SAUROPODS had excellent hearing. If dinosaurs had a good sense of hearing, they must also have been able to make sounds. We don't know what kind of sounds they made, but scientists think they may have bellowed like crocodiles. If so, a Mesozoic forest must have been a noisy place!

Soft mud oozed into openings in the skulls of some dinosaurs and formed casts of their BRAINS. These show the roots of the nerves in the brain and indicate that many dinosaurs had a keen sense of smell. The size of the nasal cavities also indicates that dinosaurs had a good sense of smell. Some scientists think that the purpose of the hollow CRESTS of LAMBEOSAURINE hadrosaurs was to lengthen the odor-sensitive area of the nose lining and thus greatly improve the sense of smell.

SHAMOSAURUS (shah-mwaw-SAWR-us) "Gobi Desert Lizard" (Chinese *shamo* = desert + Greek *sauros* = lizard, because it was found in the Gobi Desert)

One of the earliest ANKYLOSAURIDS known. This close relative of ANKYLOSAURUS was found in Early Cretaceous deposits in Mongolia. Its triangle-shaped skull is low and broad. Bony HORNS grew on the back corners of the head. This armored, four-legged plant eater is known from the skull and parts of the bony armor.

Classification: Ankylosauridae, Ankylosauria, Ornithischia

SHANSHANOSAURUS (shahn-SHAHN-o-sawr-us) "Shanshan Lizard" (Named for the area of China where it was found + Greek *sauros* = lizard)

A small Late Cretaceous CARNOSAUR about the size of DEINONYCHUS. This little BIPEDAL meat eater is known from one nearly complete specimen found in China. It was probably a very agile animal and a fast runner.

Classification: Carnosauria, Theropoda, Saurischia

SHANTUNGOSAURUS (shahn-TOONG-o-sawr-us) "Shan-tung Lizard" (Named for Shantung, China, where it was dis-covered, + Greek *sauros* = lizard)

A duck-billed ORNITHISCHIAN recently found in Late Creta-ceous deposits in China. This flat-headed 40-foot (12.2-m) HADROSAUR was one of the largest of the duck-billed dino-saurs. It was a HADROSAURINE somewhat resembling ANATOSAU-RUS. *Shantungosaurus* was BIPEDAL and ate plants.

Classification: Hadrosauridae, Ornithopoda, Ornithischia

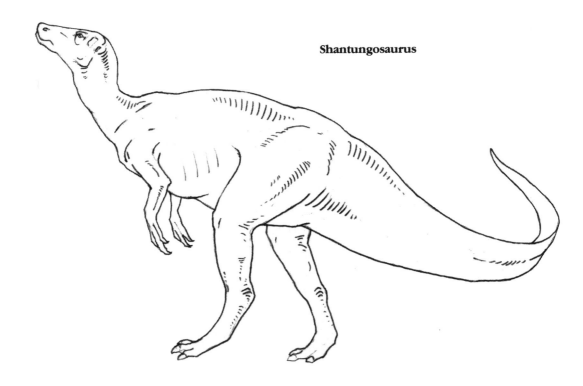

Shantungosaurus

short-frilled ceratopsians

See CERATOPSIANS.

SHUNOSAURUS (SHOO-no-sawr-us) "Sichuan Lizard" (Named for the place where it was found, Chinese *Shu* = old name for Sichuan, + Greek *sauros* = lizard)

A primitive SAUROPOD similar to BARAPASAURUS found in China. This 33-foot (10-m), four-legged plant eater lived during the Middle JURASSIC PERIOD. It was one of the most abundant species found in Sichuan, China. More than ten skeletons, including some rather complete skulls, have been found. It is believed that this dinosaur represents an intermediate stage between PROSAUROPODS and Late Jurassic sauropods.

Classification: Sauropoda, Sauropodomorpha, Saurischia

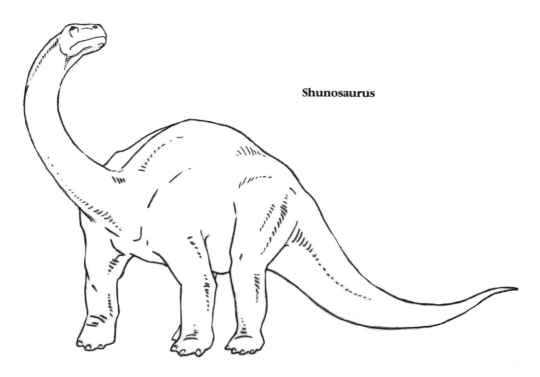

Shunosaurus

SILVISAURUS (SIL-vih-sawr-us) "Forest Lizard" (Latin *silva* = forest + Greek *sauros* = lizard, possibly referring to the place where it was found)

A primitive Early Cretaceous ANKYLOSAUR. This NODOSAURID had a clubless TAIL and a longer neck than most. Spikes protected its sides, and bony plates protected its back and tail. *Silvisaurus* was 13 feet (4 m) long. This QUADRUPEDAL plant eater is known from an incomplete skeleton found in Kansas.

Classification: Nodosauridae, Ankylosauria, Ornithischia

SINOSAURUS (SY-no-sawr-us) "Chinese Lizard" (Latin *sino-* = Chinese + Greek *sauros* = lizard, referring to the country where it was found)

A Late Triassic CARNIVORE. This animal was similar to ORNITHOSUCHUS. It was either a very primitive COELUROSAUR dinosaur or an advanced PSEUDOSUCHIAN. It is known only from jaw fragments found in China.

Classification: Coelurosauria?, Theropoda?, Saurischia?

size

Some dinosaurs were unbelievably huge—taller than a five-story building. Others were smaller than a chicken. They ranged from 2 feet (60 cm) to 120 feet (36.5 m) long.

Why did some dinosaurs get so large? Maybe they never stopped growing. It is possible that the largest lived to be more than 100 years old and never stopped growing in all that time. Many dinosaurs had large pituitary glands (glands that control growth); maybe that is why they became giants. Or maybe they got so large because solar radiation was greater during the MESOZOIC ERA than it is now, and that stimulated growth. Then again, maybe huge size was an adaptation for controlling the heat of their bodies (huge bodies cool more slowly than small ones). Scientists have many theories as to why dinosaurs grew so large, but we really don't know the answer.

The largest dinosaur we know about is a SAUROPOD called

SEISMOSAURUS. It was probably 120 feet (36.5 m) long and 60 feet (18.3 m) tall, and may have weighed more than 80 tons (72.6 metric tons). The largest THEROPOD was the huge meat eater TYRANNOSAURUS, which was 50 feet (15.2 m) long and weighed 6 tons (5.4 metric tons). The largest HADROSAUR was LAMBEOSAURUS; some specimens of this duckbill were 40 feet (12 m) long. This dinosaur was also the largest-known OR-NITHISCHIAN. TRICERATOPS was the largest CERATOPSIAN; it was 25 feet (7.5 m) long, the same size as the largest STEGOSAUR, STEGOSAURUS. The largest ANKYLOSAUR, ANKYLOSAURUS, reached a length of 25 feet (7.5 m).

The tiniest dinosaurs that have been found are a 30-inch (76-cm)-long juvenile COMPSOGNATHUS; a 10-inch (25-cm)-long baby PSITTACOSAURUS; and a robin-size, newly hatched PROSAU-ROPOD called MUSSAURUS. The smallest known adult dinosaurs we know about are the COELUROSAURS *Compsognathus,* which was about the size of a chicken, and SALTOPUS, which was about the size of a house cat.

skin

Scientists have found several fossilized impressions of di-nosaur skin. These show us what the skin of some of the dinosaurs was like. Most dinosaurs had tough, leathery skin covered with scales. Some scientists think it is possible that a few advanced dinosaurs, such as STENONYCHOSAURUS, may have had insulating covering such as fur or feathers.

HADROSAURS had leathery skin with a pebbled surface sim-ilar to that of a football. Scientists have found two mum-mified skeletons of ANATOSAURUS that clearly show skin impressions. The skin of this duckbill was textured with small bumps (or tubercles), similar to the skin of a gila monster. The skin of CORYTHOSAURUS was covered with small polygo-nal bumps, but rows of larger oval bumps covered the belly and pelvic area. The skin of LAMBEOSAURUS was similar but lacked the larger stomach bumps.

An impression of a small portion of the skin of a SAUROPOD shows that these animals had coarse, granular scales like some lizards of today. Skin impressions of the CERATOPSIAN CHASMOSAURUS show that this dinosaur was covered with rows of very large buttonlike tubercles. Some of these were 2 inches (5 cm) in diameter. They were set 5 inches (13 cm) apart and ran from the neck to the TAIL. The rows alternated with one another rather than being arranged in pairs, and the area between the rows was covered by small scales.

Impressions of the large CARNOSAUR CARNOTAURUS show that it had pebbly skin.

ANKYLOSAURS and some sauropods had heavy bony ARMOR PLATES embedded in their skin.

SORDES (SOHR-deez) "Shabby" (Latin *sordes* = shabbiness, rags, because of its long, shaggy coat of fur)

A RHAMPHORHYNCHOID that was found in Jurassic deposits in Russia. This PTEROSAUR was about the SIZE of a pigeon. Impressions left in the fine limestone where it was discovered show that this creature had long, dense, and relatively thick hair. Only the long TAIL was bare. *Sordes* probably ate fish, but we have no evidence of this.

smell, sense of
See SENSORY PERCEPTION.

species (SPEE-sheez)
See GENUS.

speed

Many people have the idea that all dinosaurs were slow creatures. Although some, such as the tanklike ANKYLOSAURS and the huge SAUROPODS, were slow, other dinosaurs were quite speedy. Sauropods probably moved no faster than 2 to 4 miles (3.2 to 6.4 km) per hour, whereas the ORNITHOMIMIDS could reach tremendous speeds. These were the "cheetahs" of the Mesozoic world. Some probably could have outrun an ostrich, and ostriches have been clocked at 50 miles (80 km) per hour. TROÖDON was probably the swiftest dinosaur.

Scientists estimate the speed of dinosaurs from the length of their strides. Many fossilized dinosaur TRACKWAYS have been found from which the stride can be measured. The faster an animal runs, the longer its strides. Scientists also can estimate the swiftness of an animal by comparing the length of its legs with known animals of comparable size. Up to a point, the longer and slenderer the legs, the faster the animal is able to run.

Some scientists estimate that ALLOSAURUS could run almost as fast as a man. TYRANNOSAURUS was somewhat slower. HADROSAURS probably could run about as fast as a modern horse. They may have been able to outrun *Tyrannosaurus,* but probably not ALBERTOSAURUS, which has generally been considered the swiftest of the large Late Cretaceous CARNOSAURS. But the swiftest carnosaur may have been ACROCANTHOSAURUS. A trackway recently found in Texas, which is believed to have been made by that dinosaur, shows that this carnosaur was capable of running 25 miles (40 km) per hour. A CERATOPSIAN could charge an attacker at speeds of up to 20 miles (32 km) per hour.

spines

Several prehistoric animals had long spines on their backbones. It is assumed that these spines supported a SKIN fold or fin similar to that of modern sailfish. These fins, or "sails," may have helped control the body temperature of the animals. If the animal stood in full sun, the fin would have warmed up quickly; in the shade, the fin would have cooled the animal more rapidly. These fins were rigid, not collapsible.

The best-known of the ancient sail-backed animals is not a dinosaur, but a Permian REPTILE named DIMETRODON. However, three dinosaurs did have similar fins on their backs. The fin of SPINOSAURUS was supported by spines 6 feet (1.8 m) high. OURANOSAURUS and ALTISPINAX also had very long spines on their vertebrae, but theirs were not as long as those of *Spinosaurus*. ACROCANTHOSAURUS had spines up to 17 inches (43 cm) long, but these probably were embedded in a thick ridge of muscles instead of supporting a fin.

spinosaurids or Spinosauridae (spy-no-SAWR-ih-dee) "Spiny Lizards" (Named after SPINOSAURUS)

A family of CARNOSAURS characterized by very long SPINES on the vertebrae. Some of the spines were as much as 6 feet (1.8 m) long. Scientists believe that these spines may have supported a skin fold, shaped like the fin of a fish, that ran along the dinosaur's back. Spinosauridae lived in North Africa during the CRETACEOUS PERIOD. *Spinosaurus* is the only positively known member of this group, although some people include the very poorly known ALTISPINAX.

SPINOSAURUS (SPY-no-sawr-us) "Spiny Lizard" (Latin *spina*

= spiny + Greek *sauros* = lizard, referring to the very long SPINES on its vertebrae)

A large CARNOSAUR of Late Cretaceous North Africa. *Spinosaurus* was 40 feet (12 m) long. It had spines 6 feet (1.8 m) tall on its back. It is assumed that these spines supported a huge fanlike sail, or fin, that stretched from the middle of the neck to just behind the hips. This fin probably helped to control the body temperature of the animal. *Spinosaurus* had a huge head and strong TEETH. This BIPEDAL meat eater is best known from an incomplete skeleton, which, unfortunately, was destroyed during World War II. Since then, however, more remains have been found.

Classification: Carnosauria, Theropoda, Saurischia

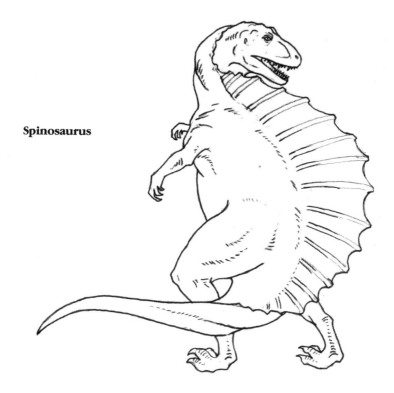

Spinosaurus

STAGONOLEPIS (stag-on-o-LEP-iss)
See AETOSAURS.

staurikosaurids or **Staurikosauridae** (stor-ik-o-SAWR-ih-dee) "Cross Lizards" (Named after STAURIKOSAURUS)

The most primitive family of THEROPODS. The staurikosaurids lived during the mid part of the TRIASSIC PERIOD in Brazil. They had long jaws and long, slender legs. Their bodies somewhat resembled those of the PROSAUROPODS. *Stauriko-saurus* is the only known member of this family.

STAURIKOSAURUS (stor-IK-o-sawr-us) "Cross Lizard" (Greek *staurikos* = of a cross + *sauros* = lizard, referring to the Southern Cross constellation, because its FOSSILS were found in the southern hemisphere)

A primitive THEROPOD of early Late Triassic times. It is the earliest-known theropod. This long-jawed CARNOSAUR had very long, slender legs and a body somewhat similar to that of a PROSAUROPOD. *Staurikosaurus* belonged to the TERATOSAURID family. Like all carnosaurs, it was a BIPEDAL meat eater. It is known from lower jaws, vertebrae, a pelvis, and hind legs found in Brazil.

Classification: Carnosauria, Theropoda, Saurischia

STEGOCERAS (steg-OS-er-us) "Covered Horn" (Greek *stego-* = roofed, covered + *keras* = horn, perhaps because the finder thought the "dome" covered a HORN) Originally called TROÖDON.

A small- to medium-size Late Cretaceous PACHYCEPHALOSAUR. The rather large BRAIN of this "dome-headed" dinosaur was covered by 3 inches (8 cm) of solid bone. The dome was divided into two parts, and males had larger and thicker domes

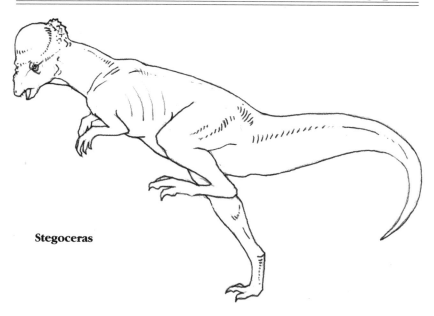

Stegoceras

than females. Small spikes fringed the back of the head, but the sides of the skull did not have the wartlike nodes found on PACHYCEPHALOSAURUS, a much larger pachycephalosaur. *Stegoceras* may have lived like wild goats of today, and males may have butted heads to defend territories or to win a mate.

Stegoceras was a BIPEDAL plant eater about the SIZE of a goat—5 to 6 feet (1.5 to 1.8 m) long, and 22 inches (56 cm) tall at the hips. It is known from nearly complete remains. Its FOSSILS have been found in Wyoming and Montana, in Alberta, Canada, and in northwestern China.

Classification: Pachycephalosauridae, Ornithopoda or Pachycephalosauria, Ornithischia

STEGOPELTA (steg-o-PEL-ta) "Plated Shield" (Greek *stego-* = covered; plated + Latin *pelta* = shield, referring to its bony armor)

Same as NODOSAURUS. This name was given to a fragmentary specimen that was found in Early Cretaceous deposits in Wyoming. Since *Nodosaurus* is the older name, it is the correct one to use.

Classification: Nodosauridae, Ankylosauria, Ornithischia

stegosaurs or **Stegosauria** (steg-o-SAWR-ee-ah) "Plated Lizards" (Named after STEGOSAURUS)

The suborder of ORNITHISCHIAN dinosaurs that had rows of plates and spikes running down their backs. Stegosaurs had small heads and tiny BRAINS (the brain of the largest was only about the size of a golf ball). The forelegs were short, and the hind legs were long. Stegosaurs carried their heads close to the ground and probably ate low ground plants. They had beaklike jaws and weak TEETH. These dinosaurs ranged from 15 to 25 feet (4.5 to 7.5 m) long and weighed up to 2.25 tons (2 metric tons). The arrangement of plates and spikes varied from one stegosaur to another, and no one knows exactly what the plates and spikes were for. Maybe they helped attract mates. Or perhaps they protected the stegosaur from large CARNOSAURS such as ALLOSAURUS. Some scientists think that the plates may have been temperature control devices. The plates had many blood vessels running through them. Sun shining on the plates would have warmed the blood flowing through them; wind blowing around the plates would have cooled the blood.

Eleven kinds of stegosaurs are known. It was once thought that these four-legged plant eaters were failures because they were short-lived. However, as a group, stegosaurs lived for more than 50 million years, and that actually is a pretty good record. The oldest stegosaur lived during the Middle Jurassic, and the latest lived in late Early Cretaceous or early Late Cretaceous times. Dacentrurus, Dravidosaurus, Kentrosaurus, Lexovisaurus, and Stegosaurus were stegosaurs.

STEGOSAURUS (STEG-o-sawr-us) "Plated Lizard" (Greek *stego-* = roofed or plated + *sauros* = lizard, referring to the plates on its back)

The only plated dinosaur ever found in North America. It has also been found in Europe. This four-legged plant eater was 11 feet (3.4 m) tall at the hips and 25 feet (7.5 m) long. Its body was about the size of an Asian elephant. *Stegosaurus* had a ridiculously small head and a golf-ball-size brain. Some people think that an enlargement of the spinal cord above the hips was a second brain, but it was not. All four-legged animals have this.

Stegosaurus was high at the hips and low at the shoulders, causing it to carry its head low. It probably ate low ground plants. Its long, heavy tail was armed with four spikes, each about 1 foot (30 cm) long. Two rows of large, thin, leaflike, bony plates arranged alternately (rather than in pairs) ran

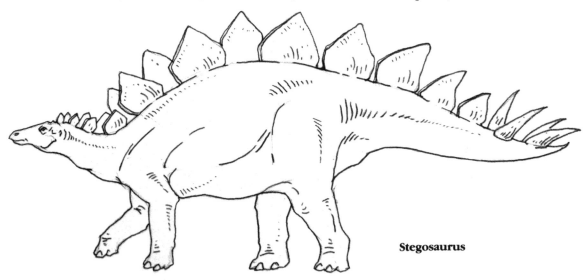

Stegosaurus

down its neck and back and partway down its tail. The largest plates were 2 feet (60 cm) wide and 2 feet (60 cm) tall. These were situated over the hips. No one knows the purpose of these plates. They might have been used to attract a mate, or as a DEFENSE mechanism—perhaps they made the animal look larger. The most recent theory is that they helped control the body temperature. (Wind flowing around the plates would have cooled the blood flowing through them.)

Stegosaurus lived during the Late JURASSIC PERIOD. Many skeletons of this dinosaur have been found in Colorado, Utah, and Wyoming. One skeleton was a baby about the size of a German shepherd dog. Another was found with its plates in position.

Classification: Stegosauridae, Stegosauria, Ornithischia

STENONYCHOSAURUS (sten-ON-ik-o-sawr-us) "Narrow-clawed Lizard" (Greek *stenos* = narrow + *onycho-* = claw + *sauros* = lizard, referring to the sicklelike CLAW on each foot)

This dinosaur is now considered to be the same as TROÖDON.

Classification: Coelurosauria, Theropoda, Saurischia

STENOPELIX (sten-o-PEL-iks) "Narrow Helmet" (Greek *stenos* = narrow + *pelex* = helmet or cap, possibly referring to the shape of the pelvis)

A small ORNITHISCHIAN. It was related to PSITTACOSAURUS. This primitive CERATOPSIAN is known only from very fragmentary material (a pelvis and hind legs) found in Early Cretaceous deposits in Germany. It was a plant eater and probably walked on two legs.

Classification: Psittacosauridae, Ornithopoda or Ceratopsidae, Ornithischia

STOKESOSAURUS (STOHKS-o-sawr-us) "Stokes's Lizard" (Named in honor of Lee Stokes, American PALEONTOLOGIST, + Greek *sauros* = lizard)

A short-snouted Late Jurassic CARNOSAUR. It is estimated that this BIPEDAL meat eater was only 13 feet (4 m) long and 5 feet (1.5 m) tall. Like all carnosaurs, *Stokesosaurus* had long, serrated TEETH. It may have been related to ALBERTOSAURUS, but it was not a TYRANNOSAUR, because it lived in the JURASSIC PERIOD. It is known from fragments found in Utah. It may be the same as ILIOSUCHUS.

Classification: Carnosauria, Theropoda, Saurischia

stomach stones
See GASTROLITHS.

STRUTHIOMIMUS (strooth-ee-o-MY-mus) "Ostrich Mimic" (Greek *strouthos-* = ostrich + *mimos* = mimic, because it resembled an ostrich)

A Late Cretaceous ORNITHOMIMID—one of the "ostrich dinosaurs." Like an ostrich, *Struthiomimus* had a long neck; long, slender—but powerful—legs; and a small head. A horny, toothless beak covered its jaws. Its eyes were quite large, as was its BRAIN.

Although *Struthiomimus* so closely resembled ORNITHOMIMUS that many scientists consider them to be the same, *Struthiomimus* was a bit smaller and had a longer TAIL. It stood 7 feet (2 m) tall and was 12 feet (3.5 m) long. Its tail was 3 feet (90 cm) longer than its very short body.

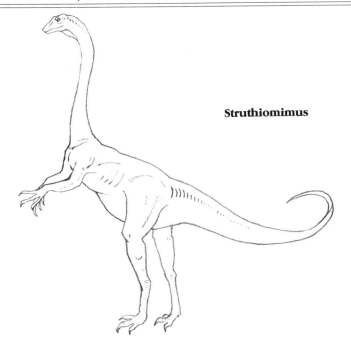

Struthiomimus

Struthiomimus had grasping fingers that were equipped with long, bearlike CLAWS. The claws may have been used to rip open logs to get at insects. This little BIPED may have been OMNIVOROUS like ostriches. It may have eaten small REPTILES, EGGS, and fruit, as well as insects. It is known from at least one complete skeleton and several partial ones found in Alberta, Canada. COELUROSAURUS may be the same as this dinosaur.

Classification: Coelurosauria, Theropoda, Saurischia

STRUTHIOSAURUS (STROOTH-ee-o-sawr-us) "Harsh Lizard" (Greek *struthnos* = harsh + *sauros* = lizard, possibly referring to its rough cranium)

The smallest known ANKYLOSAUR. This four-legged plant eater was only 5 or 6 feet (1.5 or 1.8 m) long. *Struthiosaurus* was probably the last of the NODOSAURIDAE. It is known only from incomplete material found in Late Cretaceous deposits in

Austria. Its head was unarmed, but since *Struthiosaurus* was a NODOSAURID, its sides were probably protected by large spikes, and its TAIL was clubless.

Classification: Nodosauridae, Ankylosauria, Ornithischia

STYGIMOLOCH (stij-ih-MAH-luk) "River of Hades Devil" (Latin *Stygus* = of the mythical River Styx + Hebrew *Moloch* = evil spirit, because it was found in the Hell Creek formation in Montana and because of its presumed demonic appearance)

A high-domed PACHYCEPHALOSAUR similar to STEGOCERAS. This BIPEDAL plant eater was found in Late Cretaceous deposits in Montana. There are large, elaborate HORN cores on the back of the skull of this dome-headed dinosaur. These probably formed clusters of horns on either side of the domed skull roof. Only the back part of the skull has been found to this date.

Classification: Pachycephalosauridae, Ornithopoda or Pachycephalosauria, Ornithischia

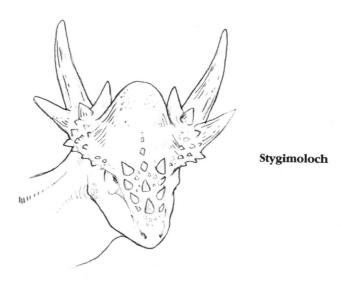

Stygimoloch

STYRACOSAURUS (sty-RAK-o-sawr-us) "Spiked Lizard" (Greek *styrax* = spike + *sauros* = lizard, referring to the spikes on its FRILL)

A short-frilled CERATOPSIAN with six long spikes along the edge of its frill. A straight HORN nearly 2 feet (61 cm) long and 6 inches (15 cm) thick grew on its nose, but only stumps grew above its eyes. Like all ceratopsians, it was a four-legged plant eater with a bulky body and a relatively short, thick TAIL. *Styracosaurus* was 18 feet (5.5 m) long and 6 feet (1.8 m) tall. It probably weighed 3 tons (2.7 metric tons). Some scientists believe it was a good runner—it may have been capable of going 20 miles (32 km) per hour. *Styracosaurus* is known from a herd of 100 individuals and at least one complete skeleton found in Late Cretaceous deposits in Alberta, Canada.

Classification: Ceratopsidae, Ceratopsia, Ornithischia

Styracosaurus

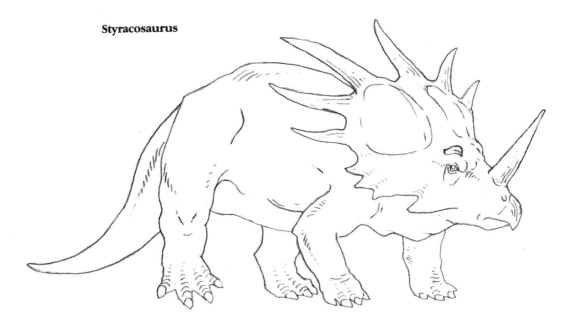

Sundance Sea (Named for the Sundance rock formation of the Rocky Mountain area)

Name given to a long, narrow arm of sea that stretched down across North America from the Arctic Ocean to southern Utah during the early part of the Late JURASSIC PERIOD. On the west side of the sea a narrow finger of highlands separated the sea from the ocean; on the east side were vast lowlands; and to the south were extensive sand dunes. Near the end of the Jurassic Period the sea retreated to the Arctic Ocean.

SUPERSAURUS (SOO-per-sawr-us) "Super Lizard" (Latin *super* = above + Greek *sauros* = lizard, because it was a very large dinosaur)

An enormous Late Jurassic SAUROPOD. It probably belonged to the DIPLODOCID family but was even larger than DIPLODOCUS. It is known only from a few gigantic bones found in Colorado—a pair of shoulder blades 8 feet (2.4 m) long, a pelvis 6 feet (1.8 m) wide, neck vertebrae 4.5 feet (1.4 m) long, and ribs 10 feet (3 m) long. If it had a long whiplike TAIL similar to that of *Diplodocus, Supersaurus* may have been 140 feet (42.7 m) long, the longest known dinosaur. It may have towered 50 feet (15.2 m) tall. Though perhaps the longest, it was not the heaviest dinosaur. This four-legged plant eater may have weighed 50 tons (45 metric tons).

Classification: Sauropoda, Sauropodomorpha, Saurischia

synapsid (sin-AP-sid) "Fused Arch" (Greek *syn* = together + *apsid* = arch)

Any animal with only one opening low on each side of its skull behind the eye sockets. The mammallike REPTILES of the

Late Paleozoic and Early Mesozoic eras were synapsids, as are present-day mammals. Dimetrodon was a synapsid.

synapsid skull

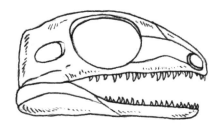

SYNTARSUS (sin-TAHR-sus) "Fused Ankle" (Greek *syn* = together + *tarsos* = part of foot, ankle, because some bones of the ankle were fused together)

A very primitive Late Triassic coelurosaur related to Coelophysis. Its four-fingered hands resembled those of *Coelophysis,* but its four-toed feet and fused ankles were more similar to those of an early ornithopod, Heterodontosaurus. *Syntarsus* weighed only about 65 pounds (30 kg) and was about 2 feet (60 cm) tall. Some scientists think it may have been insulated with primitive feathers. This very early bipedal meat eater probably ate small lizards and mammals. It is known from skeletons found in Zimbabwe and Arizona.

Classification: Coelurosauria, Theropoda, Saurischia

Syntarsus

SYRMOSAURUS (SEER-mo-sawr-us) "Trail Lizard" (Greek *syrmos* = a trail + *sauros* = lizard, because it was presumed that it dragged its TAIL)

Most of a skeleton of this ANKYLOSAUR was found in Mongolia. It is now known to be the same as PINACOSAURUS.

Classification: Ankylosauridae, Ankylosauria, Ornithischia

SZECHUANOSAURUS (su-CHWAHN-o-sawr-us) "Szechwan Lizard" (Named for Szechwan Province, China, where it was found, + Greek *sauros* = lizard)

A Late Jurassic THEROPOD. This large, two-legged meat eater lived in China and is known from most of a skeleton. It was a close relative of ALLOSAURUS and resembled that dinosaur. It was about 33 feet (10 m) long.

Classification: Carnosauria, Theropoda, Saurischia

T

tails

Dinosaurs had long, heavy, reptilian-type tails. Some BIPEDAL dinosaurs may have used their tails as braces when standing upright, but not all could have done this. For example, the tails of some, such as DEINONYCHUS and TENONTOSAURUS, were held out rigidly behind by bundles of bony, rodlike tendons that lay along each side of the vertebrae. Such rigidity improved the use of the tail as a counterbalance when the animal ran. HADROSAURS had flat tails, similar to those of alligators. This flatness may have been useful in swimming, but the main purpose of the tail (as it was with all BIPEDAL dinosaurs—both ORNITHOPODS and THEROPODS) was to balance the body when walking or running.

QUADRUPEDAL dinosaurs did not need long tails to balance their bodies while walking or running. The tails of CERATOPSIANS were relatively short, but thick and heavy. The SAUROPODOMORPHS needed long tails to counterbalance their long necks. Several SAUROPODS had whiplike tails, which could have been used as DEFENSE weapons. Some of the ANKYLOSAURS and the STEGOSAURS undoubtedly used their tails as weapons. The tails of the ANKYLOSAURIDAE were armed with heavy, macelike clubs or spikes. Stegosaurs had long spikes on the ends of their tails.

Some scientists think that the quadrupedal dinosaurs extended their tails when running, the same as the bipedal dinosaurs did. Others are convinced that the sauropods, at least, always dragged their tails on the ground. Sauropods with quite short tails and long legs have recently been discovered. These seem to support the theory that at least some sauropods extended their tails. It is hard to see how these dinosaurs could have dragged their tails.

TALARURUS (tah-lah-ROO-rus) ''Basket Tail'' (Greek *talaros* = basket + *oura* = tail, referring to the large club on its tail)

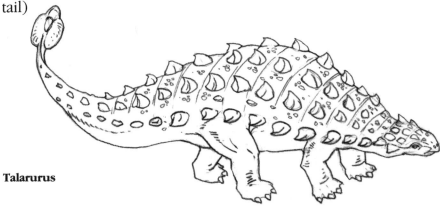

Talarurus

An early Late Cretaceous ANKYLOSAUR—the second-oldest ANKYLOSAURID known. This armored dinosaur was about 17 feet (5.2 m) long. It walked on four short legs and browsed on low ground plants. Its back, hips, and clubbed TAIL were covered with 2-inch (5-cm)-thick bony scutes (plates) and rows of sharp spikes. Its back was flexible instead of being rigid like a turtle's back. *Talarurus* is known from several partial skeletons and a partial skull found in Mongolia.

Classification: Ankylosauridae, Ankylosauria, Ornithischia

TANIUS (TAN-ee-us) (Named for an ancient Chinese state in Shantung)

A Late Cretaceous HADROSAUR (duck-billed dinosaur) closely related to ANATOSAURUS. Like *Anatosaurus, Tanius* was BI-PEDAL and ate plants. It was a HADROSAURINE and had a flat, broad head. There was a low dome or hump between its

Tanius

eyes similar to the hump found on the snout of KRITOSAURUS. This duckbill is known from a nearly complete skeleton found in eastern China.

Classification: Hadrosauridae, Ornithopoda, Ornithischia

TANYSTROPHEUS (tan-ee-STROH-fee-us) "Long Vertebrae" (Greek *tany-* = long + *stropheus* = vertebra, referring to the vertebrae of its neck)

Not a DINOSAUR, but a 20-foot (6-m)-long PROTOROSAUR that lived in Europe during the Middle TRIASSIC PERIOD. This predecessor of modern lizards was almost all neck. Its body was only 3.5 feet (1 m) long, and its tail was 6.5 feet (2 m) long. The neck of this incredible animal was 10 feet (3 m) long, but it had only ten vertebrae. Adult *Tanystropheus* ate fish and probably lived near the sea, but the young lived inland and ate plants or insects.

TARBOSAURUS (TAR-bo-sawr-us) "Terrible Lizard" (Greek *tarbo-* = terrible + *sauros* = lizard, because it was a fearsome dinosaur)

A large Late Cretaceous CARNOSAUR very similar to TYRANNOSAURUS. Some grew to be 46 feet (14 m) in length and 20 feet (6 m) or more tall. *Tarbosaurus* ran on powerful hind legs with its body parallel to the ground and its heavy TAIL extended. It had a 4-foot (1.2-m) skull and 6-inch (15-cm) daggerlike TEETH. Its arms were short; the HANDS had two fingers ending in 2-inch (5-cm) CLAWS. The claws on the three-toed FEET were 4 inches (10 cm) long. This giant meat eater is known from ten complete skeletons found in the Gobi Desert of Mongolia.

Classification: Carnosauria, Theropoda, Saurischia

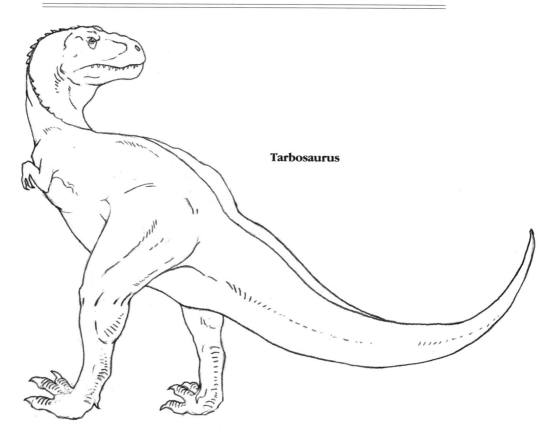

Tarbosaurus

TARCHIA (TAR-kee-ah) (Name derived from Mongolian *tar-khi* = brain, because the first specimen found was a skull)

A Late Cretaceous ANKYLOSAUR found in the Gobi Desert of Mongolia. This armored dinosaur was an ANKYLOSAURIDA. It had a triangular head, which was covered completely by bony plates, and it had SPINES above and behind the eyes. *Tarchia* is the latest and one of the largest ankylosaurs known from Asia. It may have grown to be 18 feet (5.5 m) long. Its jaws were lined with 18 TEETH. Spikes protruded from the corners of the mouth, and rows of spikes ran down its back and clubbed TAIL. This QUADRUPEDAL plant eater is known from

Tarchia

skulls, vertebral columns, spikes, plates, ribs, and other material of two separate species.

Classification: Ankylosauridae, Ankylosauria, Ornithischia

teeth

The dinosaurs never had a dental problem. As soon as one of their teeth became old or worn, it dropped out and a new one grew in its place. This continued throughout their lives. Every dinosaur tooth is quite distinctive, and scientists can usually tell by looking at a FOSSIL tooth which kind of dinosaur it had belonged to. Scientists can tell whether the animal was a plant eater or a meat eater, and sometimes they can get a good idea of the SIZE of the animal from the size of the tooth.

Meat-eating dinosaurs had sharp, pointed, bladelike teeth. CARNOSAURS had daggerlike teeth with edges that were serrated like a steak knife. The largest carnosaurs had teeth that were 6 inches (15 cm) long. COELUROSAURS had small, thin, pointed teeth with serrated edges.

Some PROSAUROPODS had both blade-shaped teeth and flat, leaf-shaped teeth (molars), indicating that they ate both plants and meat. Others had only the leaf-shaped teeth of plant eaters.

The teeth of the plant-eating dinosaurs varied a great deal, even within the same kinds of dinosaurs. For example, some SAUROPODS had weak, peg-shaped teeth that were slightly pointed on the end. Others had spatulate (spoon-shaped) teeth. Sauropods had no molars or grinding teeth. They probably swallowed their food whole.

The teeth of the CERATOPSIANS chopped plant food instead of grinding it. The lower teeth closed inside the upper, cutting tough tree branches like a pair of scissors cutting paper. ANKYLOSAURS and STEGOSAURS had small, weak teeth on the sides of the jaws. These teeth were suited only for eating tender ground plants.

The ORNITHOPODS had the most varied teeth of all the dinosaurs. Some had triangular cutting teeth to the tip of their snouts; others had only grinding teeth in their cheek region. They used their beaks to snip off branches. The HETERODONTS had both cutting teeth and grinding teeth; they had canine teeth as well. Most ornithopods had teeth arranged in single rows, but the HADROSAURS had banks of several rows of sharp, rodlike teeth packed closely together. Some species had as many as 280 teeth on each side of the upper and lower jaws— 1,120 teeth altogether! These teeth were especially suited for grinding coarse plant fibers.

TELMATOSAURUS (tel-MAT-o-sawr-us) "Marsh Lizard" (Greek *telmato-* = marsh + *sauros* = lizard, perhaps because it was thought to be a marsh dweller)

Name given to a primitive HADROSAUR skull found in Hungary. It is the only positively known European representative of the duck-billed dinosaurs. This duckbill was crestless and was a BIPEDAL plant eater. It lived during Late Cretaceous times.

A fossilized leg bone found in Holland may also be a *Telmatosaurus.*

Classification: Hadrosauridae, Ornithopoda, Ornithischia

TENONTOSAURUS (ten-ON-toh-sawr-us) "Tendon Lizard" (Greek *tenonto-* = sinew + *sauros* = lizard, referring to the ossified tendons along its backbone)

An ORNITHOPOD of Early Cretaceous North America. This 20-foot (6-m) BIPEDAL plant eater weighed 2 tons (1.8 metric tons) or more. It probably resembled IGUANODON but did not have spiked thumbs. Its TAIL was equipped with bony, rodlike tendons that held the tail rigid when *Tenontosaurus* ran. *Tenontosaurus* probably roamed vast areas—partial skele-

Tenontosaurus

tons have been found in Montana, Idaho, Wyoming, Texas, and Oklahoma. Perfect SKIN impressions were found in Texas.

Classification: Iguanodontidae, Ornithopoda, Ornithischia

teratosaurids or **Teratosauridae** (teh-rat-o-SAWR-ih-dee) "Monster Lizards" (Named after TERATOSAURUS)

The most primitive family of CARNOSAURS. These meat eaters grew to be 20 feet (6 m) long. They had massive builds, large heads, and daggerlike TEETH. Their forelimbs were about three-fourths the length of the hind and had three-fingered HANDS. Teratosaurids lived in Europe and South America during the TRIASSIC PERIOD. STAURIKOSAURUS and TERATOSAURUS were teratosaurids.

TERATOSAURUS (teh-RAT-o-sawr-us) "Monster Lizard" (Greek *terato-* = monster + *sauros* = lizard, referring to its monstrous TEETH)

This 20-foot (6-m) meat eater is generally considered to be one of the largest of the Late Triassic CARNOSAURS. It weighed more than half a ton. It is known from a skeleton found in Germany. It had three fingers, a large head, and daggerlike teeth. However, recent studies suggest that *Teratosaurus* may have been a very large THECODONT rather than a THEROPOD.

Tertiary (TER-shee-er-ee) **Period** (From Latin *tertius* = third. When this period was named, geological time was divided into three parts. The Tertiary was the third, or last, of these periods.)

The first of the two periods of the CENOZOIC ERA. The Tertiary Period is the geologic time that immediately followed the CRETACEOUS PERIOD (the last period of the MESOZOIC ERA). It lasted from 65 million years ago to 2 million years ago. No dinosaur FOSSILS have been found in rocks of this age. They had disappeared along with the PTEROSAURS, PLESIOSAURS, AMMONITES, and many kinds of plant forms at the end of the Mesozoic Era. During the Tertiary Period, mammals became the dominant life form.

Tethys (TEE-thiss) **Sea** (Named after Tethys—in Greek mythology, daughter of Oceanus)

Name of the sea or waterway that separated the two great supercontinents, LAURASIA and GONDWANALAND, during the MESOZOIC ERA. During the PERMIAN and TRIASSIC PERIODS, before the breakup of PANGAEA, Tethys was only an arm of the ocean that reached into the eastern shoreline. By the Late JURASSIC PERIOD, 140 million years ago, it had completely separated the two supercontinents.

TETRAPODITE (teh-trah-po-DY-tee) "Four-footed" (Greek *tetra* = four + *podite* = footed)

Name given to a rare type of dinosaur footprint. These footprints were found in British Columbia and Alberta, Canada. Scientists believe that they were made by a CERATOPSIAN. Ceratopsians had rather massive, four-toed hind FEET and five-toed forefeet. Both the hind feet and the forefeet had blunt CLAWS.

TETRASAUROPUS (teh-trah-SAWR-o-pus) "Four Lizard Foot" (Greek *tetra* = four + *sauropous* = lizard foot, referring to the number of toes)

Name given to four-toed footprints made by an unknown PROSAUROPOD. The footprints were found in Late Triassic rock in South Africa. They resemble the footprints named NAVAHOPUS. The dinosaur that made these TRACKS was QUADRUPEDAL and took short strides. It had four toes on both its forefeet and its hind FEET. The hind feet were long-soled. The forefeet were much smaller and had CLAWS on the first and third fingers.

THECODONTOSAURUS (thee-ko-DON-to-sawr-us) "Socket-toothed Lizard" (THECODONT + Greek *sauros* = lizard, because its teeth were set in sockets like those of thecodonts)

A very early PROSAUROPOD similar to ANCHISAURUS but more primitive. It is one of the earliest prosauropods known. FOSSILS of several individuals found in England were destroyed during World War II, but others believed to be the same dinosaur have been found in several regions of the world. This Late Triassic dinosaur was only 10 feet (3 m) long and was lightly built. Its head was small, and its TEETH were serrated. Those in front were cone shaped, like those of thecodonts, but the jaw teeth were flat like those of HERBIVORES. *Thecodontosaurus* probably ate both meat and plants. It had slender legs and FEET and, like all prosauropods, probably had a long neck and TAIL. It was QUADRUPEDAL but could also walk on two legs.

Classification: Prosauropoda, Sauropodomorpha, Saurischia

Thecodontosaurus

thecodonts or **Thecodontia** (thee-ko-DON-tee-ah) "Socket-toothed" (Greek *theke* = sheath + *odonto-* = teeth, because their teeth grew in sockets in the jaws)

Not dinosaurs, but an order of Triassic REPTILES. This is the group from which DINOSAURS, CROCODILIANS, PTEROSAURS, and possibly birds arose. Thecodonts and their descendants are called ARCHOSAURS. Most thecodonts ate meat, but some were OMNIVOROUS, eating both meat and plants. Most were QUAD-RUPEDAL, some were capable of running on two legs, and a few may have been completely BIPEDAL.

There were four suborders of thecodonts—the AETOSAURIA, the PHYTOSAURIA, the PROTEROSUCHIA, and the PSEUDOSUCHIA. Scientists think that Pseudosuchia is the only group that could have produced the ancestors of the dinosaurs. They were the most advanced thecodonts.

Thecodonts ranged from rabbit-size pseudosuchians to 30-foot (9-m) PHYTOSAURS.

therapsids or **Therapsida** (theh-RAP-sih-dah) "Beast Opening" (Greek *ther-* = beast or mammal + *apsides* = opening, because the openings in their skulls were like those in the skulls of mammals)

Not DINOSAURS, but the mammallike REPTILES from which mammals arose. These beasts lived during Late Paleozoic and Early Mesozoic times. The therapsids dominated animal life on earth for 40 million years before the rise of the dinosaurs. There were more than 300 GENERA of therapsids. They ranged from the size of a rat to the size of a rhinoceros. Some were CARNIVOROUS, and some were HERBIVOROUS; all were four-legged. They lived all over the world. MOSCHOPS was a therapsid.

THERIZINOSAURUS (ther-ih-zin-o-SAWR-us) "Scythe Lizard"

(Greek *therizo-* = reap + *sauros* = lizard, referring to its sicklelike CLAWS)

A Late Cretaceous CARNIVOROUS relative of DEINOCHEIRUS. It is known from a gigantic arm, several sickle-shaped claws, incomplete hind legs, and a tooth. The arm was 8 feet (2.4 m) long, and the claws were 2 and 3 feet (60 and 90 cm) long. The arm was shorter but more massive than the arms of *Deinocheirus*. The FOSSILS of this BIPEDAL meat eater were found in Mongolia.

Classification: Coelurosauria, Theropoda, Saurischia

theropods or **Theropoda** (theh-ROP-o-dah) "Beast-footed" (Greek *theros* = beast or mammal + *pod-* = foot. Misnamed—the feet were actually more birdlike than beastlike.)

A suborder of SAURISCHIAN dinosaurs. Members of this group were meat eaters that walked on strong hind legs with their bodies held horizontally, or parallel to the ground, and their tails outstretched to counterbalance their bodies. Most had short forelimbs with clawed HANDS that could be used for grasping. Their birdlike FEET had three long, forward-pointing toes and a backward-pointing dewclaw. The smallest theropods were chicken size; the largest were 50-foot (15-m) giants. They lived almost worldwide from Middle Triassic through Cretaceous times.

Theropods included both toothed and toothless kinds. The toothless theropods may have been OMNIVOROUS, probably eating fruit as well as meat. Toothed theropods had bladelike TEETH that were serrated like a steak knife. Scientists think that theropods were ENDOTHERMIC (warm-blooded), because they were very active and most were swift runners.

There were two major kinds of theropods: CARNOSAURS and COELUROSAURS. The carnosaurs were the large, heavily-built meat eaters. Allosaurus, Albertosaurus, and Tyrannosaurus were carnosaurs.

Coelurosaurs were small predators with hollow bones. Coelophysis and Compsognathus were members of this group. Some scientists suggest the addition of the deinonychosaurs, which would include Deinonychus and Dromaeosaurus.

Because many recent theropod discoveries do not fit neatly into these classifications, some scientists propose abolishing the Coelurosauria and Carnosauria designations and classifying all meat eaters in families under Theropoda.

Scientists describe theropods as small, medium, or large, depending on their overall length from snout to the tip of the tail. They call theropods that are up to 5 feet (up to 1.5 m) long very small. Those 5 to 10 feet (1.5 to 3 m) are called small; 10 to 23 feet (3 to 7 m), medium; 23 to 35 feet (7 to 10.5 m), large; 35 to 50 feet (10.5 to 15 m), very large; and over 50 feet (15 m), extremely large.

THESCELOSAURUS (THESS-eh-lo-sawr-us) "Marvelous Lizard" (Greek *theskelos* = marvelous + *sauros* = lizard, referring to the excellent condition of the first specimen found)

A Late Cretaceous ornithopod that closely resembled Parksosaurus and Camptosaurus. Although it was basically bipedal, this plant eater probably walked on four legs part of the time. It was 12 feet (3.7 m) long from its snout to the tip of its tail, with rather short legs, a plump body, and a small head. The hands had five fingers, and the feet had four toes. The claws were hooflike but sharp. *Thescelosaurus* may have had armor plates. It is known from a nearly complete skeleton. Its fossils have been found in Wyoming, Montana, South Dakota, and in Alberta and Saskatchewan, Canada.

Classification: Thescelosauridae, Ornithopoda, Ornithischia

Thescelosaurus

THESPESIUS (thes-PEE-see-us) "Divine Lizard" (Greek *thespesios* = divine. The reason for this name is unknown.)

A Late Cretaceous HADROSAUR. This flat-headed duckbill is known only from a partial skull and other incomplete skeletal material found in South Dakota. The skull closely resembles those of ANATOSAURUS or EDMONTOSAURUS, and some think *Thespesius* may be the same as one of them.

Classification: Hadrosauridae, Ornithopoda, Ornithischia

TICINOSUCHUS (teh-CHIN-o-sook-us) "Ticino Crocodile" (Named for the place in Switzerland where it was first found + Greek *souchos* = crocodile)

Not a DINOSAUR, but a 10-foot (3-m) PSEUDOSUCHIAN THECODONT. It was a close relative of MANDASUCHUS and probably resembled that pseudosuchian. It was basically QUADRUPEDAL but could probably run on two legs. It had sharp teeth and was probably a meat eater. This thecodont is believed by some to be the ancestor of the plant-eating SAURISCHIAN dinosaurs. Its FOSSILS have been found in Late Triassic deposits in Austria and Switzerland.

TIENSHANOSAURUS (tee-en-SHAHN-o-sawr-us) "Tien Shan Lizard" (Named for the Tien Shan Mountains in China, near which it was found, + Greek *sauros* = lizard)

An Early Cretaceous SAUROPOD that resembled EUHELOPUS in SIZE and shape. This four-legged plant eater is known from much of a skeleton found in China. It had a small head, a long neck, and a long TAIL. Its forelegs and hind legs were nearly equal in length. It was 34 feet (10 m) long.

Classification: Sauropoda, Sauropodomorpha, Saurischia

titanosaurids or **Titanosauridae** (ty-tan-o-SAWR-ih-dee) "Large Lizards" (Named after TITANOSAURUS)

The preferred name for the family of large, peg-toothed SAUROPODS (those with pencil-shaped TEETH). This major division had shorter front legs than hind legs. They were large four-legged plant eaters, 50 to 90 feet (15 to 27 m) long. They flourished in North America, South America, Europe, Asia, and Africa from Middle Jurassic through Late Cretaceous times. This group is also called ATLANTOSAURIDAE. It is divided into four subfamilies: the ATLANTOSAURINAE, the DICRAEOSAURINAE, the DIPLODOCINAE, and the TITANOSAURINAE.

A new study of sauropods combines the Titanosaurinae with the Atlantosaurinae, and the Diplodocinae with the Dicraeosaurinae, and raises the latter to family level, under the name of DIPLODOCIDAE. This new classification is not yet accepted by everyone.

titanosaurs or **Titanosaurinae** (ty-tan-o-SAWR-ih-nee) "Large Lizards" (Named after TITANOSAURUS)

A subfamily of Titanosauridae dinosaurs. This group was very much like the DIPLODOCINAE, but had six vertebrae in the pelvic area instead of five. Some had ARMOR PLATES. They ranged in size from 50 to 60 feet (15 to 18 m) long. They lived during the CRETACEOUS PERIOD and have been found in Africa, Europe, India, South America, and the United States. HYPSELOSAURUS, LAPLATASAURUS, SALTASAURUS, and TITANOSAURUS were members of this subfamily.

TITANOSAURUS (TY-tan-o-sawr-us) "Titan Lizard" (Named after the Titans, a family of giants in Greek mythology, + Greek *sauros* = lizard, because it was a large dinosaur)

A Late Cretaceous SAUROPOD. This four-legged plant eater resembled DIPLODOCUS, but was smaller, heavier, and had six vertebrae in the pelvic area instead of five. Its neck and TAIL were more like those of CAMARASAURUS. *Titanosaurus* was one of the last of the sauropods, and it may have had ARMOR PLATES. A nearly complete skeleton found in Argentina lacked only a skull. *Titanosaurus* was 60 to 66 feet (18 to 20 m) long.

Classification: Sauropoda, Sauropodomorpha, Saurischia

Titanosaurus

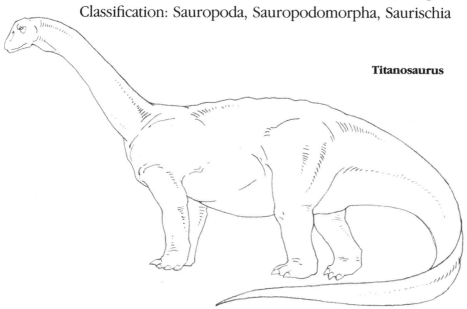

321

TORNIERIA (tor-NEE-ree-ah) (Named in honor of T. Tornier, German paleontologist)

A Late Jurassic SAUROPOD of the TITANOSAURINAE subfamily. It is known only from fragments found in Tanzania. The SIZE of these FOSSILS suggests that this four-legged plant eater was a *very* large creature—its height at the shoulders may have reached 20 feet (6 m). *Tornieria*'s forelimbs were the same length as the hind.

Classification: Sauropoda, Sauropodomorpha, Saurischia

TOROSAURUS (TOHR-o-sawr-us) "Piercing Lizard" (Greek *toros* = piercing + *sauros* = lizard, referring to its HORNS)

One of the last of the CERATOPSIANS. Its FRILL was longer than that of any other ceratopsian. Its skull, from the tip of the horny beak to the back edge of the frill, was 8.7 feet (2.6 m) long. The frill was 5.5 feet (1.7 m) wide and extended well back of the animal's shoulders. This dinosaur's head was larger in proportion to the SIZE of the body than that of any other known land animal.

Torosaurus was probably 20 feet (6 m) long and weighed about 5 tons (4.5 metric tons). Its nose horn was small, but

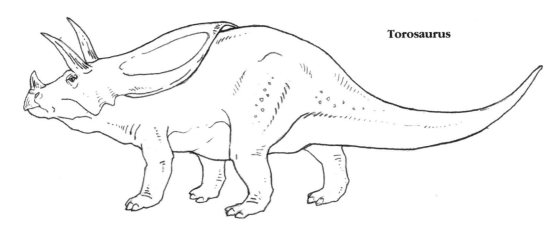

Torosaurus

the horns on its brow were 2 feet (60 cm) long. *Torosaurus* walked on four legs and ate low vegetation, which it chopped with scissorlike TEETH.

Torosaurus lived in Late Cretaceous North America and endured to the very end of the period. Its FOSSILS have been discovered in Wyoming, Texas, and Alberta, Canada, but a complete skeleton has not been found.

Classification: Ceratopsidae, Ceratopsia, Ornithischia

TORVOSAURUS (TOHR-vo-sawr-us) "Savage Lizard" (Latin *torvus* = savage + Greek *sauros* = lizard, referring to its lethal CLAWS and TEETH)

A large and heavily built Late Jurassic CARNOSAUR. It was about 35 feet (10.7 m) long and may have weighed as much as 6 tons (5.4 metric tons). *Torvosaurus* was different from other known meat eaters. It was more massive than the other Jurassic carnosaurs, and its arms were shorter—about the length of a man's arms. However, the arms were much longer than those of the TYRANNOSAURS, and were more powerful. The HANDS had three short, stout fingers equipped with wicked 12-inch (30-cm) claws that were longer than the claws of any other Jurassic THEROPOD. It had shorter and more massive jaws than any other carnosaur. They were lined with enormous teeth. *Torvosaurus* resembled MEGALOSAURUS more than it did any other theropod. Like TYRANNOSAURUS, *Torvosaurus* probably could not run swiftly because of its weight, and it was probably a scavenger. This BIPEDAL meat eater is known from an incomplete skeleton found in Colorado.

Classification: Carnosauria, Theropoda, Saurischia

TRACHODON (TRAK-o-don) "Rough Tooth" (Greek *trachys* = rough + *odon-* = tooth, referring to the rough surface formed by dozens of tiny denticles on the tooth crown)

Name given to a single HADROSAUR tooth found in Late Cretaceous rock in Montana. *Trachodon* is now considered to be the same as ANATOSAURUS. Since the name *Anatosaurus* is based on more complete information, it is the preferred one.

Classification: Hadrosauridae, Ornithopoda, Ornithischia

trachodont (TRAK-o-dont) "Rough Tooth" (Named after TRACHODON)

Any duck-billed dinosaur; a name sometimes used in place of HADROSAUR.

tracks, trackways

Scientists have discovered thousands of dinosaur tracks that were left in Mesozoic mud. These fossilized footprints tell many things about the animals that made them. From tracks scientists have learned things they could not have learned in any other way.

Tracks have been found that show when dinosaurs sat or rested. Others show the animals swimming or floating. A recent discovery shows that a THEROPOD had been floating in water, pushing itself along with one foot. This provides evidence that theropods sometimes went into water. Scientists once thought that SAUROPODS and HADROSAURS could escape predators by taking to the water, but perhaps this was not true. In England whole trackways of MEGALOSAURUS have been found. Scientists have learned almost as much about this dinosaur from its tracks as from its FOSSIL bones.

From tracks scientists can tell whether an animal was BIPEDAL or QUADRUPEDAL. They can determine whether the animal sprawled like an alligator or walked erect like an elephant.

By measuring the distance between footprints, scientists can estimate how fast the dinosaur was going. Long strides indicate the animal was traveling rapidly. Gigantic three-toed CAR-NOSAUR tracks found in a coal mine in Colorado show that the animal that made them had a very long stride. Three-toed footprints recently uncovered by a flash flood in Texas reveal that 15 large carnosaurs that passed that way in Early Cretaceous times were in a great hurry. The strides are the longest known. By using a formula based on the distance between the tracks and the size of them, a scientist has estimated that these dinosaurs were running nearly 25 miles (40 km) per hour. We can't be sure what dinosaur made the tracks, but it is thought that they were made by ACROCANTHOSAURUS, a carnosaur whose fossils have been found in similar rock nearby. Whether these animals were chasing something, running from something, or just romping cannot be determined.

Some tracks give clues to the way dinosaurs lived. Tracks in Canada indicate that carnosaurs hunted in packs. A sauropod trackway in Texas shows that 23 individuals were traveling in the same direction. Smaller individuals were most often in the center of the group. This indicates HERDING and also suggests that adult sauropods protected their YOUNG. (See PARENTAL CARE.) Another trackway in Texas shows the prints of a sauropod that was being followed by a three-toed carnosaur. The carnosaur footprints are impressed on top of those of the sauropod. Scientists think that the carnosaur may have been stalking the sauropod. Still another group of tracks shows herding in COELUROSAURS. These footprints are in the Connecticut Valley in the eastern United States. They indicate that several members of the same species were traveling together. Long trackways left by hadrosaurs in Canada show that hadrosaurs traveled in herds and that they walked side by side. Young hadrosaurs appear to have herded in groups of similar-size individuals.

Scientists can't be exactly sure which kind of dinosaur made a footprint or trackway unless they find a fossil skeleton nearby that has FEET that match the footprints. But scientists can determine whether the track was made by a sauropod, a carnosaur, a coelurosaur, or a hadrosaur, because they know what kind of foot each of these types of dinosaurs had.

Triassic (try-ASS-ik) **Period** (From Latin *trias* = triad, three, referring to the three successive series of rocks in Germany that are of this age)

The first of the three periods of the MESOZOIC ERA. This geological time period began 225 million years ago and ended 190 million years ago. Dinosaurs appeared in the middle of this period. Other major land animals of the period were amphibians and THERAPSIDS. The THECODONTS were the dominant life form. ICHTHYOSAURS and NOTHOSAURS inhabited the oceans. During the Late Triassic, the first mammals and earliest CROCODILIANS and turtles appeared.

TRIASSOLESTES (try-ass-o-LESS-teez) "Triassic Robber" (Triassic + Greek *lestes* = robber, referring to the stratum in which it was found)

A small COELUROSAUR that lived in Argentina during the earliest part of the Late TRIASSIC PERIOD. This little BIPEDAL meat eater was about the size of PODOKESAURUS and probably closely resembled that dinosaur. It is known from an incomplete skull, lower jaw, and cervical vertebrae.

Classification: Coelurosauria, Theropoda, Saurischia

TRICERATOPS (try-SAYR-ah-tops) "Three-horned Face" (Greek *tri* = three + *keratops* = horned face, because it had three HORNS)

The largest and heaviest of the CERATOPSIANS. It was 25 feet (7.5 m) long and 9.5 feet (2.9 m) tall. It weighed 5 tons (4.5 metric tons). It had a smooth, solid FRILL; a short, thick nose horn; and two enormous 40-inch (102-cm), forward-curved brow horns. This four-legged plant eater lived in western North America during Late Cretaceous times.

Triceratops was one of the very last of the horned dinosaurs to develop and one of the last of the dinosaurs to become extinct. (See EXTINCTION.) It had no real enemies. It was an aggressive animal and was well protected by its horns, frill, and tough, leathery SKIN.

Triceratops had a turtlelike beak and scissorlike TEETH. Large numbers of *Triceratops* must have roamed western North America, because several whole skeletons have been found in Montana, Wyoming, and Alberta, Canada.

Classification: Ceratopsidae, Ceratopsia, Ornithischia

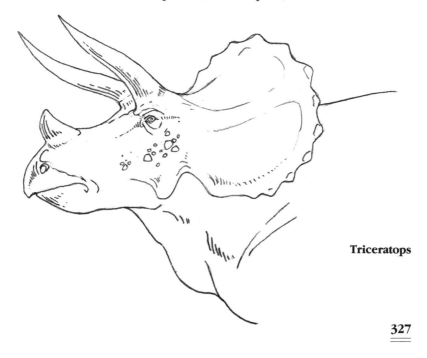

Triceratops

TROÖDON (TROH-o-don) "Wound Tooth" (Greek *troo* =
to wound + *odon-* = tooth, referring to its serrated teeth)

This small, Late Cretaceous COELUROSAUR was one of the
first dinosaurs named in North America. The name was based
on a single tooth, and this led to much debate as to what
kind of dinosaur it was. It was once thought to be a dome-
headed dinosaur, now known as STEGOCERAS. In 1980 scientists
found several adults, juveniles, NESTS, and EGGS in Montana
that were identified as being those of *Troödon*. We now know
that *Troödon* was a coelurosaur and is apparently the same
dinosaur as STENONYCOSAURUS. Since *Troödon* is the older
name, it is the correct scientific name for both dinosaurs.

This BIPEDAL meat eater was only 6 feet (1.8 m) long. It was
probably one of the most dangerous of the Late Cretaceous
animals. It closely resembled DROMAEOSAURUS and, like that
dinosaur, had hollow bones, a large BRAIN, and large eyes. Its
eyes were spaced far apart, so it was probably able to judge
distances accurately. Scientists think it was the most intelligent of the dinosaurs. (See INTELLIGENCE.)

Troödon

It was a swift runner and probably could outrun any other dinosaur. Its FEET were equipped with sicklelike CLAWS, and its HANDS had grasping fingers. It may have caught prey larger than itself. It probably hunted in packs. Adults found near nests and juveniles indicate *Troödon* may have cared for its YOUNG. (See PARENTAL CARE.) Some scientists think that *Troödon* must have been warm-blooded, because it was so active. It also has been found in Alberta, Canada, and along the north shores of Alaska. This dinosaur so closely resembled SAUROR-NITHOIDES of Mongolia that some scientists think they, too, may be the same.

Classification: Coelurosaura, Theropoda, Saurischia

TROÖDONTID (troh-o-DON-tid)
See TROÖDON.

TSINTAOSAURUS (CHIN-dah-oo-sawr-us) "Ts'ingtao Lizard" (For Ts'ingtao, China, where it was found, + Greek *sauros* = lizard)

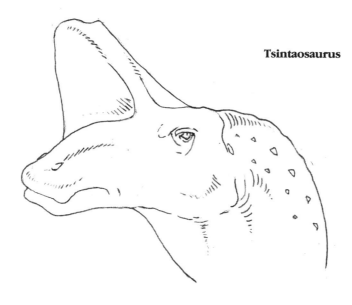

Tsintaosaurus

A Late Cretaceous HADROSAUR whose FOSSILS were found in China. This LAMBEOSAURINE duckbill had a hollow, spikelike CREST that projected upward and slightly forward like a HORN. However, it seems to have been covered by SKIN instead of horn covering, so it probably was not a weapon. Some scientists think that a flap of skin may have stretched from the crest to the middle of the nose. It may have been a sex display device. This BIPEDAL plant eater is known from a nearly complete skeleton.

Classification: Hadrosauridae, Ornithopoda, Ornithischia

TUOJIANGOSAURUS (twah-JEEAHNG-o-sawr-us) "Tuojiang Lizard" (Named for the Tuojiang River, where it was found, + Greek *sauros* = lizard)

The first STEGOSAUR found in Asia. It is known from a nearly complete skeleton found in China. This Late Jurassic plated dinosaur resembled STEGOSAURUS but had narrower, more conical plates. It had 15 pairs of plates running down its back and TAIL, with two pairs of sharp, defensive spikes on the tail.

Tuojiangosaurus

This 23.5-foot (7.2-m)-long, 8.4-foot (2.6-m)-tall stegosaur probably ate low, tender branches and lush ground plants.

Classification: Stegosauridae, Stegosauria, Ornithischia

TYLOCEPHALE (ty-lo-SEF-ah-lee) "Knob Head" (Greek *tylos* = knob + *kephale* = head, referring to its domed head)

A recently discovered PACHYCEPHALOSAUR. This dome-headed dinosaur is known only from a partial skull and several other skeletal parts found in Mongolia. The skull was thick and decorated with small spikes similar to those on the skull of STEGOCERAS. Like all pachycephalosaurs, *Tylocephale* walked on two legs and ate plants. Scientists estimate that this animal was about 7 feet (2 m) long.

Classification: Pachycephalosauridae, Ornithopoda or Pachycephalosauria, Ornithischia

TYLOSAURUS (TY-lo-sawr-us) "Knot Lizard" (Greek *tylos* = knot or knob + *sauros* = lizard. The reason for this name is not known.)

Not a DINOSAUR, but one of the largest known of the MOSASAURS. This seagoing lizard lived in the NIOBRARA SEA during the Late CRETACEOUS PERIOD. It was 20 to 40 feet (6 to 12 m) long and had a long, slim body. It had huge jaws; sharp, conelike teeth; and flipperlike hands and feet. It was a savage hunter and ate fish and shellfish. *Tylosaurus* FOSSILS have been found in Kansas.

TYPOTHORAX (ty-po-THOH-raks)
See AETOSAURS.

tyrannosaurids or **Tyrannosauridae** (ty-ran-o-SAWR-ih-dee) "Tyrant Lizards" (Named after TYRANNOSAURUS) Also called TYRANNOSAURS.

The family of Late Cretaceous CARNOSAURS. The tyrannosaurs were the largest and the last of the meat eaters. They had huge heads, long TEETH, very short arms, and two short fingers with long CLAWS. Tyrannosaurs had heavier, more powerful bodies than earlier carnosaurs. Some weighed as much as 6 tons (5.5 metric tons), and the largest were 50 feet (15 m) long. They probably could not run swiftly because of their great weight. It is possible that they were scavengers, eating carcasses. They have been found in North America, Mongolia, India, and Japan. Some lived along the north shores of Alaska. ALBERTOSAURUS, ALECTROSAURUS, DASPLETOSAURUS, TARBOSAURUS, and TYRANNOSAURUS were tyrannosaurs.

tyrannosaurs (ty-RAN-o-sawrz)
See TYRANNOSAURIDS.

TYRANNOSAURUS (ty-RAN-o-sawr-us) "Tyrant Lizard" (Greek *tyrannos* = tyrant + *sauros* = lizard, because of its great size and wicked TEETH and CLAWS)

The last and largest known CARNOSAUR. This huge meat eater measured up to 50 feet (15 m) from the tip of its enormous jaws to the end of its TAIL. It was 18.5 feet (5.6 m) tall and weighed 6 tons (5.4 metric tons). It ran with its massive tail extended to balance its 4-foot (1.2-m) head. Its monstrous 3-foot (90-cm) jaws were lined with 60 daggerlike teeth that were 3 to 6 inches (8 to 15 cm) long. *Tyrannosaurus* had long, strong hind legs, and its huge FEET were equipped with

8-inch (20-cm) talons. However, its arms were very short—only about 30 inches (76 cm) long. They were so short that *Tyrannosaurus* could not even scratch its chin! But the HANDS, like the feet, were armed with long, strong claws.

This ferocious BIPEDAL dinosaur stalked its prey across western North America during Late Cretaceous times. It probably preferred to eat young duckbills or other prey that was easy to catch. Seven complete skeletons have been found in Montana. Its FOSSILS have also been found in Wyoming, New Mexico, and South Dakota. A close relative, TARBOSAU-RUS, lived in Mongolia.

Classification: Carnosauria, Theropoda, Saurischia

Tyrannosaurus Rex

U

UGROSAURUS (ug-ro-SAWR-us) "Ugly Lizard" (Scandinavian *ugro* = ugly + Greek *sauros* = lizard)

A late Late Cretaceous CERATOPSIAN found in Montana. It was a short-snouted ceratopsian that appears to have had a large FRILL and a broad, robust snout with a large, raised knob similar to that of PACHYRHINOSAURUS. This four-legged plant eater is known only from fragments.

Classification: Ceratopsidae, Ceratopsia, Ornithischia

ULTRASAURUS (UHL-truh-sawr-us) "Very Large Lizard" (Latin *ultra* = excessive + Greek *sauros* = lizard, because of its enormous size)

Name originally applied to the FOSSILS of one of the largest known dinosaurs, a huge, Late Jurassic SAUROPOD found in Colorado. The fossils of this four-legged plant eater include a 9-foot (2.7-m) shoulder blade (the largest dinosaur bone ever found), 4- and 5- foot (1.2- and 1.5-m) vertebrae, and a few other bones. The shoulder blade is 25 percent larger than that of any known BRACHIOSAURUS. It was estimated that this dinosaur was 100 feet (30.5 m) long, 50 or 60 feet (15 or 18 m) tall, and may have weighed 80 tons (72.6 metric tons). It was taller than a five-story building.

Some people think this dinosaur may have been a large *Brachiosaurus,* but not everyone agrees. The name will remain valid, however, regardless, because a similar sauropod was found in Korea and officially named *Ultrasaurus tabriensis.* The finder believed it was the same GENUS as the American sauropod, but it has since been determined that the Korean sauropod was a much smaller dinosaur. Since the Korean

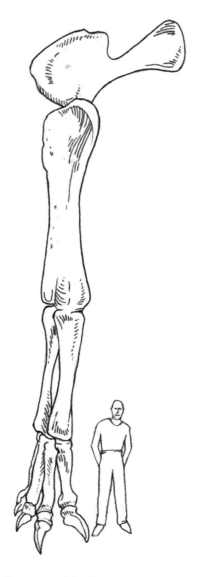

Ultrasaurus

species was officially named before the American species, the name *Ultrasaurus* belongs to the Korean dinosaur, and the American dinosaur must be renamed, unless it is proved to be just a large species of *Brachiosaurus*.

Classification: Sauropoda, Sauropodomorpha, Saurischia

unnamed species

New dinosaurs are discovered every year, both in the field and in museum collections. Most dinosaur fossils do not receive names as soon as they are found, because first they must be removed from the rock encasing them. This is hard and tedious work and can take many years. Often they are simply stored in the museum collection room until someone has the time to clean them up. Then many more years may be required to examine all known similar specimens to make sure the new discovery is indeed a new and different dinosaur. Finally a report must be written, describing the find and giving it a name.

Recently discovered dinosaurs that are still unnamed include an ANKYLOSAUR found in Antarctica, a new, large CARNOSAUR found in China, a TITANOSAURIDAE SAUROPOD in Argentina, an Early Cretaceous DIPLODOCIDAE sauropod known from a 6-foot (1.8-m) pelvis and long-spined vertebrae found in Colorado that may have been even larger than SEISMOSAURUS, and a 10-foot, 100-million-year-old HYPSILOPHODONT found in Jurassic rock in Texas. This last dinosaur is known from six nearly complete adult skeletons and a NEST of ten chicken-size juveniles.

UNQUILLOSAURUS (un-KWIL-o-sawr-us) "Unquillo Lizard" (Named for the area where it was found + Greek *sauros* = lizard)

A Late Cretaceous CARNOSAUR that appears to be closely related to TYRANNOSAURUS. It is known only from very fragmentary material but is important because it establishes that these large THEROPODS were in Argentina, where its FOSSILS were found.

Classification: Carnosauria, Theropoda, Saurischia

V

VALDOSAURUS (VAL-doh-sawr-us) "Wealden Lizard" (Latin *valdo* = weald, a woodland, + Greek *sauros* = lizard, referring to the Wealden rock formation, where it was found)

An ORNITHOPOD of Early Cretaceous England. This BIPEDAL plant eater was closely related to and resembled DRYOSAURUS and was probably a descendant of that dinosaur. It is known only from very fragmentary material.

Classification: Hypsilophodontidae, Ornithopoda, Ornithischia

VECTISAURUS (VEK-tih-sawr-us) "Isle of Wight Lizard" (Latin *vectis* = name for Isle of Wight, where it was found, + Greek *sauros* = lizard)

An Early Cretaceous ORNITHOPOD known only from fragmentary material found on the Isle of Wight. It may be the same as IGUANODON.

Classification: Iguanodontidae, Ornithopoda, Ornithischia

VELOCIRAPTOR (veh-loss-ih-RAP-tor) "Swift Robber" (Latin *velocis* = swift + *raptor* = robber, referring to its speed and its grasping hands)

Velociraptor

A COELUROSAUR similar to DEINONYCHUS, but this fierce little meat eater lived several million years later, during the Late CRETACEOUS PERIOD. *Velociraptor* was about the SIZE of a man. It had long, three-fingered HANDS and sicklelike talons on each foot. Like *Deinonychus,* this BIPED had long, slender legs and could run swiftly. Its FOSSILS were found in Mongolia, where it had died in a death struggle—its hands were gripping the skull of a PROTOCERATOPS, and one of its awful CLAWS was embedded in the belly of its prey.

Classification: Coelurosauria, Theropoda, Saurischia

VOLKHEIMERIA (volk-HY-mer-ee-ah) (Named in honor of Wolfgang Volkheimer, Argentine PALEONTOLOGIST)

A Middle Jurassic SAUROPOD. This dinosaur was similar to CETIOSAURUS but was more primitive. In fact, it is one of the most primitive sauropods known. Like all sauropods, it walked on four pillarlike legs, ate plants, and had a long neck and TAIL. It is known from an incomplete skeleton found in Argentina. This is a very recent discovery and has not yet been thoroughly studied.

Classification: Sauropoda, Sauropodomorpha, Saurischia

VULCANODON (vul-KAN-o-don) "Volcano Tooth" (Named after Vulcanus, the Roman god of fire, + Greek *odon-* = tooth, because it was found in sandstone between two lava flows)

An Early Jurassic PROSAUROPOD resembling MELANOROSAURUS. This four-legged plant eater was found in Zimbabwe. It is one of the last and largest of the prosauropods. In fact, some believe it was a primitive SAUROPOD instead of a prosauropod. It was 40 feet (12 m) long from the tip of the snout to the end of its long TAIL. It probably weighed more than an elephant. Like all prosauropods, *Vulcanodon* had a small head and a long neck. It also had elephantlike legs. It is known from incomplete material.

Classification: Prosauropoda, Sauropodomorpha, Saurischia

W

WANNANOSAURUS (wahn-NAHN-o-sawr-us) "Lizard from Wannan" (Named for Wannan, China, where it was found, + Greek *sauros* = lizard)

A primitive, flat-headed PACHYCEPHALOSAUR from Cretaceous China. This BIPEDAL, plant-eating dome-headed dinosaur was very small, probably no more than 39 inches (99 cm) long. It is known only from a skull (with jaws), a femur, tibia, and other fragments.

Classification: Pachycephalosauridae, Ornithopoda or Pachycephalosauria, Ornithischia

WUERHOSAURUS (woo-er-ho-SAWR-us) "Wuerho Lizard" (Named for the village in China near the site where it was found + Greek *sauros* = lizard)

Until recently, the only positively identified STEGOSAUR of the Cretaceous age. Until its discovery, it was thought that the stegosaurs had become EXTINCT by the end of the JURASSIC PERIOD. It was found in Early Cretaceous rock in northwestern China. It is known only from fragments. Like all stegosaurs, it was a QUADRUPEDAL plant eater.

Classification: Stegosauridae, Stegosauria, Ornithischia

X

XENOTARSOSAURUS (zeen-o-TAHR-so-sawr-us) "Lizard with a Strange Ankle" (Greek *xeno-* = strange + *tarsos* = ankle + *sauros* = lizard, because its anklebones were fused, uncommon in large theropods)

A large, Late Cretaceous THEROPOD found in Argentina. This two-legged meat eater is known only from two vertebrae and a leg, minus the foot. The leg, which is 46 inches (1.2 m) long, resembles that of CARNOTAURUS, a close relative, but is much better preserved.

Classification: Carnosauria, Theropoda, Saurischia

XIAOSAURUS (sheeyow-SAWR-us) "Dawn Lizard" (Chinese *xiao* = dawn + Greek *sauros* = lizard)

A small HYPSILOPHODONT found in Middle Jurassic deposits in China. It was 5 feet (1.5 m) long and had a short, deep skull. This BIPEDAL plant eater is known from most of the skeleton of a 40-inch (1 m)-long juvenile.

Classification: Hypsilophodontidae, Ornithopoda, Ornithischia

Y

YALEOSAURUS (YAYL-ee-o-sawr-us) "Yale's Lizard" (Named in honor of Yale University + Greek *sauros* = lizard)

Name given to several PROSAUROPOD FOSSILS found in Late Triassic rock in Connecticut. They are now known to be the same as those of ANCHISAURUS, and since the name *Anchisau-*

rus was given first, it is the preferred name for this dinosaur.

Classification: Prosauropoda, Sauropodomorpha, Saurischia

YANGCHUANOSAURUS (yahng-CHWAHN-o-sawr-us) "Yang-ch'uan Lizard" (Named for Yang-ch'uan, China, where it was found, + Greek *sauros* = lizard)

A Late Jurassic or Early Cretaceous CARNOSAUR. *Yangchuanosaurus* was closely related to ALLOSAURUS. It was about 26 feet (8 m) long and had a 32-inch (80-cm) skull. It had short arms and three-fingered HANDS. It walked on two strong legs with its heavy TAIL extended to balance its huge head. The jaws of this large meat eater were lined with daggerlike TEETH. A nearly complete skeleton of *Yangchuanosaurus* was found in China.

Classification: Carnosauria, Theropoda, Saurischia

Yangchuanosaurus

YAVERLANDIA (yah-ver-LAND-ee-ah) (Named for Yaverland Battery on the Isle of Wight, where it was found)

A very primitive PACHYCEPHALOSAUR (dome-headed dinosaur) discovered in Early Cretaceous rock on the Isle of Wight. The skull roof of this turkey-size ancestor of STEGOCERAS had thickened into two small, rather flat domes. It is known only from this skull roof, but like all pachycephalosaurs, it was probably a BIPEDAL plant eater.

Classification: Pachycephalosauridae, Pachycephalosauria, Ornithischia

young

Little is known about baby dinosaurs. Discoveries of their remains are extremely rare. Their immature bones were too fragile to fossilize readily. However, enough young dinosaurs have been found to give us some idea of dinosaur development. The FOSSIL record seems to indicate that specialized traits did not develop until the animals were half-grown.

PROTOCERATOPS is one dinosaur that is known from every stage of development. EGGS, hatchlings, and half-grown and adult individuals of this dinosaur have been found. Young *Protoceratops* had very poorly developed FRILLS. The frills did not become fully developed until the animals were about half-grown. Skeletons of several other young CERATOPSIANS show that their HORNS were not well developed until they were half-grown, either.

MAIASAURA (a HADROSAUR) is also known from hatchlings to adults. The hatchlings were 18 inches (46 cm) long. Month-old babies were about 3 feet (1 m) long or about one-tenth of the SIZE of the adults, while "adolescents" were half the adult size. Young hadrosaurs did not develop CRESTS until they were half-grown. In immature hadrosaurs, the bills were less broad than in adults, and there were fewer rows of TEETH. Similarly, young PACHYCEPHALOSAURS had shallower domes than the adults, and baby STEGOSAURUS did not have plates.

Young CARNOSAURS had larger heads, bigger eyes, and longer legs in comparison to their body size than did adults. These characteristics probably improved their ability to catch prey and to escape larger predators. Several half-grown ALBERTO-SAURUS have been found, and ALLOSAURUS is known from juveniles 10 feet (3 m) long to full-grown adults. These young individuals were about one-fifth of adult size and were well past the hatchling stage. Hatchlings were probably no more than 30 inches (76 cm) long (or about one-tenth of adult size).

Several young SAUROPODS have been found. The youngest, a hatchling CAMARASAURUS, is known only from its upper jaw, and its size is unknown. Remains of an approximately one-month-old baby APATOSAURUS indicate that it was 6 feet (1.8 m) long, 18 inches (46 cm) tall, and probably weighed 75 pounds (34 kg). It would have reached only to the ankle of a full-grown adult. Its fossils have only recently been found at the University of Oklahoma and have not yet been fully studied. Before these discoveries, the most complete and smallest sauropod known was a 16-foot (4.9-m) juvenile *Camarasaurus* skeleton. This animal was about one-fourth the size of a full-grown adult. Although the size of the hatchling is unknown, from the size of known sauropod eggs, hatchlings could not have been more than 30 inches (80 cm) long or weighed more than 17 pounds (7.7 kg).

Baby armored dinosaurs are known from five very young PINACOSAURUS found huddled together in China. Their tails had not yet developed clubs, and their ARMOR PLATES had just begun to develop.

The smallest and youngest dinosaur known to date is a newly hatched PROSAUROPOD called MUSSAURUS. This tiny dinosaur was about the size of a robin. It had a tiny head, a long neck, a long TAIL, and heavy legs. The second-smallest dinosaur is a baby PSITTACOSAURUS. Wear on its teeth indicates it was not a hatchling. This tiny dinosaur was only about 10 inches (25 cm) long—its body was half the size of a pigeon's. It had enormous eyes and a large braincase.

Other known juvenile dinosaurs include a turkey-size CAMPTOSAURUS and a 30-inch (75-cm)-long COMPSOGNATHUS. Several very young COELOPHYSIS are also known.

YOUNGOOLITHUS (YAHNG-o-o-lith-us) "Young's Stone Eggs" (Named in honor of C. C. Young, Chinese PALEONTOLOGIST, + Greek -oon = EGG + *lithos* = stone)

Name given to dinosaur eggs and a footprint found in China. The eggs were in a clutch of 16. A three-toed left footprint was clearly impressed upon three of the eggs. Scientists think the footprint was made by the dinosaur that laid the eggs. The eggs were elongated and nearly pointed on each end. They were found in Cretaceous rock.

YÜNNANOSAURUS (yun-NAHN-o-sawr-us) "Yünnan Lizard" (Named for Yünnan Province in China, where it was found, + Greek *sauros* = lizard)

An Early Jurassic PROSAUROPOD. This four-legged plant eater is smaller and less heavily built than MELANOROSAURUS. It is quite similar to LUFENGOSAURUS but smaller and does not have coarsely serrated TEETH like those of most prosauropods. Its teeth are more like those of the sauropod BRACHIOSAURUS—cylindrical and somewhat flattened from side to side. Its skeleton, however, is nearly the same as that of ANCHISAURUS.

Yünnanosaurus

Yünnanosaurus apparently ate only plants. It is known from an almost complete skeleton.

Classification: Prosauropoda, Sauropodomorpha, Saurischia

Z

ZATOMUS (zah-TOH-mus) "Very Sharp" (Greek *za-* = very + *tomos* = sharp, referring to the character of the tooth)

Name given to a single CARNOSAUR tooth found in North Carolina. This tooth is similar to those of TERATOSAURUS. It is the only evidence, other than footprints, that large THEROPODS

lived in eastern North America during the Late TRIASSIC PE-
RIOD.

Classification: Carnosauria, Theropoda, Saurischia

ZEPHYROSAURUS (ZEF-er-o-sawr-us) "West Wind Lizard"
(Named after Zephyros, god of the west wind in Greek mythology, + Greek *sauros* = lizard, because it was discovered
in western North America)

An Early Cretaceous ORNITHOPOD recently found in Montana. It was closely related to HYPSILOPHODON. *Zephyrosaurus*
was 6 to 8 feet (1.8 to 2.5 m) long. Its skull was 6 inches (15
cm) long. This animal was a BIPEDAL plant eater. It is known
from a partial skull that included the braincase and a jaw, a
few ribs, and broken vertebrae.

Classification: Hypsilophodontidae, Ornithopoda, Ornithischia

ZIGONGOSAURUS (dzih-GOONG-o-sawr-us) "Zigong Lizard" (Named for Zigong, China, near where it was found, +
Greek *sauros* = lizard)

A euhelopodid SAUROPOD found in Late Jurassic deposits of
China. This four-legged plant eater probably grew to be 35
feet (10.7 m) long and weighed about 20 tons (18 metric
tons). It is known from a nearly complete skeleton.

Classification: Sauropoda, Sauropodomorpha, Saurischia

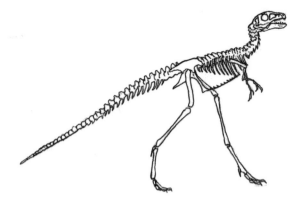

baby Albertosaurus skeleton

FOR FURTHER READING

Bakker, Robert T. *The Dinosaur Heresies.* New York: William Morrow and Company, Inc., 1986.

Charig, Alan J. *A New Look at the Dinosaurs.* New York: Mayflower Books, 1979.

Colbert, Edwin H. *The Age of Reptiles.* New York: W. W. Norton & Co., 1965.

———. *The Year of the Dinosaur.* New York: Charles Scribner's Sons, 1977.

Desmond, Adrian J. *The Hot-Blooded Dinosaurs.* New York: Warner Books, 1977.

Gould, Stephen Jay. "The Great Dying." *Natural History,* October 1974, pp. 22–27.

———. "Were Dinosaurs Dumb?" *Natural History,* May 1978, pp. 9–16.

Horenstein, Sydney. *Dinosaurs and Other Prehistoric Animals.* New York: Strawberry Books, 1978.

Jacobs, Louis L., ed. *Aspects of Vertebrate History.* Flagstaff: Museum of Northern Arizona Press, 1980.

Kielan-Jaworowska, Zofia. *Hunting for Dinosaurs.* Cambridge: The MIT Press, 1969.

Kurtén, Björn. *The Age of the Dinosaurs.* New York: McGraw-Hill Book Co., 1968.

Langston, Wann, Jr. "Pterosaurs." *Scientific American,* February 1981, pp. 122–136.

Long, Robert. *The Last of the Dinosaurs.* San Francisco: Bellerophon Books, 1978.

Long, Robert A., and Samuel P. Welles. *All New Dinosaurs.* San Francisco: Bellerophon Books, 1975.

McIntosh, John S. *Dinosaur National Monument.* Phoenix: Constellation Phoenix, Inc., 1977.

McLoughlin, John C. *Archosauria: A New Look at the Old Dinosaur.* New York: The Viking Press, 1979.

Moody, Richard. *A Natural History of Dinosaurs.* London: Chartwell, 1977.

———. *The World of Dinosaurs.* New York: Grosset & Dunlap, 1977.

Morell, Virginia. "Announcing the Birth of a Heresy." *Discover,* March 1987, pp. 26–51.

Norman, David. *The Illustrated Encyclopedia of Dinosaurs.* New York: Crescent Books, 1985.

Olshevsky, George. "Dinosaur Renaissance." *Science Digest,* August 1981, pp. 34–43.

Ostrom, John H. *The Strange World of Dinosaurs.* New York: G. P. Putnam's Sons, 1964.

———. "A New Look at Dinosaurs." *National Geographic,* August 1978, pp. 152–185.

Russell, Dale A. *A Vanishing World.* Ottawa: National Museum of Natural Sciences, 1977.

———. "The Mass Extinctions of the Late Mesozoic." *Scientific American,* January 1982, pp. 58–65.

Sattler, Helen Roney. *Dinosaurs of North America.* New York: Lothrop, Lee & Shepard Books, 1981.

Stout, William. *The Dinosaurs.* New York: Bantam Books, 1981.

Tweedie, Michael. *The World of Dinosaurs.* New York: William Morrow & Co., 1977.

Wadsworth, Nelson. "Colorado's 100-foot Dinosaur! Is It the World's Largest?" *Science Digest,* April 1973, pp. 77–81.

West, Susan. "Dinosaur Hunt." *Science News,* November 3, 1979, vol. 116, pp. 314–315.

REFERENCE, BY LOCATION, OF DINOSAUR DISCOVERIES

Reference by Location

Reference by Location

Reference by Location

MEXICO
Albertosaurus, 37–39
Apatosaurus (Brontosaurus), 53–55
Gorgosaurus, 153
Hypacrosaurus, 170
Kritosaurus, 180–181
Labocania, 182
Lambeosaurus, 183–184

MICHIGAN
Acrocanthosaurus, 34

MISSOURI
Parrosaurus, 235

MONGOLIA
Alectrosaurus, 39
Alioramus, 40
Amtosaurus, 44
Archaeornithomimus, 56
Avimimus, 62
Bactrosaurus, 63
Bagaceratops, 64
Chilantaisaurus, 91
Deinocheirus, 108–109
Deinodon, 109–110
Dyoplosaurus, 123
Elmisaurus, 129–130
Erlikosaurus, 133
Gallimimus, 148
Garudimimus, 149
Goyocephale, 153
Homalocephale, 166
Hulsanpes, 168–169
Iguanodon, 174
Ingenia, 176
Microceratops, 200–201
Mongolosaurus, 203
Nemegtosaurus, 210–211
Opisthocoelicaudia, 216–217
Ornithomimus, 220–221
Oviraptor, 225–226
Pinacosaurus, 239
Prenocephale, 246–247
Probactrosaurus, 247
Procheneosaurus, 248
Protoceratops, 253–254
Psittacosaurus, 257
Quaesitosaurus, 261
Saichania, 267–268
Saurolophus, 271–272
Saurornithoides, 277–278

Segnosaurus, 283
Shamosaurus, 285
Stegoceras, 294–295
Syrmosaurus, 305
Talarurus, 306–307
Tarbosaurus, 308
Tarchia, 309–310
Therizinosaurus, 316–317
Titanosaurus, 321
Tylocephale, 331
Velociraptor, 337–338

MONTANA
Albertosaurus, 37–39
Ankylosaurus, 49–50
Apatosaurus (Brontosaurus), 53–55
Avaceratops, 61–62
Brachyceratops, 72–73
Ceratops, 84
Claosaurus, 93
Deinodon, 109–110
Deinonychus, 110–111
Hadrosaurus, 157–158
Lambeosaurus, 183–184
Maiasaura, 191–192
Microvenator, 201–202
Montanaceratops, 204–205
Nanotyrannus, 209
Ornithomimus, 220–221
Orodromeus, 223
Palaeoscincus, 229–230
Panoplosaurus, 231–232
Parksosaurus, 234–235
Pleurocoelus, 243–244
Stegoceras, 294–295
Stygimoloch, 301
Tenontosaurus, 312–313
Thescelosaurus, 318
Trachodon, 323–324
Triceratops, 327
Troödon, 328–329
Tyrannosaurus, 332–333
Ugrosaurus, 334
Zephyrosaurus, 346

MOROCCO
Rebbachisaurus, 263

NEW JERSEY
Coelurosaurus, 98
Dryptosaurus, 122–123

Reference by Location

Reference by Location

Reference by Location

HELEN RONEY SATTLER grew up on a farm and was a schoolteacher and children's librarian before she became a full-time writer and researcher. Her own love of puzzles and nature, and her grandson's interest in dinosaurs, helped spur her on to becoming a leading science writer for children. She has written more than thirty books, among them the award-winning *Dinosaurs of North America; The Book of Eagles; Whales, the Nomads of the Sea;* and the first edition of *The Illustrated Dinosaur Dictionary.*

Ms. Sattler has traveled widely and now lives in Oklahoma.

JOYCE POWZYK also grew up on a farm and has spent much of her life exploring and studying the natural world. She has traveled and studied in Africa, Guatemala, Costa Rica, New Zealand, Australia, and Tasmania. Her award-winning books include *Wallaby Creek; Tasmania, a Wildlife Journey;* and *Tracking Wild Chimpanzees.*

Ms. Powzyk lives in North Carolina and is working on her Ph.D. in physical anthropology.

Other books by Helen Roney Sattler
illustrated by Joyce Powzyk

Tyrannosaurus Rex and Its Kin

Books by Helen Roney Sattler

Baby Dinosaurs
The Book of Eagles
Dinosaurs of North America
Hominids: A Look Back at Our Ancestors
Giraffes, the Sentinels of the Savannas
Pterosaurs, the Flying Reptiles
Recipes for Art and Craft Materials
Sharks, the Super Fish
Train Whistles
Whales, the Nomads of the Seas

Books by Joyce Powzyk

Tasmania: A Wildlife Journey
Tracking Wild Chimpanzees
Wallaby Creek

The main text of this book was typeset by Maple-Vail Book Manufacturing Group in 12/16 ITC Garamond Light and ITC Garmond Bold type. The title was set in Players type, and other display type in ITC Kabel bold. The jacket was typeset by Pulsar Graphics. The color insert was printed by United Lithographers, Inc., on 80-pound Westvaco Sterling Litho Gloss paper. The balance of the book was printed by Maple-Vail Book Manufacturing Group on 80-pound Willman Finch Opaque Vellum paper. The jacket and cover were printed by New England Book Components.

The black-and-white drawings were executed using pencil on Bristolboard. T. R. Rowney's watercolor paint and colored pencil were used on T. H. Saunders watercolor hot-press paper for the paintings.

DESIGNED BY JOANN P. HILL